EAT, LAUGH, TALK!

THE FAMILY DINNER PLAYBOOK

52 Weeks of Easy Recipes,
Engaging Conversation,
and Hilarious Games

We dedicate this book to our families and to all families who take delight in food, fun, and conversation about things that matter.

FAMILIUS

THE FAMILY DINNER PROJECT.ORG

Published by Familius LLC, www.familius.com

Familius books are available at special discounts for bulk purchases, whether for sales promotions or for family or corporate use. For more information, contact Familius Sales at 559-876-2170 or email orders@familius.com.

Library of Congress Cataloging-in-Publication Data
2019903710

Print ISBN 9781641701648
Ebook ISBN 9781641701785

Printed in China

Edited by Katharine Hale, Peg Sandkam,
and Brooke Jorden
Cover design by David Miles and Zach Marell
Book design by Zach Marell

10 9 8 7 6 5 4 3 2 1

First Edition

CONTENTS

PREFACE

Dinner often feels like another mountain to climb in a work week filled with mountains.

If you agree with that statement, you'll be so happy you opened this book. We at The Family Dinner Project (TFDP) have worked for ten years toward a singular goal: to help families gather for dinner over food, fun, and conversation. Why are we so invested in family dinner? We're motivated by extensive scientific research that shows there are significant benefits extending far beyond nutrition and physical health. The psychological, cognitive, and emotional well-being of kids and parents is greatly enhanced by eating together. Even academic performance is improved. Through our work with thousands of families spanning ethnic, racial, geographic, and socio-economic groups, TFDP aims to help make family dinner doable and enjoyable. This book brings you fifty-two weeks of meals, games, and conversation starters in the hope that you and your family will experience the many benefits of a shared meal.

Here at TFDP, we take a flexible, fun approach to changes in your family dinner routine. This isn't about regimen or rules. We want you to feel comfortable and liberated from the many things that can make dinner so challenging.

Here are our core principles:

THIS IS NOT ABOUT PERFECT.

Many people become paralyzed at the thought of trying to include a family dinner in their complicated schedules because they're imagining their version of perfect. Whether it's a home cooked gourmet meal, a perfectly set table, or everyone dressed well and behaving like angels, most people have certain standards they think make family dinner a valuable and worthy experience. And those standards, which are impossible to achieve with today's busy lives, can lead us to conclude: If it's not perfect, why bother?

We at TFDP encourage you to forget "perfect" so you can enjoy family dinner. Your meals don't all have to be home-cooked. You don't need to have family dinner every night. And guess what? The shared meal doesn't even need to be dinner. This is about small steps and modest, achievable goals. If your family currently doesn't eat any meals together and you get to one a week, that's a win.

WE ARE NOT THE FOOD POLICE.

Food is at the center of a shared family meal, but TFDP isn't built around any kind of prescriptive eating. Of course, nutrition matters. We're proponents of fruits and vegetables over sugar and saturated fat. But we choose our recipes with the following criteria: ease, affordability, taste, and versatility.

We're not worried about the meals being perfectly nutritious, but we know that we can all always do better. For example, we advise checking labels for sugar content when buying sauces and salad dressings because the hidden sugars can exceed the recommended daily allotment. For those who want to reduce saturated fat, olive oil can be substituted for many recipes calling for butter. We also offer recipes for a variety of dietary needs, including gluten-free and vegetarian meals. And because it can be hard for one meal to please everyone, we provide recipes that allow for customization, such as tacos and pizza, where everyone can build the dish that suits them.

WE ARE REALISTIC ABOUT TECHNOLOGY.

Imagine a family harmoniously sitting around a candlelit table without a ringtone or screen in sight, and no one angling to sneak a peek at their phone. That's not the world we live in. We at TFDP won't tell you that technology has no place at the table, because it's part of the tapestry of modern life. We recognize that technology at the table can sometimes serve as a bridge to conversation by breaking down barriers and opening up communication. Instead of a blanket ban, we offer options to modify and minimize its use so that it doesn't hijack this important time. Think of it this way: We all spend so much of our day connected to our phones and screens. If you keep their place at the table short and sweet, it'll be easier to focus your attention on your family.

WE ARE ALL ABOUT THE FUN.

Families tell us that they come to the table for the food, but they linger and keep coming back if they have fun and good conversation during their time together. We encourage families to play with each other, and we have suggestions about how to make this happen. Parents with younger children will find games to engage antsy toddlers and keep them at the table longer. Kids and parents of all ages enjoy games like "Would You Rather," classics like "Telephone," and competitions like "Iron Chef." The point is to lighten the mood, let go of the tension, and have fun together.

We at The Family Dinner Project believe so strongly in what we do because we've seen and experienced the many benefits of family dinner firsthand. We've written this book to help make shared meals a reality for all families. In these pages, we share some of the science supporting the benefits of family dinner, but most importantly, we show you how to take steps to bring your family together for food, fun, and conversation. There is no one-size-fits-all when it comes to family dinner, so we've come up with suggestions for many scenarios and challenges based on our experiences working with families across America.* This book provides a number of examples of how real families make dinner happen in their homes.

We think TFDP's first core principle is the most important and the key to moving forward: This is not about perfect. If you can make small improvements that result in eating together as a family, you're doing great. Instead of another mountain to climb, you'll have a real oasis for your family.

Lynn Barendsen; Brianne DeRosa; Anne K. Fishel, PhD; Shelly London; and Cindil Redick-Ponte

*In the following family stories, some pseudonyms have been used by request.

INTRODUCTION

By Anne K. Fishel, PhD

Before phoning her ex-husband about their co-parenting plans this week, Jill needs to check whether she's scheduled to work nights at her nursing job. She wants to make sure that their eight-year-old son, Henry, will be having dinner every evening with either his mom or dad. Getting the co-parenting plan in place is the easy part. The real challenge is dinner. Too often, she and Henry run out of things to talk about in the first five minutes. When she asks about his school day, she's met with the universal answer. "He tells me 'fine,' and then we might be quiet for the rest of the meal," Jill says. "It's not very lively or interesting with just two people at the table." A lot of nights, they flip on the TV or each bring a book to the meal and read silently. Jill wishes that dinner could feel more enjoyable and valuable, rather than two people just trying to get through it.

Ellen and Brian are parents to three teenage children. The couple works in the city and, at the end of each day, brave an hour of traffic to get home. They arrive at their suburban house exhausted and often cranky. The kids juggle their own after-school jobs, as well as music lessons, soccer practice, and drama rehearsals. It's a rare night when all five are home at the dinner hour. Although Ellen and Brian both grew up enjoying nightly family dinners, they are at a loss as to how to make them happen for their family. "I really hate to cook, and what's the point if everyone is too busy to sit down together?" Ellen says. Brian adds, "I think that teenagers would rather just eat in their room, playing a game, texting with a friend. They need time to decompress too." Most nights, someone picks up take-out food on the way home and each family member eats alone, usually in front of a TV or computer.

Whether urban or suburban, small or big, economically comfortable or struggling, families across America find it challenging to have dinner together. If you are one of them, this book is for you.

For so many people, the mere thought of family dinner—planning, cooking, and wrangling—brings a sense of dread. Parents have demanding work schedules, often getting home exhausted. Kids have never been more scheduled and bogged down with homework, sports, and rehearsals. We are a busy, hurried, tired people. It's no wonder that dinner often ends up on the back burner, despite parents' best intentions to find time to talk and relax together over a shared nightly meal.

So even though the vast majority in a recent survey of thousands of parents endorsed the idea that eating family dinners together is a good idea, fewer than half

of American families will actually be gathering around the table tonight or any night this week. In the United States, about 70 percent of meals are eaten outside the home and about 20 percent are eaten in the car.[1]

We've written this book to make family dinners doable and enjoyable. Our simple, practical blueprints were created based on our work with thousands of families across the United States. We've done a ton of heavy lifting so you don't have to.

HOW DID WE GET HERE?

In 2010, a band of people from a range of backgrounds—parents, non-parents, and grandparents; single and married; and with collective professional experience that included education, family therapy, conflict resolution, research, food, design, social work, marketing, and communication—gathered in Cambridge, Massachusetts. We were united by the desire to unlock the many benefits of family dinners, and to provide practical resources, inspiration, and family-tested tips online and in person to families across the country. We wanted to help people like you—that is, busy, overwhelmed parents—feel that a family dinner was well within your reach. Not a gourmet extravaganza with heirloom vegetables and perfect table manners, but a "good-enough" meal with plenty of ways to make the atmosphere warm and engaging. We created The Family Dinner Project to help you and your family connect over food, fun, and conversation about things that matter.

I am proud to say that I was one of those original founders of The Family Dinner Project. As a family therapist for thirty years, I have been a longtime advocate of family dinners, going so far as to profess that I could almost be out of business if family dinners were more prevalent.[2] That's because dinners are essential to a family's mental health. The research backs me up. Twenty years of scientific studies document that nightly dinners are good for

the body, brain, and spirit of family members. Let's take a quick spin through the science that supports these benefits.

Good for the Body

For starters, home-cooked dinners tend to have fewer calories and smaller portions than restaurant or take-out meals. Plus, when we eat at home, we're less likely to consume fried and fatty foods, or to wash down our meal with a sugary soft drink. It's not just what we skip by eating at home, but what we're more likely to eat: Kids who eat family dinners consume more fruits, vegetables, protein, fiber, and vitamins.[3] Researchers have even linked family dinners to lower rates of obesity.[4]

While these nutritional benefits may seem quite obvious, others are more surprising. Some studies show a connection between regular family dinners and reduction of symptoms in medical conditions such as asthma.[5] There are several possible explanations for this. Children who eat nightly dinners have lower levels of anxiety—a symptom sometimes associated with asthma—and parents have a nightly opportunity to check in with their child about medication compliance. Yet another explanation: Home-cooked meals have fewer preservatives, a significant asthma-inducing allergen.

Teens who eat at home have better cardiovascular health.[6] Health benefits continue paying dividends into early adulthood. Kids who grow up eating with their families go on to be young adults who eat healthfully and are less likely to be overweight.[7] So family dinners during childhood are an investment in lifelong health.

Good for the Brain

There are cognitive benefits associated with family dinner for children of all ages. Yes, it may contribute to smarter kids! For young kids, conversation at the dinner table is a great vocabulary booster—even better than reading aloud.[8] Consider this: When parents recount their days or discuss current events, they use ten times as many advanced words compared to the vocabulary in picture books. Even young children can decipher the meaning of sophisticated words by hearing them in the context of a story. When my kids were preschoolers, I recounted the following anecdote to them: "Coming home today from the subway, I slipped on a patch of ice and bruised my knee. A postal clerk was passing by and helped me up. I was pretty shaken up, and he tried to console me. He even reached in his satchel and pulled out a dog biscuit!" "Postal clerk," "bruise," "shaken up," "console," "satchel," and "biscuit" are not commonly heard by preschoolers, but they are understandable in the context of this little story. As an extra bonus, children who know more words tend to read earlier and more easily than kids with slimmer vocabularies.[9]

Yet another benefit is academic performance. Eating regular family dinners is associated with higher grades and achievement scores in school-aged children.[10] Having regular family dinners is a stronger predictor of academic accomplishment than doing homework, playing sports, or making art.[11] Researchers report that teens who eat dinner at home five to seven times a week are twice as likely to earn As in school, compared to those who eat with their families fewer than three times a week.[12]

Good for the Spirit

A pile of studies links regular family dinners to reductions in high-risk teenage behaviors such as substance abuse,[13] smoking, eating disorders,[14] and behavioral problems in school.[15] In one large-scale study of teens, researchers found that regular family dinners were also associated with lower rates of depression and suicidal thoughts.[16] Another study found that teens who had been victims of cyberbullying bounced back more quickly if they participated in nightly family meals.[17]

Dinners with the family have been found to be a more powerful deterrent against high-risk adolescent behaviors than church attendance or getting good grades.[18]

It's not just that family dinners curtail dangerous behaviors—they also promote positive ones. When adolescents have frequent family dinners, they are more likely to have an upbeat mood and a more optimistic view of the future as compared to their peers who don't eat with parents.[19]

WHY DOES FAMILY DINNER HAVE SUCH AN IMPACT?

The secret sauce of family dinner isn't a juicy roast chicken, a perfectly cooked lasagna, or any kind of sauce. It's actually not about specific foods at all. The real power of family dinner is that it provides a reliable time for parents and kids to connect with one another. Think about it: You separate from your kids each morning and spend about eight to ten hours apart. To eat dinner together is to reconvene, to talk and learn about one another. Dinnertime can be an opportunity for you to detect early problems or conflicts in your child's life. And if you and your child spend a good deal of time communicating via text message, it's a chance for face-to-face conversation. Children who feel known by their parents, who have a chance to talk and feel heard, are less prone to depression and anxiety.[20]

Dinner is also a great forum for you and your kids to tell stories, which is the main way we all make sense of the world. Researchers have found that children who know the stories of their own families are more resilient and have higher self-esteem.[21] Stories about family members who have overcome adversity, fallen in love, immigrated to a new country, had a mischievous pet, lost a job, or started fresh—all these can help kids feel connected to something bigger than themselves. When your kids are young, they often enjoy hearing stories from your childhood. Family stories

offer kids perspective about paths and choices they can take—and proof that adults didn't arrive in the world all-knowing and fully capable. Embedded in stories are lessons about mistakes, risks, and growth. And, of course, stories are an opportunity for humor and laughter.

As an extra bonus, kids who know how to *tell* stories are also better readers. To draw kids out, ask lots of "how" and "why" questions, rather than questions that can be answered simply with yes or no. In addition, to build empathy and emotional intelligence, asking questions about how people feel helps cultivate a child's storytelling abilities.

WHAT *IS* A FAMILY DINNER, ANYWAY?

Many parents wonder what "counts" as a family dinner and if they are doing enough to get the benefits. Here are some questions I've been asked at community dinners and in my family therapy practice:

1. What if only one parent is home for dinner?

A ten-year-old boy whose father was deployed to Iraq asked me at a community dinner held at the Hanscom Air Force Base, "Does it count as family dinner with my father away?" I told him emphatically, "Of course! It's a family dinner with you and your mother at the table." As long as there are two family members eating together, experiencing connection, and enjoying one another, that is a family dinner. And it can include extended family!

2. What if it's take out?

If the meal is eaten with conversation and storytelling, it's a family dinner. A take-out dinner may not have the same nutritional value as a home-cooked meal because restaurant food tends to be higher in fat, salt, and sugar. But remember that the food is secondary. The human interaction and connection are paramount.

3. What if the TV is on?

Research suggests that kids tend to eat more calories and fewer fruits and vegetables when the TV is on.[22] And when the TV is on, or when family members are constantly checking their gadgets, it detracts from everyone feeling that they are important and worth listening to. If you and your family occasionally watch a TV program during dinner (such as a special event), or watch the news together, that can be a natural opportunity to spark conversation beyond the usual school day report.

4. What if we can only pull off having dinner once a week, but the research says that it should be five times a week? Should we just forget about it?

No! Often when families have one great meal or one "good enough" meal, they find that they want to have more of them. Even one positive dinner a week can be very beneficial to you and your family.

5. Does it have to be dinner?

No, it doesn't! In any average week, there are at least sixteen possible times for families to eat together: seven breakfasts, seven dinners, and two weekend lunches. A nighttime snack when you and your kids take a break together, eat fruit, and sip hot chocolate, for example, is another chance to connect and enjoy one another. The goal is not to achieve a magic number. The goal is to find as many opportunities as you can and to make the most of them.

WHAT GETS IN THE WAY AND WHAT HAVE WE LEARNED FROM FAMILIES AND RESEARCHERS?

The impediments to family dinner are pretty universal, regardless of income, family composition, or ages of children. These obstacles will almost certainly be familiar:

- Lack of time.
- The hard work of making dinner.

- Picky eaters.
- Too much tension and conflict at the table.
- Teens not wanting to eat with their parents.

The research summarized at the beginning of this introduction provides the answers to *why* family dinners are so important. At community dinners held by The Family Dinner Project in firehouses, schools, clinics, libraries, military bases, homeless shelters, and after school programs, we've talked to thousands of parents about *how* they've overcome these common obstacles. While the meat of this book—the fifty-two weeks of recipes, games, and conversations from real families—provides many creative solutions, here is an appetizer, a preview of some of those work-arounds.

1. There's just no time.

Kids and parents both feel rushed, stretched thin by hectic work and school schedules, and exhausted by screens that keep us tethered to work around the clock. Against this sped-up backdrop, we need a chance to slow down and decompress more than ever. And to state the obvious, we all have to eat to live, so why not make the most of that fact and eat together?

FLEXIBLE COURSES

If one parent can't get home until 8:00, and there are small children who get hungry by 5:00, you might want to consider feeding your family in overlapping shifts. For example, offer your kids a plate of cut-up vegetables, cheese, and some fruit. Then they can be invited to join a full dinner later with you and/or your partner. Or, the kids could eat a whole dinner earlier and the family can sit down together for dessert.

Don't forget breakfast or late-night snack.

We're quite partial to dinner, but any chance for food, fun, and conversation that is reliable and regular may work better for some families. Several years ago, we realized that if you don't hit the "snooze" on your alarm clock in the morning, there are seven additional minutes for breakfast. We came up with a breakfast program that includes:

- A piece of toast smeared with peanut butter and decorated like an animal with fruit pieces, or a make-it-yourself yogurt parfait.
- A morning playlist of favorite songs, or note pads on the table to write notes for one another's lunch boxes.
- Look-ahead conversation starters, like forecasting the day with weather analogies.

Additionally, families have often found that making breakfast foods like pancakes or scrambled eggs for dinner can be a big time-saver and stress reliever—and kids love the switcheroo.

PUSH BACK ON THE CULTURE OF COMMITMENTS

Some families get together and take a stand against excessive time commitments at their kids' schools. We've met some who talked to a soccer coach or band leader to ask if the schedule could be changed so that kids could participate in family dinners. We've heard of parents insisting that their children let go of an activity that meets during the dinner hour because the nightly mealtime is more important than an extracurricular activity. If your family is feeling overbooked, you may want to review your commitments and see if any can be adjusted.

2. It's too much work.

Historically, women have shouldered the lion's share of family prep. Today, men are much more likely to participate. Between 1965 and 2008, men nearly doubled the amount of time they spent cooking; 42 percent of men now cook.[23] Of course, total equality in the kitchen has not been achieved, but family dinner can provide an opportunity to move in that direction. It's a good idea to get your kids to help out too, both to teach them life-sustaining skills of cooking and because it's good for their well-being. In a survey of 1,000 children ages eight to eighteen, researchers found that kids' participation in clean-up was correlated with good feelings.[24] In fact, pitching in on the workload was found to be as helpful as having a good conversation.[25] Since the main benefits of family dinner come from what happens once the food comes to the table, here are some ideas about how to lighten the labor.

MAKE DOUBLE BATCHES

This is a practice used by many families to great success. Over the weekend or on a night when there is a little extra time and energy, make a double or triple batch of a soup, stew, or chili. Freeze the extra batches. Then, when the meal is defrosted the following week, it's as though you have a sous chef who did the work for you.

COOK WITH WHAT'S ON HAND

If you get in the habit of keeping your pantry stocked with staples such as pasta, tomato sauce, Parmesan cheese, eggs, rice, and lemons, prep time can be dramatically reduced. Every cook needs to have a few meals that can be thrown together with essentials that put you completely at ease and eliminate the need for a cookbook or grocery store run. Sauté an onion and whatever veggies you have on hand, crack some eggs into the pan, shred some cheese, and pop the whole thing in the oven for ten minutes. This is a one-pan meal I can make in my sleep. Many parents have a trusty, go-to pasta dish, or a farro or rice bowl with leftover vegetables that will do in a pinch.

USE SHORTCUTS

Since the benefits of family dinner don't depend on food being made from scratch, why not use some shortcuts, like store-bought rotisserie chicken, pre-cut vegetables, or frozen pizza dough? Lots of families have come to rely on slow cookers and instant pots, which can be huge time savers. And it's hard to argue with any meal that comes from a single pot and reduces cleanup!

3. My family has "picky eaters," and I can't figure out how to make one meal for everyone.

About 14 to 20 percent of parents report that preschoolers are often or always selective with their food.[26] Sometimes there are medical or developmental reasons for selective eating, but those tend to be the exception.

Broadly speaking, young children have very little control over their lives, and food is one arena where they can exercise some agency. If there are no medical reasons for your child's pickiness, here are some strategies to try.

KEEP FOOD TALK TO A MINIMUM

The best advice I've heard about picky eating came from a nutritionist, Ellyn Satter, who suggests that it's a parent's job to choose *what* healthy food to serve, and *when* and *where* it's going to be eaten. But it's a child's job to decide *whether* and *how much* to eat.[27] Even though it can be challenging, parents should try to refrain from commenting about how much or how little is being eaten. In fact, the less said about the food, the better. Even seemingly positive commentary can backfire, as it can be heard as taking charge of the eating experience, rather than letting kids decide for themselves what and how much they want to eat.

MODEL YOUR ENJOYMENT

As a parent, you are a model and guide for your child in terms of discerning what's safe, interesting, and worthwhile. This extends to the dinner table. When you eat a broad range of food and do so with gusto and enthusiasm, your kids will often follow along. At the very least, if you rave about a food, you can often prompt your child to take a bite or two of something new.

DON'T REWARD "GOOD" FOODS WITH DESSERT

It's one of the most instinctive things to do as a parent: Reward kids with dessert. But when you resort to bribing, cajoling, or rewarding, there's inevitably more tension at the table, and things can quickly get derailed. Researchers say that when kids are told that if they eat their peas, they can have ice cream for dessert, there is a double whammy—the peas become less desirable and the ice cream more so.[28]

MAKE THE STRANGE FAMILIAR

Children like familiar foods. That's why they smile as infants when they taste something they were exposed to *in utero*.[29] It is also why nutritionists offer the Rule of Fifteen—children need to see a food show up on their plate as many as fifteen times before parents should give up on offering it.[30] After a food shows up that many times, it can start to feel like an old friend. You may also use an everyday food as a bridge to a new food. If your child likes strawberries, he may also like raspberries, or if she happily eats string beans, she may try a few carrots that are accompanying those string beans. Even if your child initially picks out the interloping carrots, these new vegetables will be more recognizable and less suspect.

DESCRIBE THE NEW TASTE

Ask your child to offer three words to describe the new food. In asking this question, you're focusing your child's attention on the food rather than allowing her to automatically reject it.

ENCOURAGE TACTILE PLAY OF FOOD

Encourage young children to play with food, like smearing oil on vegetables for roasting, making dough into letters, or putting raspberries onto their fingertips. Studies have shown that playing with food can lead to kids being less fearful of trying new foods.[31]

INTRODUCE NEW FOODS EARLY

Food pickiness tends to peak during toddlerhood, so try to introduce new foods as early as possible. If your child becomes more selective from ages three to eight, try not to label him or her as picky, but remember to keep offering new foods and expect that tastes may change over time. The key is not to stop exposing your child to new foods and flavors.

INVOLVE KIDS AS STAKEHOLDERS

Children who participate in any aspect of food preparation—picking the herbs from a plant, choosing a recipe, going to the grocery store, helping to cook, setting the table, or clearing the dishes—are more likely to want to eat the meal on offer. In a Columbia University study of 600 kids ages five to eleven, those who took part in a cooking class were much more likely to eat the foods they had made than those who didn't take the class.[32]

CUSTOMIZE MEALS

Rather than becoming a short-order cook trying to please several picky palettes, try making a basic dish that can be customized or altered by each person. We love crêpes, tacos, pizzas, or a basic rice soup for this reason. All of these can be a base that everyone in the family can personalize to their tastes. An extra bonus here is that a selective eater can be exposed to a range of foods, which will hopefully become familiar and inviting over time.

CUT DOWN ON SNACKING

This is the number-one recommendation given by pediatricians. We are a culture of snackers. Snacking by children has been on the rise and may be the reason for increased pickiness.[33] Simply put, if your kids come to dinner hungry, they are more likely to eat what is served.

STAY OUT OF FOOD STRUGGLES

Many parents have told us that when a child doesn't like the meal on offer, they offer a dull alternative. The alternative should be something that the child can get or make himself, such as yogurt with fruit or a bowl of cereal. And you might want to set limits on how many times per week a child can go with the alternative so that children hold on to the expectation that they will enjoy what parents offer.

4. It's just not fun to have dinner—we have tension and conflict.

The benefits of dinner really depend on a warm atmosphere at the table that gives opportunities for everyone to talk, be heard, and feel accepted. It shouldn't feel like detention. Conflicts about the food, tensions about gadget use at the table, and over-vigilance about manners can all cause discord. For most families, playing games, discussing thought-provoking topics, and telling stories can keep the focus on enjoyment. For some families, larger issues such as abusive behavior or addiction bring unpredictability and anger outbursts to the family dinner table that undermine any benefits to family members. Family dinner alone will not solve these problems; substance abuse treatment or other forms of therapy will be needed before children and adults can enjoy a nightly meal together. Still, many of these tips can be adapted to fit most families so that tension can be reduced while the focus is placed on having fun and lively conversations.

GET AGREEMENT ON MEALS

It's hard enough to put food on the table night after night, but when your efforts are met with belly-aching about the dinner, it's extremely frustrating and dispiriting. One approach to stave off food complaints is to compile a list of "family faves," meals that everyone agrees they genuinely enjoy. The list can be posted on the fridge and updated from time to time as tastes change.

GO EASY ON TEACHING MANNERS

It's hard for kids to relax at dinner if they are constantly being corrected. And it's tiresome for you to be the manners police. I think what's most important is to limit the manners monitoring to the ones that promote respectful listening and speaking, like not interrupting or not talking with your mouth full. These are behaviors that all of you can work on, so the kids don't have to be singled out.

AVOID TOPICS THAT USUALLY RESULT IN FIGHTS

You can establish a ground rule at the table to "stay away from the bummers." It's better to discuss hot-button things like a poor grade, a missed curfew, or a messy room after dinner, on a full stomach, without an audience. Remind yourself that dinner is a time to reconnect with your child, make memories, and form bonds. That said, many kids can find things to tussle about no matter how benign the conversation topics. When tensions start to rise, you can ask everyone to hit the pause button: "Bummer alert! Let's talk about something else!" If things escalate, try saying, "Let's all talk a deep breath or walk around the room for a minute."

PLAY GAMES

Games, particularly non-competitive ones, can be jump-starters to conversation at the table and give children as well as adults a chance to relax and have fun. Some games offer an alternative to asking "How was your day?" For example, in Two Truths and a Tall Tale, players tell three stories, two about the day and one that's made up. Everyone guesses which one is fictional. Throughout this book, there are games to accompany every recipe. They're for every age and for gatherings of any size.

5. Our teens would rather watch their screens or eat with their friends than with us.

A moody teen who refuses to talk is a common pop-culture cliché. But scientific surveys of thousands of teens paint a different picture. Most teens actually value their relationships with parents and want to spend time with them.[34] This is also true at dinner. About 80 percent of teenagers report that they'd rather have dinner with their families than by themselves or with friends.[35] And when adolescents are asked to list their favorite activities, family dinner ranks high on that list.[36]

TALK WITH YOUR TEENS

Teens say that dinnertime is the time of day when they're most likely to talk with their parents. Time in the car is second best, but that's usually without the benefit of eye contact and without other family members aboard. Having a nightly opportunity to connect offers a life raft on the stormy seas of adolescence, and it may explain the protective function of family dinners in reducing high-risk behaviors in teens.

USE DINNER AS A BRIDGE TO THEIR WORLDS

One of the pleasures of parenting teens is allowing them to expand your world by learning about their music, interests, and friends. Though it may seem daunting, encourage your teens to participate in making dinner, or make one on their own. It could be something that he or she ate from a food truck, had at a friend's house, or saw on a cooking show. Your adolescent may want to make something from a cuisine that is new to the family, or share a new vegan dish. They may be willing to make a playlist of their favorite songs to play during dinner or clean-up, and even talk about some of these choices. In addition, you and your teenagers might like to create a weekly ritual where they invite a friend to dinner or dessert.

SHARE YOUR OWN DAILY DILEMMAS

Your teens benefit from you sharing your real-life challenges, particularly as these challenges resonate with theirs. When your child receives a disappointing grade, it's a chance for you to share your own brush with setbacks. Teen years are a time when kids often feel a greater distance from parents. Narrow the distance by humanizing yourself, being vulnerable, and sharing difficulties from your own teen years. You might also choose to share a dilemma faced at work, such as misfiring an email to a group meant to go to just one person. Seek your teen's opinion. Ask, "What would you have done?"

LIMIT TECHNOLOGY AND AGREE ON RULES

In a recent survey about technology use, parents were found to use screens at the dinner table twice as often as their children.[37] A starting point at the dinner table is for parents and kids to agree on the rules. For some families, there may be a strict no-tech policy, with the idea that dinner should be a time when you focus on each other. You might agree to use technology in a limited fashion—such as consulting phones to resolve factual disagreements that come up at dinner—while others may share interesting photos or emails at the table as a way to talk about their days.

ONTO THE BOOK
At The Family Dinner Project, we frequently hear stories from families about their resourceful, often ingenious hacks to these common obstacles. In this book, you will read some of these stories. We're confident you will be inspired, as we have been, by the many creative strategies used by families to make dinner happen despite feeling tired, overworked, challenged by different palates, or uncertain that their teens really want to dine with them. Getting dinner planned, shopped for, cooked, and cleaned up night after night can strain your stamina, resources, and patience. But we've learned that even small changes that allow for family dinner will help you reap the many benefits of a shared meal. You'll feel connected and maybe even energized. This is why we're arming you with easy, affordable ways to keep at this worthwhile—if sometimes tedious—pursuit.

Since it is food that brings families to the table, we offer you fifty-two weeks of delicious recipes. These recipes are from TFDP team members and from families who have participated in The Family Dinner Project. Most can be made in under thirty minutes! But this is more than just a cookbook. Once the meal is taken care of, you and your family will reap all the other benefits to body, brain, and spirit that derive from the atmosphere at the table. To help you better enjoy your dinners, have more fun, and engage in stimulating, interesting, and meaningful conversations, we've included a game to play and a conversation starter to accompany each week of recipes in this book.

There will always be days and dinners that are harder than others. But we believe that we can make family dinner easier for you. Take heart in knowing that any incremental changes that help bring your family together over a shared meal are providing an array of wonderful benefits that go way beyond the table.

PART I
THEY'RE TOO PICKY!

Picky eating. As a parent, you may read this and think, "Is there any other kind?" Kids who don't discriminate against some (or even many) foods are the exception. Ask any parent and most can reel off their child's "no-fly zone" foods. Just because food pickiness is common doesn't mean there are easy solutions. Parents often tell us that wrangling fussy taste buds can zap all the joy out of family dinner.

Over the years, we've developed some smart tips for helping manage this very common phase of childhood. Many of them come from families we've met who have their own brilliant solutions for minimizing or eliminating picky-eating drama. Try some of these ideas at your table and see how your family dinners change when you're not battling over every bite.

LET EVERYONE BUILD THEIR OWN DINNERS

Andrea and Matthew were tired of the dinner table battles with their picky preschoolers. "Many times, I will make a meal only to have the kids refuse it, which sends me back into the kitchen to make another meal I know they will eat. It's exhausting making two meals every night!" As a military family constantly juggling the realities of unpredictable schedules, possible deployments, and work with on-base family organizations, they had only so much energy left to devote to dinnertime debates.

If you've ever watched a family member pick through a dish to try to remove the smallest speck of onion, then you know how irritating it can be—for both adults and kids—to have a lovingly prepared meal met with "I don't like this!" But as Andrea and Matthew discovered, allowing their picky little ones to have some choices at meals made dinner more peaceful for the whole family. "Instead of trying to force [them] to eat the one vegetable I prepared, they can choose between a couple of different options. They might only eat a bite or two, but I consider that a success!" Andrea said.

Build-your-own dinners reduce stress for the cook while making dinner seem more appealing to selective diners. Everyone is encouraged to make their own choices from an array of options, relieving you of having to make two separate dinners. From tacos to salad bars, sandwiches to pizzas, you'll find plenty of ideas in this section for creative and healthy dinners that put everyone at the table in control of their own dinner destiny.

FOOD

Start with this totally customizable dinner of lettuce wraps that your family can fill with chicken and noodles. Stir-frying vegetables in batches is quick and lets you work with one ingredient at a time, so no one ends up having to pick around something they don't want. Finish the meal with personalized pineapple "sundaes" so irresistible, no one will miss the ice cream.

CHICKEN NOODLE LETTUCE WRAPS

SERVES 4-6

These Asian-inspired wraps are quick and easy to make, thanks to the use of rice noodles. We call for mushrooms and carrots in the recipe, but you can use your family's favorites or provide a variety of toppings so everyone at the table can customize their own lettuce wraps!

INGREDIENTS

2 tablespoons coconut oil

1 1/2 pounds boneless, skinless chicken breasts or thighs, cut into 1 inch cubes

4 cloves garlic, minced

12 ounces fresh mushrooms (any variety), sliced

4 ounces brown rice noodles (sometimes called mei fun noodles)

1/4 cup soy sauce, preferably low sodium

2 tablespoons honey

1 head romaine lettuce

1 cup shredded carrots

INSTRUCTIONS

Heat the coconut oil in a large skillet over medium-high heat. Add the chicken and garlic. Sauté for 3–4 minutes until the chicken starts to turn opaque.

Add the mushrooms, stir, and continue to sauté until the chicken is fully cooked, about 8 minutes total.

While the chicken is cooking, place the rice noodles in a large bowl and pour boiling water over them until they're fully covered. Cover the bowl (a dinner plate works well for this) and allow the noodles to steep in the hot water until they're cooked, about 5 minutes. Drain thoroughly.

Whisk the soy sauce and honey together and pour over the chicken mixture. Add the cooked noodles and toss to combine.

Fill individual lettuce leaves with the chicken and noodle mixture. Top with shredded carrots or whatever other toppings your family enjoys.

STIR-FRIED VEGETABLES
SERVES 4-6

In this stir-fry recipe, we're recommending you cook each vegetable separately so that you can plate and present them individually and let family members combine them as they like. You can certainly cook them all together in one big batch if that suits you.

INGREDIENTS

3 tablespoons canola or vegetable oil, divided

1 large red bell pepper, julienned

2 cups snow peas

1 medium zucchini, thinly sliced

2 cloves garlic, minced

2 teaspoons fresh ginger, grated

1/2 cup soy sauce

INSTRUCTIONS

Heat 1 tablespoon of oil in a large skillet just until shimmering. Add the bell pepper strips and cook, stirring constantly, for 2–3 minutes or just until pierceable with a fork but still firm. Remove the bell peppers to a bowl and set aside.

Add another tablespoon of oil to the skillet and heat until shimmering. Stir-fry the snow peas for 3–4 minutes until pierceable but firm, and remove to a separate bowl.

Heat the final tablespoon of oil in the skillet and stir-fry the zucchini slices for 1–2 minutes until softened. Remove to a bowl and set aside.

Add garlic, ginger, and soy sauce to the hot skillet. Cook the sauce for 2 minutes, stirring constantly to prevent sticking. Divide the warm sauce evenly between the three different bowls of vegetables and toss to coat before serving.

PINEAPPLE SUNDAES
SERVES 4

These pineapple sundaes are fun and indulgent. You can experiment with some of the flavors—try raspberry jam instead of strawberry, different types of chopped nuts (or other crunchy toppings if there are allergies), hot fudge instead of chocolate hazelnut spread, and so on.

INGREDIENTS

1 cup plain Greek yogurt

2 tablespoons strawberry jam

4 rings cored pineapple, fresh or canned

1/2 cup chocolate hazelnut spread

1/4 cup toasted cashews, chopped

INSTRUCTIONS

In a small bowl, mix together the Greek yogurt and strawberry jam until combined.

Microwave the chocolate hazelnut spread for 45 seconds to 1 minute, just until pourable.

Place one pineapple ring on a plate or in a wide, shallow bowl. Scoop about 1/4 cup of the yogurt mixture into the center of the ring.

Drizzle 2 tablespoons of the chocolate hazelnut spread over the yogurt and pineapple ring, then top with a sprinkling of chopped nuts.

FUN Since we live in an era of ratings ("Please rate your experience . . ."), encourage your kids to rate their meals. This can turn dinnertime complaints into constructive comments when kids can play "restaurant critic." It allows them to share their opinions about foods they like and dislike, but helps them articulate their thoughts beyond "I like/don't like this."

HOW TO PLAY

Give each person at the table a comment card and pencil. You can use index cards or scrap paper. Have them answer the following questions:

What Do You Think of This Dish?

1 = No, Thank You

2 = I Would Give It Another Try

3 = It's Okay

4 = I Like It

5 = I Love It!

What do you like best about this dish?

What would make this dish better?

Go around the table and let everyone share their responses.

CONVERSATION

Though it's hard, try to remember that picky eating in children is often only partly about the food. More often it stems from a desire for kids to take control and make their own choices. We developed these conversation starters with the concept of choice in mind.

(AGES: 2-13)

- If you could choose different names for your pets or stuffed animals, what would you suggest?

- If you did the grocery shopping, what would you choose to buy?

- What are three things you have to do every day, whether you like it or not? What would happen if you chose not to do those things?

- If you could eat only one food for the rest of your life, what food would you choose? Why is it important that we eat more than just our one or two favorites all the time?

- Have you ever made a decision that you wished you could go back and change later? What was it? What different choice would you have made?

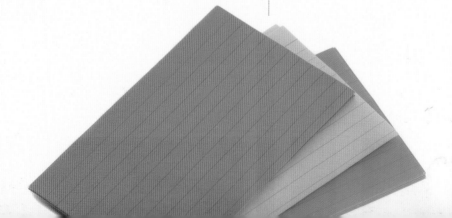

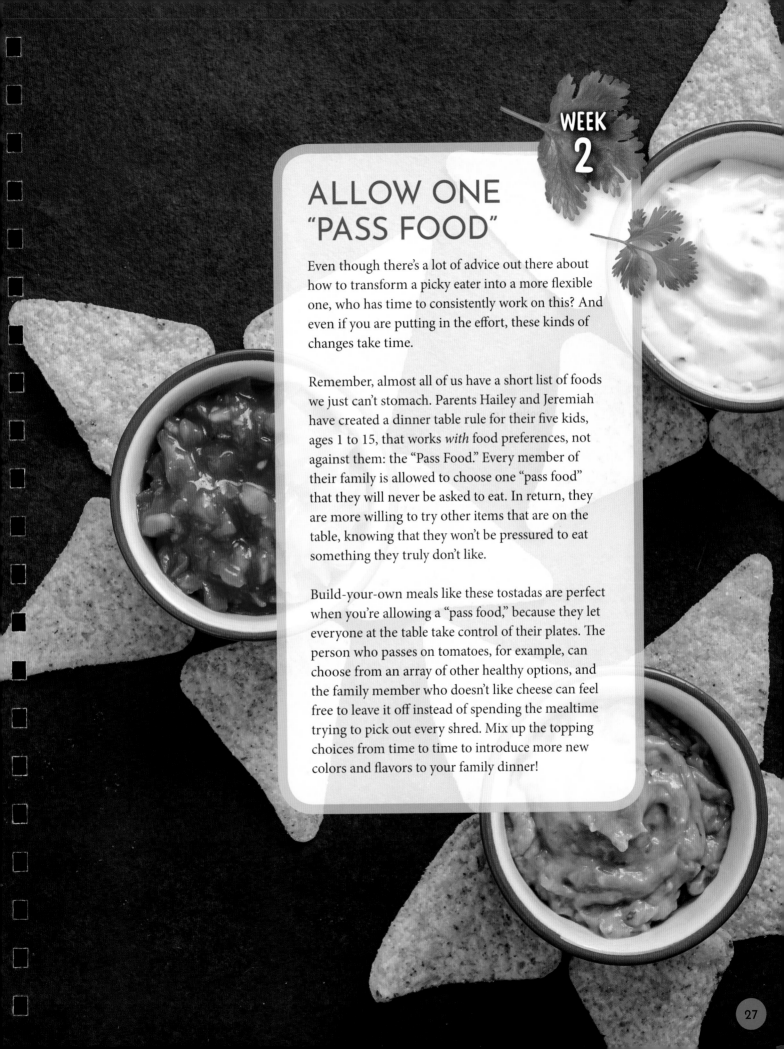

ALLOW ONE "PASS FOOD"

Even though there's a lot of advice out there about how to transform a picky eater into a more flexible one, who has time to consistently work on this? And even if you are putting in the effort, these kinds of changes take time.

Remember, almost all of us have a short list of foods we just can't stomach. Parents Hailey and Jeremiah have created a dinner table rule for their five kids, ages 1 to 15, that works *with* food preferences, not against them: the "Pass Food." Every member of their family is allowed to choose one "pass food" that they will never be asked to eat. In return, they are more willing to try other items that are on the table, knowing that they won't be pressured to eat something they truly don't like.

Build-your-own meals like these tostadas are perfect when you're allowing a "pass food," because they let everyone at the table take control of their plates. The person who passes on tomatoes, for example, can choose from an array of other healthy options, and the family member who doesn't like cheese can feel free to leave it off instead of spending the mealtime trying to pick out every shred. Mix up the topping choices from time to time to introduce more new colors and flavors to your family dinner!

FOOD
Consider the topping suggestions for these tostadas just a guideline, and feel free to substitute similar items that your family might prefer. We suggest serving the tostadas with a colorful and easy slaw that you can make up to two days ahead of time. Finish the meal with a plate of apple "nachos" for dessert that can be customized to your family's tastes.

TOSTADAS
`SERVES 6`

With tostadas, everyone gets access to the same ingredients, but each person picks only the ones that he or she wants. The toppings listed here are suggestions only. You can add anything you like, including avocado, different types of beans and cheeses, leftover meats, and lots of different vegetables.

INGREDIENTS

1/2 cup vegetable oil

12 corn tortillas

2 15-ounce cans refried beans

8 ounces shredded Monterey Jack cheese

4 cups shredded lettuce

2 medium tomatoes, chopped

2 avocados, chopped

Salsa

Sour cream

INSTRUCTIONS

Heat oil in a heavy skillet on medium-high heat. When oil is hot (a drop of water immediately sizzles), place one or two tortillas in the pan. Turn them over soon after adding to the oil, and every minute or so until crisp and slightly browned. Each tortilla will take 3–4 minutes. After removing tortillas from the oil, lay them on a paper towel to drain.

Warm beans over low heat, stirring frequently.

When beans are hot, spread 1–2 tablespoons on each fried tortilla. Place bean-covered tortillas on each person's plate.

Arrange cheese, lettuce, tomatoes, salsa, sour cream, and any other condiments in bowls. Let your family members create a masterpiece.

LiME CONFETTi SLAW
SERVES 6-8

This slaw can be made up to two days ahead of time and refrigerated. The flavors get better as it sits, so it's worth making in advance. Besides, having the slaw ready to go means that dinner can be made in a snap.

INGREDIENTS

1 small head cabbage, shredded

1 head radicchio, shredded

4 carrots, peeled and shredded

2 red bell peppers, julienned

3 green onions, thinly sliced

1/4 cup chopped cilantro

Juice of 2 limes

1/2 cup mayonnaise

2 tablespoons olive oil

Salt and pepper to taste

INSTRUCTIONS

Mix together the vegetables and herbs.

In a jar, shake together the lime juice, mayonnaise, and olive oil. Add salt and pepper to taste.

Combine the dressing with the vegetables. Serve immediately or cover and refrigerate.

APPLE NACHOS
SERVES 4

These apple "nachos" are a sweet treat for dessert or a family snack. Have fun experimenting with different toppings to find the combinations your family likes best.

INGREDIENTS

2 medium apples, sliced

1/2 cup peanut butter

Chocolate or caramel syrup (optional)

2/3 cup chopped strawberries, raspberries, or both

1/3 cup miniature chocolate chips

1/4 cup roasted sunflower seeds

INSTRUCTIONS

Arrange the apple slices on a large plate as if layering tortilla chips for nachos.

Microwave the peanut butter between one and one-and-a-half minutes, stirring every thirty seconds, just until pourable.

Drizzle the warm peanut butter all over the apples. Add drizzles of chocolate or caramel syrup, if using.

Let family members top the "nachos" with fruit, chocolate chips, sunflower seeds, and any other topping choices you can think of.

FUN

One of our most popular table game suggestions is "Would You Rather?" Kids and adults of all ages love to squirm as the scenarios get more difficult, and the sillier the choice, the better! To add another dimension to the game, ask everyone at the table to explain their choice.

HOW TO PLAY

Choose scenarios from our list or make up your own. Take turns asking "Would You Rather" questions and letting others answer.

Would You Rather . . . ?

. . . own your own boat or your own plane?

. . . sweat melted cheese or always smell a skunk?

. . . be able to fly or be invisible?

. . . speak every language in the world or play every instrument?

. . . live in the future or in the past?

. . . be the best player on a losing team or the worst player on a winning team?

. . . live in the city or the country?

. . . walk the Great Wall of China or float down the Amazon River?

. . . live without a telephone or a television?

. . . meet the president of the United States or your favorite movie star?

. . . be a rabbit or a horse?

. . . go to the beach or go skiing?

. . . be famous and poor or be unknown and rich?

. . . win an Academy Award or an Olympic Gold Medal?

. . . take a vacation on an exotic island or in a romantic city?

. . . eat a bowl full of crickets or a bowl full of worms?

. . . lose your sense of taste or your sense of smell?

. . . raise chickens for eggs or sheep for wool?

. . . live on a houseboat or in an RV?

. . . live in space or under the sea?

. . . have feet for hands or hands for feet?

. . . have a head twice as big or half as small as the one you have now?

. . . be totally covered in hair head to toe or completely bald?

. . . shoot spaghetti out of your fingers or sneeze meatballs?

. . . always have to enter rooms backwards or always have to somersault out?

. . . always have the same song stuck in your head or always have the same dream at night?

. . . have a unicorn horn or a squirrel tail?

CONVERSATION

It's human nature to complain, but science has shown that constant negativity is bad for both our mental and physical health. Positivity, on the other hand, can improve our long-term health—not to mention the moods of everyone around us. Help your family start a habit of spreading positivity with these conversation starters.

(AGES: 8-13, 14-100)

🌸 Every once in a while, there's a news story about a kid who did something positive after being bullied. For example, a high school junior went viral for sticking Post-It notes with encouraging messages on her classmates' lockers. A middle-school boy responded to teasing by making a habit of opening the door for everyone at his school each day and greeting them with a kind word and a smile. Have you ever turned a negative situation into an opportunity to be positive? Tell us about it.

🌸 How could you become a role model for kindness? Are there other "kindness role models" you look up to?

🌸 Has anyone ever surprised you by doing something kind for no good reason? Did you "pass it on" by doing something kind for someone else?

🌸 Is it easier to remember a negative comment or a positive one? Why do you think that is?

🌸 Sometimes when something challenging happens, we have a hard time finding the "silver lining" or "flipping the script" to think about it from a more positive point of view. Can you think of a recent event in your life that seemed negative, but where you might be able to find a silver lining?

🌸 When famous people or celebrities do something kind for someone, it often gets a lot of publicity. Do you feel more inspired when a famous person commits an act of kindness or when someone you personally know does a kind thing?

ALWAYS SERVE ONE "PREFERRED" FOOD

While some families take the "pass food" approach, Elizabeth and Trampus swear by the "one preferred food" method. They make sure there's at least one item on the table each night that their picky eaters will enjoy.

Because their two children are busy athletes and the family is rushing to and from practices and games three to five nights a week, they've made the conscious decision to emphasize spending time together as a family rather than focusing on food choices. They strive to make dinners easy and relatively healthy, but don't worry about being too elaborate.

In order to continue to encourage their kids to try new foods and expand their choices, the preferred items the family serves are usually simple: bread, a bowl of fruit, or a plate of sliced cucumbers, for example. Or they might set out an array of vegetables that the kids can use to top individual pizzas or tacos. Offering these "safe" foods alongside whatever main dish the parents have prepared helps kids feel comfortable coming to the table, because right away they see that there's something they know they'll enjoy eating. And while there are the occasional evenings where a child might choose to eat only the bread and cucumbers and reject the rest of the meal, more often than not Elizabeth and Trampus have found the opposite with their three kids. Nibbling on their "safe foods" while watching others enjoy something more adventurous has actually led their kids to want to try a wider variety of dishes.

FOOD
This souvlaki menu has a little bit of something for everyone: bread and chicken for the most cautious palates, toppings that can be piled on or left off, and simple side salads. We've chosen dilled cucumber and cherry tomato salads for this dinner because you can easily leave a few undressed cucumber slices and tomatoes and present them in their own little dishes for kids who prefer a simpler presentation. Over time, odds are they'll get curious about tasting your "grown up" version of the vegetables.

CHICKEN SOUVLAKI
SERVES 4

Take a shortcut on busy evenings by substituting pre-cooked chicken in this recipe, such as a rotisserie chicken from the supermarket.

INGREDIENTS

4 pita breads

1 teaspoon dried oregano

1/2 teaspoon dried thyme

1/4 teaspoon freshly ground black pepper

1 tablespoon fresh lemon juice

1/4 cup extra-virgin olive oil, plus 2 tablespoons for sautéing the chicken

4 boneless, skinless chicken breasts, cut into 1 inch strips

1/2 cup plain yogurt

1 small cucumber, diced

1 1/2 tablespoons fresh dill, minced

INSTRUCTIONS

Heat oven to 200 degrees F. Wrap the bread in foil and place in oven.

In a large bowl, combine the oregano, thyme, pepper, and lemon juice. Slowly add the oil in a steady stream, whisking constantly until incorporated.

Pour the vinaigrette over the chicken and let marinate for 10 minutes at room temperature.

Heat remaining olive oil in a large skillet over medium-high heat. Transfer the chicken, not the liquid, to the skillet and heat, turning occasionally, until cooked through, about 5 minutes.

In a small bowl, combine the yogurt, cucumber, and dill. Spread the bread with some yogurt sauce and top with the chicken.

DILLED CUCUMBER SALAD
`SERVES 4`

Because this salad is really a quick pickle, you can make it several days in advance and store it in a jar in the refrigerator. However, it will get tangier and the flavors will be stronger the longer it sits, so enjoy it fresh if you prefer a milder taste.

INGREDIENTS

1 English cucumber, peeled and thinly sliced

1 tablespoon coarsely chopped fresh dill

4 tablespoons rice vinegar or apple cider vinegar

Salt and pepper to taste

INSTRUCTIONS

Combine all ingredients in a bowl. Add salt and pepper to taste.

Cover and refrigerate until ready to serve.

CHERRY TOMATO SALAD
`SERVES 4`

Feel free to keep the feta cheese and olives separate from the rest of the dish and allow diners to add them to their own plates at the table.

INGREDIENTS

1 pint cherry tomatoes, halved

1/2 small red onion, thinly sliced

1/4 cup crumbled feta cheese

1/4 cup pitted Kalamata olives

2 tablespoons extra-virgin olive oil

Juice of 1 lemon

Salt and pepper to taste

INSTRUCTIONS

Combine the tomatoes, onion, feta, and olives in a bowl.

Drizzle the lemon juice and olive oil over. Stir to combine.

Taste. Add more salt or pepper if needed.

FUN

Classic games are classics for a reason—they're always fun to play! Introduce your family to the old "Telephone" game at the dinner table tonight.

HOW TO PLAY

Have one person think of a sentence or phrase and have him whisper it into the next person's ear. When the last person hears the phrase, she repeats it to the group and the person who started the game can see how close it was!

CONVERSATION

Dinner conversation doesn't need to be topical. Elizabeth and Trampus find that their kids really enjoy using their imaginations during dinner conversations, and yours might too. You can find out with these conversation starters designed to get the imagination going.

(AGES: 2-7, 8-13)

- What is the best vacation you could imagine?
- In a movie about your life, who would play you? Your best friends? Your family?
- If you founded a new country, what would you call it? What would the flag look like?
- If you had super powers, what would they be? How would you use them to help people?
- If you had a pet dragon, what would you name it? What would you and your dragon do together?

PUT THE KIDS IN CONTROL

Have you ever been so frustrated with picky eaters that you've wanted to say, "Go ahead and make dinner yourselves"?

Jacqui, a mom of three, has been there—and she's realized that letting the kids make their own meal can be a good plan. "I probably found The Family Dinner Project by Googling how to get them to eat what they're served," she jokes, adding that for a long time, her three kids (ages 6 to 12) would refuse dinner and beg for pizza or macaroni and cheese. In her household, the rule that works best is that the kids will try everything she's serving, but are allowed to swap their plate for a different choice they make for themselves. Knowing that they can get up and make a sandwich or bowl of cereal if they truly dislike dinner has made the kids less resistant to trying new foods, and they're learning some self-sufficiency skills in the process.

If you're thinking of trying this approach, we recommend working on the kids' kitchen skills by having them take part in making the main meal as well. Besides, if your kids do end up opting out of the main meal to make a sandwich instead, that sandwich-making will go a lot more smoothly if they've been developing basic cooking skills with you.

FOOD

This menu builds on a favorite flavor for Jacqui's kids—pesto—in an easy, one-pan dinner format that older kids can make with just a little supervision from you. Kids of all ages can help peel and mash potatoes, and a bake-together recipe for pumpkin muffins could just be the thing that keeps them from getting up to make a sandwich after all!

ONE PAN PESTO CHICKEN WITH VEGGIES
SERVES 4

This easy sheet pan dinner was shared with us by our friends at SNAP4CT. It's healthy, budget-friendly, and a great recipe for helping older kids build cooking skills.

INGREDIENTS

2 medium sweet potatoes, peeled and chopped (about 2 cups)

12 ounces Brussels sprouts, trimmed and halved

2 tablespoons olive oil

2 teaspoons garlic powder

1 pound boneless, skinless chicken breasts

1/4 cup basil pesto

Salt and pepper

INSTRUCTIONS

Preheat oven to 350 degrees F.

Place sweet potatoes and Brussels sprouts on opposite sides of a large baking sheet.

Pour olive oil and garlic powder over each set of veggies. Season with salt and pepper. Toss to coat evenly.

Place chicken in the center of your baking sheet. Coat both sides with basil pesto.

Place baking sheet in the oven and cook for 30–40 minutes, or until the juice of the thickest chicken breast runs clear.

GARLIC MASHED POTATOES
SERVES 4

Adding garlic to mashed potatoes gives a little zing to a family favorite. Over time, you can experiment with the amount of garlic you add to find the right level for your family's tastes. Other mix-ins like chopped chives, lemon zest, or cheese are also a fun way to try out different taste sensations.

INGREDIENTS

4-5 large Yukon Gold potatoes (about 2 pounds), peeled and cut into 1/4 inch rounds

8-12 cloves of garlic, peeled

4 tablespoons unsalted butter, softened

6-10 tablespoons whole milk

Salt and pepper

INSTRUCTIONS

Put the potatoes and garlic cloves into a large saucepan. Cover with cold water.

Put a lid on the pot, bring to a boil, and reduce to a simmer. Simmer the potatoes and garlic cloves 15–20 minutes until easily pierced with a fork. Drain well.

Wipe out the pot to dry it. Add the potatoes and garlic back to the hot pot and allow to sit for 2–3 minutes to allow any additional water to evaporate.

Add the butter and 6 tablespoons of milk to the potatoes. Mash well with a potato masher. Add more milk, 1 tablespoon at a time, until you reach the desired consistency.

Season with salt and pepper to taste and serve warm.

HARVEST PUMPKIN SPICE MUFFINS

MAKES 12 MUFFINS

This moist, spicy pumpkin muffin recipe was provided by our friends at the Home Baking Association (homebaking.org). They encourage families to help kids learn basic skills by baking these muffins—scooping and leveling dry ingredients, cracking eggs, and mixing thoroughly and carefully.

INGREDIENTS

2 cups whole-wheat flour

3 tablespoons yellow cornmeal

2/3 cup packed brown sugar

1 tablespoon baking powder

1 teaspoon ground cinnamon

1/4 teaspoon baking soda

1/4 teaspoon salt

1/4 teaspoon ground ginger

1/4 teaspoon ground nutmeg

1/8 teaspoon ground cloves

1 cup pumpkin puree

1/2 cup milk

1/4 cup unsalted butter, melted

2 tablespoons vegetable oil

1 large egg

INSTRUCTIONS

Preheat oven to 400 degrees F. Line twelve muffin cups with paper liners or grease the muffin tins.

Measure dry ingredients (flour through cloves) into a medium bowl. Whisk to combine.

Using an electric mixer on medium speed, beat pumpkin, milk, butter, and oil together for 2 minutes. Add the egg and beat until fluffy.

Stir the dry ingredients into the wet ingredients until combined; no need to beat.

Use an ice cream scoop to scoop batter into the muffin cups, filling 2/3 full.

Bake the muffins for 18–20 minutes, or until a toothpick in the center comes out clean.

Remove muffins from pan and cool on a wire rack.

FUN
Another excellent way to build kids' competence in the kitchen is by introducing an element of challenge. Try playing "Iron Chef" to expose the whole family to new flavors and ideas while practicing basic cooking skills.

HOW TO PLAY

One family member selects two or three ingredients. Another family member—or a team!—then creates and cooks a meal using those ingredients. Sample ingredients: pasta, a vegetable, and an herb.

Or for a more challenging version: Choose a single ingredient and devise a menu that uses this ingredient in three recipes (as an appetizer, main dish, dessert, etc.). Some suggestions: a fruit (apples, berries), a spice (cinnamon, pepper), or something that adds flavor without dominating (lemon, shallot).

CONVERSATION

Helping kids go outside of their comfort zones bravely and safely can start small with a new food at dinner, but extend to trying a new activity, facing a fear, or tackling a challenge they didn't think they could master. Support them in developing their sense of exploration with these conversation starters that center around trying new things.

(AGES: 8-13, 14-100)

- What's something you've done in your life that you thought you could never do?
- Share a story from your own life about being bold. How did it turn out?
- Tell us about a time when you tried something new—a food, an activity, or a new way of doing things. What did you learn from that experience?
- What motivates you to try new things?
- What new skill do you wish you could learn?

MAKE THE OLD STANDARDS INTO NEW FAVORITES

As kids' food preferences expand, you can start to introduce more items by slowly changing the way that familiar foods are presented. You can change things up by adding a little garlic to the mashed potatoes one night, trying a new dressing for the salad, or mixing whole-wheat pasta into the familiar pasta. Let them share their opinions about the differences between these new presentations and the familiar favorites they're used to, and continue experimenting from time to time so they get used to the idea that foods don't have to only look and taste one specific way.

This whole dinner is inspired by the idea of presenting familiar favorites in a new way. Burgers, fries, and shakes are a kid-friendly selection of foods, but each one of these recipes is a twist on the expected. Instead of plain burgers, or the usual burger with melted cheese on top, try serving burgers with the cheese stuffed inside. Roasted sweet potato wedges can take the place of conventional fries. Round out the meal with a smoothie that's got the cold, creamy goodness of a milkshake and a naturally sweet, delicious peach flavor.

FOOD

These inside-out burgers are a good opportunity to offer a simple choice while still serving one intended main dish. Let kids choose what kind of cheese they want to put inside their burgers, and if you're feeling really creative, try adding small amounts of other ingredients, like crumbled bacon or finely chopped herbs. Mix different colors and varieties of potatoes—sweet, yellow, and purple, for example—for yet another way to gently expand horizons. Or ask the kids to suggest new fruits to add to the smoothies for different color and taste sensations.

INSIDE-OUT BURGERS
SERVES 4

These burgers are a fun twist on a classic family favorite! You can easily omit the cheese stuffing for anyone who prefers their burgers plain.

INGREDIENTS

1 pound ground beef, 85-90% lean

1/2 teaspoon garlic powder

1 teaspoon salt

1/2 teaspoon ground black pepper

1/4 cup cheese. Shredded cheddar, Swiss, soft goat cheese, or blue cheese are all good options.

4 burger buns

Burger toppings (lettuce, tomato, bacon, etc.)

INSTRUCTIONS

Preheat a grill, grill pan, or griddle.

In a small bowl, combine the garlic powder, salt, and pepper.

In a large bowl, mix the ground beef with half of the seasoning mix.

Divide the ground beef into four equal portions. Shape each into a ball.

Use your thumb to make an indentation in each ball. Place 1 tablespoon of your desired cheese in each indentation, then carefully shape the meat around it so the cheese is completely encased inside the ball of meat.

Flatten each ball and shape into a patty.

Sprinkle the remaining seasoning mix evenly over the patties.

Grill the burgers for 3–4 minutes per side for medium rare. Allow them to rest for a few minutes before serving.

Serve the burgers on your favorite buns with lettuce, sliced tomato, and condiments of your choice.

ROASTED SWEET POTATO WEDGES
SERVES 4-6

Skip the French fries and go for these colorful, nutritious sweet potato wedges instead.

INGREDIENTS

2 medium sweet potatoes, washed and cut into 1/2-inch thick wedges

1/4 cup olive oil

1 teaspoon salt

1/2 teaspoon pepper

1/2 teaspoon sweet paprika

INSTRUCTIONS

Preheat oven to 400 degrees F.

Pile sweet potato wedges in the center of a rimmed baking sheet. Drizzle with olive oil. Season with salt, pepper, and paprika. Toss to coat evenly.

Spread the potato wedges out into a single layer on the baking sheet. Try not to let them touch if possible.

Roast the sweet potatoes for 15 minutes. Stir, then return to the oven and roast for another 10–15 minutes, until the potato wedges are easily pierced with a fork and have a slightly crisp, golden exterior.

TASTES-LIKE-SUMMER PEACH SMOOTHIE
MAKES 1-2 SMOOTHIES

Peaches make a delicious, creamy smoothie, but you can also invent your own creation depending on the fruits that you have on hand. Since you're adding frozen peaches and ice cubes, you can use an unfrozen banana as needed. Just remember that whenever you see a banana getting a bit overripe on your counter, you can peel, slice and pop it into the freezer for future smoothies!

INGREDIENTS

2/3 cup plain yogurt

1/3 of a very ripe banana, peeled, sliced, and frozen

1 cup frozen, sliced peaches

1/3 cup orange juice

2 teaspoons honey

4 ice cubes

INSTRUCTIONS

Put the yogurt in a blender. Add banana, peach, and orange juice.

Put the lid securely on the blender and blend on high speed until smooth.

Turn the blender off. Add a squirt of honey and blend again.

With the machine running, remove the center part of the blender lid and drop in a few ice cubes. Blend until ice is crushed.

FUN
Using the theme of cooking and the part that each ingredient plays in making an enjoyable dish, try playing a round of Story by Sentence at the dinner table.

HOW TO PLAY

One family member begins a story and talks for no more than a minute. The next family member continues the story and so on. Some ground rules:

Everyone participates

No one goes on for too long

No one can change events radically during his or her turn (For example, "No, that's not what happened!" is a story-killer, not a story-continuer!)

If suggestions are needed to get warmed up, begin by brainstorming together a few things that should be included in the story: a city, a type of terrain (mountains, seashore, woods), some animals, an event (sports event, historical occasion, entertainment experience), a color, a food, and so on.

CONVERSATION

Sometimes what seems comfortable and familiar changes in ways that become difficult for us—not only with food, but with our opinions about friendships too. Check in with your family members about friendships and social dynamics with these conversation starters.

(AGES 8-13)

- Have you ever been teased by a friend? How did that make you feel? How did you respond?

- Have you or a friend ever left someone out on purpose? How did that feel? What's the difference between rude behavior, mean behavior, and bullying behavior?

- Have you ever seen someone bullied? What did you do? What could you do differently next time?

- What are the qualities you look for in a good friend? Do you always exhibit those qualities yourself?

RESPECT EXPERIMENTATION (WITHIN REASON)

Terri was ready to "stop feeding them at all and let them figure it out!" Her two teenagers' sudden insistence on pursuing vegetarian diets had put a huge strain on family mealtimes. As a single parent, Terri was entirely in charge of meals except for the few items her kids had mastered cooking. Unfortunately, her kids' decision to go vegetarian took all of those kid-friendly cooking projects off the menu.

To make matters worse, no matter what Terri cooked, her kids seemed to turn up their noses. Their limited palates were leading her to worry about their nutrition. "It'd be one thing if they actually liked vegetables, but the only green thing either one of them will eat is broccoli pizza." Important sources of plant-based protein like beans and lentils were also a non-starter, leaving the teens with menus based largely on three time-honored adolescent food groups: bread, cheese, and packaged snacks.

Terri's teens certainly aren't the only adolescents we've ever met who decided to dabble in vegetarianism (or some other dietary change that conveniently departs from the typical family menus). As frustrating as it can be to suddenly have a whole new set of food restrictions to accommodate, arguing with a teen who's determined to remove meat from the menu is more likely to result in a headache for you than a change of heart for them.

Still, it's important to set some guidelines that will help ensure your fledgling plant-eaters eat at least a reasonably balanced diet. For example: Bread is not dinner, but bread dipped in a creamy eggplant casserole can be dinner. Plain macaroni and cheese is okay, but macaroni and cheese with a dose of vegetables—even hidden ones—is better. And if they're going to insist on a vegetarian diet, they need to find at least one preparation of plant-based protein they'll eat. Bonus points if it's something the whole family, meat-eaters and not, can enjoy.

FOOD

Try building vegetable powerhouses into familiar comfort food for your young vegetarian. Even if you have a mostly meat-eating family, these fun veggie-packed recipes are likely to be a hit with the whole household.

LENTIL SLOPPY JOES
SERVES 4-6

You can also make a half-meat version of these sandwiches if there are family members who prefer theirs that way. Just brown 1/4–1/2 pound of ground beef in a separate skillet, season with salt and pepper, and stir in some of the lentil filling.

INGREDIENTS

1 tablespoon olive oil

1 cup diced onion

1 large red bell pepper, diced

2 medium carrots, shredded

4 cups cooked lentils*

1 tablespoon chili powder

1 teaspoon ground cumin

1 teaspoon salt

1/4 teaspoon pepper

4 tablespoons ketchup

2 tablespoons brown sugar

1 tablespoon Dijon mustard

1 tablespoon apple cider vinegar

Sandwich buns

*If using canned lentils, drain and rinse first.

INSTRUCTIONS

In a deep skillet over medium heat, sauté onion in olive oil until very soft and slightly golden brown. Add the bell pepper and carrots and cook, stirring until the bell pepper begins to soften.

Add the lentils and stir. Season with chili powder, cumin, salt, and pepper. Cook for 2–3 minutes.

Add ketchup, brown sugar, mustard, and vinegar to the skillet. Stir well. Simmer for 10 minutes, stirring occasionally. If the mixture seems dry, add a little water to it. The lentils should be saucy but not runny.

Taste and adjust seasonings if needed. Serve on warm buns.

BAKED EGGPLANT CASSEROLE

SERVES 4-6

This mashed eggplant dish is an old family comfort food recipe provided by one of our team members. Eat as-is or pair it with slices of crusty bread for dipping.

INGREDIENTS

1 large eggplant or 2 small eggplants

2 tablespoons olive oil

1 large sweet onion, chopped

1 cup Italian-style breadcrumbs, divided*

2 large eggs

Salt and pepper to taste

1-2 tablespoons unsalted butter

*You can make this recipe with any other type of breadcrumbs you prefer. Potato bread or brioche will give a slightly sweeter flavor to the dish that some families might enjoy. Experiment to see what you like best!

INSTRUCTIONS

Preheat oven to 350 degrees F. Generously butter a 9-inch pie plate or casserole dish and set aside.

Peel the eggplant and cut into rounds about 1-inch thick, then quarter the rounds. Place the eggplant pieces in a large pot, cover with water and boil until easily pierced with a fork, but not falling apart.

While the eggplant is cooking, sauté chopped onion in olive oil until golden brown, about 10 minutes.

Drain the cooked eggplant and return to the hot pot. Mash with a potato masher until relatively smooth, with no large chunks of eggplant remaining.

Stir the sautéed onions into the mashed eggplant, along with 1/2 cup of breadcrumbs. Season with salt and pepper to taste.

Add the eggs and beat with a wire whisk until the mixture is smooth and fluffy.

Transfer the eggplant mixture to your prepared baking dish. Top with the remaining 1/2 cup of breadcrumbs. The eggplant mixture should be about 1/2 inch thick in the dish; if it's too thick, try separating it into two pans. Dot the top with small pats of butter.

Bake the eggplant for 45–60 minutes, until the top is golden brown and crunchy.

PUMPKIN MACARONI AND CHEESE

SERVES 6-8

Adding pumpkin to the creamy sauce gives this macaroni and cheese a nutritious lift, without taking away from the rich, silky texture that kids love.

INGREDIENTS

1 pound penne pasta

2 tablespoons unsalted butter

2 tablespoons all-purpose flour

1 1/2 cups milk

1 cup pumpkin puree

Salt and pepper

1 teaspoon mustard powder

1 tablespoon fresh sage, chopped

8 ounces sharp cheddar cheese, shredded

1/2 cup dry breadcrumbs

1/2 cup Parmesan or asiago cheese, grated

INSTRUCTIONS

Preheat oven to 350 degrees F.

Cook pasta according to package directions. Drain, then return to the pot and set aside.

Melt butter over low heat in a medium saucepan. Whisk in the flour and stir for about 1 minute. Add the milk and stir until no flour lumps remain. Bring to a simmer and cook until thickened.

Add pumpkin, salt, pepper, mustard powder, and sage. Mix well. Add the cheddar cheese. Stir until the cheese is melted and the sauce is smooth and creamy.

Pour the sauce over the pasta and mix well.

Transfer the pasta to an ungreased 9-by-13–inch baking dish. Sprinkle the breadcrumbs and Parmesan or asiago over the top. Bake, uncovered, for 15–20 minutes.

Allow to cool for 5–10 minutes before serving.

FUN   Invite a cast of characters to your family dinner!

HOW TO PLAY

Each person thinks of a famous person, book character, or movie character. They then behave as that character at the dinner table, taking on their mannerisms and voice, and using well-known quotations as best they can. See if you can guess who's sitting at the dinner table with you!

CONVERSATION

When older kids are trying to assert their independence—whether through food choices, clothing styles, or other sometimes-trying methods—it can present a good opportunity to have a conversation about rights, privileges, wants, and needs.

(AGES 8-13, 14-100)

- What's the difference between a want and a need? What are some things you think you need on a daily basis that you might actually be able to go without for a while?

- It feels good to get everything you want, but are there downsides to getting what you want sometimes? Give an example.

- How is a right different from a privilege?

- Are there certain privileges you don't have that you think you should be granted? How could you earn those privileges?

- Do you think you should have to work to earn the things you need? What about the things you want? What are some ways that we all "work" in this family to get our wants and needs met?

PART II
WE'RE TOO BUSY!

One parent we know compared family mealtimes to a game of Whack-a-Mole, saying, "Just when I think I can get everybody sitting down together, another commitment pops up and there goes one of the kids away from the table again." There's no question that the window of time after school and work and before going to bed is incredibly tight, and it is jammed with things that need to get accomplished. One of the most common frustrations parents share with us is that there just doesn't seem to be enough time to fit in a family meal during that window.

We can't clear your calendar for you, but we can share with you some of the time-tested strategies we've learned from families who have managed to fit dinner into their busy schedules. Many of these ideas are ones The Family Dinner Project team members use in their own homes, so we're confident that one or more of these solutions can work for you.

NO ONE EATS ALONE

Beth and Gary of Washington state have a lot of mouths to feed. As parents to five boys ages 7–25, they have several layers of challenges. For one, there's not always going to be time to gather all seven members of their family for a meal. Therefore, they've instituted one "golden rule" of family dinner: No one eats alone.

If the rest of the family will be late at work, school, and sports practices, the youngest child might get to eat earlier, while an adult joins him at the table to share some fun and conversation. Then the family encourages him to join their later meal for 10 or 15 minutes to play a game or join in the conversation topic at hand. Similarly, if another family member has to join the meal late or eat after everyone else is done, at least one parent or sibling will be sure to join that person at the table to socialize.

One way Beth says she makes it all work with competing schedules and big appetites is to always serve buffet-style and to keep healthy grab-and-go options continuously available. She has jars of homemade muffins, cookies, and breads on hand and adds cutting boards filled with fruits, vegetables, and nuts to every meal. One particularly helpful strategy for a family that juggles multiple schedules is to make sure to plan a main course that holds well and reheats easily, and pair it with self-serve sides.

FOOD
Beth's broccoli soup recipe makes an easy and budget-friendly main course that can stay warm in a slow cooker or be easily reheated on the stovetop as different family members come and go. A tasty variation on cornbread and a fruit salad can both be made in advance and dished up for sides, snacks, or a fruity dessert whenever someone's ready for a quick bite.

CREAM OF BROCCOLI SOUP
SERVES 4

This soup recipe was shared with us by Beth Swanson and the Mom's Network of Walla Walla, Washington, where it's a popular go-to meal for busy families.

INGREDIENTS

4 tablespoons butter

1 1/2 cups chopped onion

1 medium green pepper, diced

1/2 cup chopped broccoli

2 1/2 cups chicken or vegetable stock

2 cups milk

1/2 cup sour cream

1 bay leaf

Dash of allspice, thyme, or basil

INSTRUCTIONS

Sauté onions in butter with bay leaf.

Add green pepper, broccoli and stock. Cook about 10 minutes, covered, until the vegetables are very tender.

Put in blender and puree little by little with milk. Texture should be smooth.

Whisk in sour cream and seasoning.

CONFETTI CORNBREAD
MAKES 12 CORNBREAD WEDGES
OR SQUARES

Our friends at the Home Baking Association provided this recipe for a colorful and tasty take on the classic cornbread. Let kids get in on the action by grating cheese and measuring and mixing ingredients.

INGREDIENTS

1 cup cheddar cheese, shredded

1/3 cup green onions, chopped

1/3 cup red or yellow bell peppers, chopped*

3 tablespoons butter

1 cup white or yellow cornmeal

1 cup all-purpose or white whole-wheat flour

2 tablespoons sugar

2 1/2 teaspoons baking powder

1/2 teaspoon salt

1 large egg

1 cup low-fat milk

*You may substitute fresh or frozen sweet corn for bell peppers if you prefer.

INSTRUCTIONS

Wash and chop the vegetables. Shred the cheese.

Preheat oven to 425 degrees F. While the oven preheats, melt the butter in a 9-inch cast-iron skillet or square baking pan inside the oven. This will help grease the pan and also prepare the butter. Once the butter is melted, remove pan from oven.

In a medium mixing bowl, whisk together cornmeal, flour, sugar, baking powder, and salt. Make a small well in the center of the dry ingredients.

In a small mixing bowl, beat the egg. Add the milk and melted butter. Beat well.

Pour the wet ingredients into the well in the center of the dry ingredients. Stir together just until evenly moistened.

Stir in the cheese and chopped vegetables. Do not beat or overmix. Pour the batter into the prepared skillet or baking pan.

Bake for 25–30 minutes, until golden brown and set in the center. A toothpick inserted in the middle should come out clean or with just a few moist crumbs clinging to it.

WALDORF FRUIT SALAD

SERVES 6

This fruit salad is a combination of sweet and mildly savory. If your family isn't wild about celery and lettuce with their fruit, you can always omit the vegetables, but we like the refreshing flavor and added crunch. This recipe was given to us by our friend Chef Robin.

INGREDIENTS

1/2 cup plain, nonfat yogurt

2 tablespoons fresh lemon juice

2-3 medium apples, washed, cored, and chopped

1 cup celery, thinly sliced

1 cup red seedless grapes, sliced

1 cup walnuts, chopped

Lettuce, washed and torn into pieces

INSTRUCTIONS

In a medium bowl, whisk together the yogurt and lemon juice.

Mix in the apple, celery, grapes and walnuts.

Serve on a bed of fresh lettuce.

FUN
When you can't get everyone to the table at the same time, you'll want the fun to be ready whenever you are. One low-key way to keep the good times rolling is to start a Joke Jar for your table.

HOW TO PLAY

Let each member of the family write favorite jokes on slips of paper and put them into an empty Mason jar, jelly jar, or can. When you think a good joke or two might lift everyone's spirits, bring the jar to the table and take turns drawing slips and telling the jokes.

Need help getting started? Here are some favorite jokes from kids we know:

Why did the chicken cross the plate? To become the winner, winner, chicken dinner!

Why didn't the skeleton cross the road? Because he didn't have the guts!

What's a cow's favorite movie? The Sound of Moo sic!

CONVERSATION

When family members of all ages are coming and going, it's nice to provide a sense of consistency for everyone with pre-set conversation starters. One idea is to let family members interview each other. You might find out some new things about each other that wouldn't come to light in the hustle and bustle of a big family meal.

- Talk about a time when you tried something new. What was it? What happened?
- What was your favorite tradition when you were a child? How have you passed that down to future generations (or how will you)?
- Tell me your favorite story about our family. Why do you like this story in particular?
- Do you know any stories about your grandparents when they were kids?
- Tell me something about yourself that you think I might not know.

IT DOESN'T ALWAYS HAVE TO BE DINNER

For many families, a regular evening gathering may be too difficult to schedule. In talking to thousands of families, we've found that breakfast or a weekend brunch can be a more realistic choice when work and after-school schedules take up too much space in the evenings.

Making space for family breakfasts "reminded me to slow down and enjoy the morning, instead of rushing around so much," said Katie, a mom of two. Justine, a Massachusetts parent who has tried family breakfasts, found that the practice encouraged her to get items like lunch-packing and backpack-checking done at night, leaving time in the mornings for face-to-face interaction with her family—and a less stressful morning routine.

Family breakfast can certainly be a simple bowl of cereal or toast and fruit. As with dinner, what you serve doesn't matter as much as spending the time to connect with one another. But if you have a little extra time, this family breakfast menu can make the occasion feel just a little bit special. You can make the yogurt dip and assemble the French toast casserole the night before. Or you can even bake the French toast in advance, then warm up individual servings in the microwave for a quick morning boost. And, of course, if you're planning to have family dinner rather than family breakfast, there's no need to flip past this menu. We've never met anyone who didn't like breakfast for dinner.

FOOD

A sweet and savory flavor combination takes French toast to the next level. While it's baking, slice some fresh fruit to go with a simple yogurt dip. You can also make bacon, hash browns, or other typical breakfast side dishes to round out this meal.

CHEDDAR AND APPLE FRENCH TOAST BAKE

SERVES 4

Great for a family dinner or a family breakfast, this French toast dish is a quick throw-together with a balance of sweet and savory flavors. Serve it plain with bacon, ham, or turkey to make it more savory; pour maple syrup over the top and garnish with berries to bring out the sweetness.

INGREDIENTS

1 tablespoon unsalted butter, plus more for greasing the pan

2 medium apples, thinly sliced. Rome or Honeycrisp work particularly well.

2 tablespoons brown sugar

1/2 cup milk

4 large eggs

1/2 teaspoon ground cinnamon

1/8 teaspoon ground nutmeg

8 slices challah or brioche bread, 1/2 inch thick

1 cup sharp cheddar cheese, shredded

INSTRUCTIONS

Preheat the oven to 400 degrees F. Lightly butter an 8-by8-inch baking dish and set aside.

Melt the tablespoon of butter in a medium skillet. Add the sliced apples and brown sugar and cook, stirring occasionally, for 5–7 minutes or until the apples are softened.

In a medium bowl, whisk together the milk, eggs, cinnamon, and nutmeg.

Spread the cooked apple mixture evenly over the bottom of the prepared baking dish.

Layer the bread on top of the apple mixture with the bread slices standing up at a slight angle. Sprinkle cheese evenly between the slices.

Pour the egg and milk mixture evenly over the bread. Press down firmly with hands to help it soak.

Bake the French toast for 20–25 minutes until the bread is lightly golden brown and the liquid is absorbed. Slice and serve warm with apples spooned over the top.

CINNAMON YOGURT DIP WITH FRESH FRUIT

SERVES 4-6

This easy fruit and yogurt dessert comes from the USDA and the Pennsylvania Nutrition Education Program. Experiment with different fruits and different flavor mix-ins for your yogurt dip to spice things up.

INGREDIENTS

1 apple

1 orange

1 banana

1/4 cup orange juice

1 cup vanilla yogurt

1/2 teaspoon ground cinnamon

INSTRUCTIONS

Core and slice the apple. Slice banana into circles. Peel the orange and break it into sections.

Pour the orange juice into a small bowl.

Dip the fruit pieces into the orange juice to prevent browning.

Arrange on a plate.

Mix the yogurt and cinnamon in a small bowl.

Use the yogurt as a dip for the fruit.

FUN

Being able to recognize emotions is an important social skill for kids. It not only helps them to build empathy for others, but it can even make them more aware of their own feelings and encourage the development of self-regulation skills. "Guess That Emotion" is a fun way to playfully build emotional awareness at the table.

HOW TO PLAY

Have one person leave the table for a minute. Once she leaves, the rest of the family decides on an emotion (or you can pick out of a hat).

Some examples include:

Happy

Angry

Sad

Mad

Excited

Nervous

When the missing family member returns to the table, the rest of the family eats and acts with that feeling in mind. For example, if the emotion is "worry," someone might say, "I have so much homework tonight I'm never going to get to sleep." Or you can make it a bit more challenging for older kids by allowing only body language or facial expression to convey emotion.

CONVERSATION

If you're having a family breakfast, why not have a conversation geared towards starting the day off on the right foot? Try these "good morning" questions with your family.

(AGES 2-7, 8-13)

- What was the first thing you thought about when you woke up this morning?
- What's one thing you're hoping for or looking forward to about today?
- What was your most vivid dream last night?
- What's one thing you can do to brighten someone's day?
- Is there any part of today you're nervous or anxious about? How can we help you feel more confident?

PLAN AHEAD
FOR SUCCESS

Most parents we've met either love meal planning or hate it. Some delight in the organization and adventure of it all and receive deep satisfaction from the process. Others see it as nothing but a tedious time-suck that takes time from much more pleasurable activities. Whichever side you're on, it's hard to deny that planning ahead is one of the best ways to keep family dinner stress at bay. Knowing what you plan to serve, shopping accordingly, and having everything on hand when you walk in the door at night improves the odds that you'll be able to get a meal on the table and gather the family to enjoy it.

Even nutrition professionals, like Montana dietician Danielle, sometimes struggle to manage meal planning. As a busy working mother of two young children, she sometimes forgets to plan ahead, "and then I'm rushing to figure something out on my way home from work." The after-work dinner rush adds stress and tension, especially if it ends up involving an extra stop at the grocery store. Danielle tries to commit to writing up a menu for the week whenever possible.

But no matter how well Danielle plans her meals, she needs them to be quick and easy to prepare while still giving plenty of attention to her boys, ages two and five. We've designed this menu to be fast, with lots of opportunities to keep the kids involved and entertained.

FOOD

While parents work on cooking the chicken taco filling and chopping ingredients for the quinoa salad, turn on some music for the kids and let them have a dance party that also does double duty: whipping the cream for dessert!

QUICK TRICK CHICKEN TACOS
SERVES 4-6

The perfect dinner for a rushed evening, these chicken tacos are packed with vegetables and take only minutes to cook. Try adding different vegetables like zucchini or tomatoes and vary your toppings for an endless parade of options.

INGREDIENTS

1 pound boneless, skinless chicken thighs, cut into 1 inch strips

1 tablespoon olive oil

1 teaspoon salt

1/2 teaspoon black pepper

1 medium onion, thinly sliced

1 large red bell pepper, sliced into strips

1 cup corn kernels, fresh or frozen

3/4 cup salsa

Juice of 1 lime

Flour tortillas

Shredded lettuce and sliced avocado (optional)

INSTRUCTIONS

Heat the olive oil in a large skillet over medium-high heat.

Add the chicken strips and sprinkle with salt and pepper. Cook until browned on one side, about 3 minutes.

Flip the chicken over and add the onions and bell pepper strips to the pan. Cook, stirring occasionally, for another 2-3 minutes until the vegetables begin to soften slightly.

Add the corn and salsa to the pan. Stir well then cover and simmer for 5 minutes.

Remove from the heat and stir in the lime juice. Serve in flour tortillas with avocado and shredded lettuce.

QUINOA SALAD
SERVES 4-6

This quinoa salad recipe was provided by our friend Chef Robin, who notes that you can add almost anything you like to your version. If you've never cooked quinoa before, note that it's important to thoroughly rinse and drain the grains before cooking to avoid a bitter taste. Just place the uncooked quinoa in a fine mesh strainer and rinse under cold running water for 2-3 minutes, until the water runs nice and clear.

INGREDIENTS

1 cup quinoa

2 cups corn kernels, fresh or thawed from frozen

1 15-ounce can black beans, rinsed and drained

1 red or green bell pepper, chopped

2 green onions, chopped

1/2 cup parsley or cilantro, chopped

1 mango, peeled and diced

2 tablespoons Italian dressing

Juice from half a lime

Salt and pepper to taste

INSTRUCTIONS

Rinse the quinoa and cook according to package directions.

Let the quinoa cool, then mix together with all the other ingredients.

Add salad dressing and toss to coat thoroughly. Serve right away, or refrigerate until ready to serve.

BERRIES AND WHIPPED CREAM
SERVES 4-6

You can make this simple dessert into a fun activity by whipping the cream in a whipped cream dance party!

INGREDIENTS

1 pint whipping cream, chilled

1 tablespoon confectioner's sugar

4 cups berries of your choice

Splash of vanilla extract (optional)

INSTRUCTIONS

If whipping the cream traditionally, pour the chilled cream into a large bowl. Using an electric mixer, whip at medium speed for 2–3 minutes until it starts to thicken. Gradually increase the speed to high, adding a tablespoon of sugar at a time, until the whipped cream has achieved soft peaks. Fold in the vanilla, if using. Alternately, see the dance party method in the "fun" section for a different spin on whipping the cream.

Divide the berries among individual serving bowls. Top with generous dollops of whipped cream.

FUN
This whipped cream dance party is one of the most popular activities at our Community Dinner events. One of our favorite moments at any dinner is watching kids of all ages (and some kids at heart) take over the dance floor with their containers of cream!

HOW TO PLAY

Pour a pint of chilled whipping cream into a tightly lidded container—we recommend something with a screw-on cap if possible. And since kids are involved, plastic or stainless steel is preferable to glass. For the best results, add some metal agitator balls or small marbles to the containers. They're not strictly necessary, but they really speed up the whipping process.

Add a splash of vanilla extract and a tablespoon of confectioner's sugar to the cream, then screw the lid onto the container securely. Turn on some dance music and hand the container to the kids. Encourage them to jump, dance, and shake the container as hard as they can to the music. It may take a few songs and possibly an assist from the adults, but you'd be surprised how a dance party can result in a great batch of whipped cream.

CONVERSATION

Build the little ones' "helping muscles" with a conversation about becoming a good helper.

(AGES 2-7)

- What are some things you need grown-ups to help you with that you think you could learn to do all by yourself?
- What's one thing that happened today that made you feel like a good helper?
- What jobs do you like to help with the most?
- Are there times when you don't like to help? Why not?
- What is one thing you could do to help at school or home tomorrow without being asked?

TAKE IT TO GO

Often, families are in the same location during the dinner hour, but not able to take the time to sit and eat together. This is especially true of families like Barbie and Shane's. Their kids have busy sports schedules year-round. On practice and game nights, the whole family might be at the field during practice or game times, but dinner can turn into a hurried afterthought with everyone grabbing a bite to eat at different times to ensure that the activity schedule stays on track.

Most of the time, Barbie tries to handle the dinner rush by planning ahead and making something in the slow cooker, but it's not always possible to hold off dinner until after a late activity. Packing up a quick meal and taking it on the run is one way for the family to continue to connect over meals—without compromising the kids' schedules.

You can adapt the dinner-on-the-go model to any number of circumstances. Bring a meal to the workplace of a parent who's scheduled for a late shift and join them during their break. Open up packed dinners outside the dance recital or school concert before the event begins. Whatever your situation, a picnic could be the solution that makes dinner together a possibility within a seemingly impossible schedule.

FOOD
A twist on a classic chicken salad makes great sandwiches for a picnic dinner, or it can be eaten just as it is. Make cut-up vegetables a little more interesting with an easy curry dip and pop a few yogurt parfaits into your bag for a sweet treat.

CHICKEN SALAD WITH CRANBERRIES
SERVES 4

For an easy, unique twist on chicken salad, we recommend this simple recipe from the USDA Food and Nutrition Service. This is just a starting point—you can vary it by adding any dried fruits and nuts you like, and we encourage trying all different kinds of salad dressing to create the flavor combinations you like best.

INGREDIENTS

1 1/2 cups cooked, diced chicken

1 cup dried cranberries or cherries

2 tablespoons sliced almonds

1/2 cup vinaigrette dressing*

1 head lettuce, chopped

*Our method for making vinaigrette dressing is included on page 140. You can also use any store-bought dressing that your family prefers.

INSTRUCTIONS

Toss chicken, cranberries, and almonds with dressing.

Serve on a mound of chopped lettuce, or use for sandwiches.

CURRY VEGETABLE DIP
SERVES 4-6

This recipe is slightly modified from the original, provided by the USDA Food and Nutrition Service. Serve with sliced vegetables or pita chips.

INGREDIENTS

8 ounces Greek yogurt

1/4 cup shredded carrot

2 tablespoons green onion, minced

1 tablespoon mayonnaise

1 teaspoon sugar

1/4 teaspoon curry powder

Salt and pepper

INSTRUCTIONS

Mix ingredients in a bowl.

Chill until ready to serve.

YOGURT PARFAITS

SERVES 4

Yogurt parfaits are a perfect and quick sweet treat. They're endlessly customizable. You can manage the amount of sugar in your parfaits by choosing a plain or lightly sweetened yogurt brand, or by varying the types of toppings you offer.

INGREDIENTS

4 cups plain or vanilla yogurt

1 cup crushed graham crackers, dry cereal, or granola

1/2 cup chopped nuts or miniature chocolate chips

2 cups chopped berries, bananas, or both

INSTRUCTIONS

Place 1/4 cup of yogurt in the bottom of each of four cups.

Mix the graham crackers or cereal with the nuts or chocolate chips.

Add a layer of fruit and a sprinkling of the dry ingredients.

Follow with another 1/4 cup of yogurt, more fruit, and more dry ingredients. Continue layering, ending with a final sprinkle of crushed graham crackers or granola for a crunchy top.

FUN Why not plan an imaginary picnic while you're enjoying the real thing? This well-known alphabet game is fun and easy to play at the table, in the car, or on the sidelines at a game.

HOW TO PLAY

"I'm going on a picnic and I'm bringing . . ." The first person to go completes the sentence with a word that starts with *A*. The next person repeats what the first person said and adds a word that starts with *B*. Continue through the alphabet until you can't think of any more things to bring on your picnic!

CONVERSATION

A picnic is the perfect time to think about the world around you. Cultivate your kids' sense of responsibility for their environment with these eco-friendly conversation starters.

(AGES 2–7, 8–13)

- The three Rs of environmentalism are reduce, reuse, recycle. Can you think of an example of how our family practices each one?

- Are there any ways in which you think our family could do a better job being environmentally friendly?

- What are three actions we can start doing regularly that would be good for the earth?

- What are some ways in which you see your school or other places in our community practicing eco-friendly habits?

- Imagine you were building a whole new planet for people to live on. What would it be like? What other species would live there? How could you make sure your planet was taken care of by the people and animals?

FIND NEW WAYS TO CONNECT

Getting everyone to the dinner table can be a challenge for any family, but what happens when the challenge is further complicated by a work schedule that takes one parent away from the table for months at a time?

Heather and Eric and their four kids have dealt with continued changes in their family schedule due to Eric's military service. In addition to all the usual calendar conflicts familiar to most busy families, they've also moved every two to three years to countries around the globe and dealt with regular deployments that keep Eric away from home for six months or more at a time. With Eric gone, Heather says, "It's difficult for me to be motivated to cook dinner and not just make the kids mac and cheese, but I realize more than ever that we'll need family dinners to deal with the stress of my husband being gone."

Their situation also means that they live far away from family members who could help. Instead, they have learned to rely on one another and on the family dinner routine. Having a reliable time to connect helps them stay close-knit even as they navigate life in different countries and the challenges of deployment. One of their suggestions was to use technology to help ease the strain of separation. Several military families we know have shared with us that when a loved one is away for an extended period, using video apps to occasionally allow the absent person to "participate" in family dinners is a comforting and fun way to keep the connection going.

FOOD

Heather and Eric's kids love to eat this crispy Japanese pork dish that they enjoyed frequently while the family was stationed in Japan. Here we're recommending you serve it over a bed of steamed rice with a side of roasted broccoli. Roasting brings out different flavors in vegetables and often makes them more appealing than plain steaming or boiling, so it's a good technique to try if you have reluctant vegetable eaters.

KATSUDON

SERVES 6-8

Dashi powder is usually available in the international section of most supermarkets. If you can't find it there, you can look for it at an Asian grocery or order online.

INGREDIENTS

6-8 thin pork cutlets

4 large eggs

1/2 cup flour

1 cup panko

1 1/2 cups water

1 teaspoon dashi powder

2 tablespoons sugar

2 tablespoons honey

6 tablespoons soy sauce

1 white onion, thinly sliced

Cooking oil

INSTRUCTIONS

Beat two of the eggs in a shallow dish and set aside.

Place the flour in another shallow dish and the panko in a third.

Dredge each pork cutlet first in flour, tapping off the excess; then dip in beaten egg; and finally coat thoroughly in panko.

Coat a large skillet lightly with oil and place over medium heat.

Fry the pork cutlets until golden brown all over, turning once. Remove to a wire rack to cool slightly, then cut into 1/2 inch strips.

In a medium bowl, mix the dashi powder, water, sugar, honey, and soy sauce. Pour 3/4 of the sauce into the pan, reserving the rest for garnish.

Add the sliced onions to the sauce in the pan. Cook for about 10 minutes or until the onions are tender.

Add the sliced pork and cook until the sauce begins to thicken slightly.

Beat the remaining two eggs and pour over the pork. Cover the pan immediately and cook for 1 minute to set the eggs.

Serve over rice, adding the reserved sauce on top.

STEAMED RICE

SERVES 6

This method will work with any widely available white rice: Basmati, Jasmine, Carolina, or converted.

INGREDIENTS

2 cups long-grain white rice

1 tablespoon unsalted butter

3 cups water

1 teaspoon salt

INSTRUCTIONS

Place rice in colander or fine-mesh strainer and rinse under running water until water runs clear. Place colander over bowl and set aside.

Heat butter or oil in large saucepan over medium heat. Add rice and cook, stirring constantly until grains become chalky and opaque, 1 to 3 minutes.

Add water and salt. Increase heat to high and bring to boil, swirling the pot to blend ingredients. Reduce heat to low. Cover and simmer until all liquid is absorbed, 18 to 20 minutes.

Turn off heat and remove lid. Place a kitchen towel, folded in half, over the saucepan and replace the lid. Let stand 10 to 15 minutes. Fluff with fork and serve.

ROASTED BROCCOLI
`SERVES 4`

TFDP friend and cooking instructor April Hamilton shared this recipe with us. To learn more about April and explore her recipes and ideas, visit Aprilskitchencounter.com.

INGREDIENTS

1 head fresh broccoli, trimmed and cut into florets

1 tablespoon olive oil

Coarse salt and freshly ground pepper

INSTRUCTIONS

Heat a rimmed baking sheet in the oven as you preheat it to 425 degrees F.

Toss the broccoli florets (and sliced stems, if you like) with the olive oil in a large bowl.

Sprinkle with salt and pepper and toss again.

Remove the hot baking sheet from the oven and carefully place a sheet of parchment paper on it, then pour out the broccoli into an even layer.

Roast the broccoli for 15 minutes, or until desired degree of doneness. Ideally, the broccoli will be just tender with some crusty browned edges.

FUN
If you'll be using technology at your dinner table to help connect with an absent family member, take advantage of the face time to play a game of Charades.

HOW TO PLAY

One person chooses a category, like "book titles" or "movies." That person then thinks of something that fits into that category and acts it out without words. The others guess what they're enacting.

CONVERSATION

When family members are far away, it can be comforting to connect to family stories as a reminder of all of the things we share. Sharing family stories also makes kids more resilient, which is especially beneficial during tough times. These conversation starters can help you share your family history.

(ALL AGES)

- What is the earliest story you know about one of your ancestors?
- Do you know some of the jobs your parents had when they were young?
- What three words would you use to describe our family?
- How did your parents or grandparents meet?
- Is there anything unique about our family that you're really proud of?

MAKE IT SNACK-SIZED

We often think of possible family mealtimes as being breakfast, lunch, and dinner, but when life gets busy, sometimes it's just important to sneak in an opportunity to share food, fun, and conversation whenever you can. One tip we've learned from families over the years is that as kids get older and life gets busier, a shared snack time—either before evening activities hit, or late in the evening when everyone finally gets home—can be the only moment during a jam-packed week when parents and kids connect.

The idea of hanging out together sharing snacks is appealing. After all, snacking usually feels less formal than a meal, and you can dip and munch almost anywhere, not just at the table. Also, an assortment of healthy snacks can make up a full meal with relatively little fuss and often a lot less cooking, making the family snack time—or snacks-for-dinner—an easy, relaxing way to end a long day. Here we've suggested an array of snacks that are simple to make, so you can try one or all of them for your next shared snack time.

FOOD

Dipping, spreading, and crunching are some of the most essential elements of a rewarding snack time. Get serious about snacking with recipes for homemade hummus, a sweet and savory baked cheese spread, and easy homemade pumpkin butter.

HUMMUS PLATE

SERVES 4-6

You can certainly use store-bought hummus in a pinch, but this homemade version is fast and easy. Play with flavors by adding more garlic (or using roasted garlic for a different twist), sun-dried tomatoes, or drained roasted red peppers.

INGREDIENTS

1 15-ounce can chickpeas

1 lemon

1 clove of garlic

3 tablespoons olive oil

2 tablespoons sesame tahini

1 teaspoon sea salt

4 pitas, cut into triangles

3 cups assorted chopped vegetables, such as carrots, celery, and red bell peppers

INSTRUCTIONS

Open can of chickpeas and pour about half the liquid into a measuring cup. Set aside this extra liquid for later.

Pour chickpeas into blender.

Squeeze the juice of one lemon into a bowl (or less, if you prefer it less lemon-y). Toss out any seeds and pour the liquid into the blender.

Peel one clove of garlic and drop into blender.

Add tahini, olive oil, and salt (it's best to start with less and add more if you want).

Blend all ingredients until smooth.

If the hummus is too thick, add some of the liquid saved in the measuring cup and blend again.

Serve with pita triangles and sliced vegetables for dipping.

BAKED CHEESE WITH JAM AND NUTS

SERVES 6

Cheese and fruit are a natural pairing. Make your snack time "fancy" with this easy method for making a sweet and savory baked cheese spread.

INGREDIENTS

8 ounces soft cheese (Brie, goat cheese, and cream cheese all work well)

3/4 cup fig or raspberry jam, separated

1/2 cup chopped, toasted pistachios or almonds

1/4 cup fresh raspberries or golden raisins

Crackers or crusty bread for serving

INSTRUCTIONS

Preheat oven to 400 degrees F.

Place cheese in a small casserole dish or pie plate. If using Brie, carefully remove the top portion of the rind to expose the soft cheese underneath, leaving a 1/4-inch border all the way around.

Spread 1/2 cup of jam on top of the cheese.

Microwave remaining 1/4 cup of jam for 30–45 seconds, until slightly runny. Stir the nuts into the warm jam to glaze them.

Pile the nuts on top of the cheese. Bake the cheese for 15–20 minutes, until soft and slightly runny but not totally melted (watch carefully, as cheeses and ovens can vary widely!).

Top the warm cheese with berries or golden raisins and serve with crackers or slices of crusty bread for spreading.

EASY PUMPKIN BUTTER
SERVES 6-8

This simple recipe for pumpkin butter makes a perfect dip for apples, but it's also great spread on toast, pancakes, or waffles. Store it in an airtight container in the refrigerator and it will keep for up to two weeks—if you don't eat it all up before then!

INGREDIENTS

1 15-ounce can pumpkin puree

3/4 cup apple cider

1/4 cup pure maple syrup

2 teaspoons ground cinnamon

1/2 teaspoon ground nutmeg

1/4 teaspoon ground cloves

INSTRUCTIONS

Combine all the ingredients in a medium saucepan.

Cook over medium heat, stirring occasionally with a whisk, until the pumpkin butter is thick and smooth, about 10 minutes.

Allow the pumpkin butter to cool before using it for dipping or spreading.

FUN

Set the tone for a laid-back hangout session by playing Celebrity, a challenging game that taps into pop culture.

HOW TO PLAY

This is a game of naming people in the public eye. The trick is this: The first letter of the celebrity's last name dictates what the first letter of the next person's first name must be. For example, if someone names "George Washington," the next person might say "Walt Disney," or another celebrity whose name begins with *W*. Keep going until someone gets stumped. Special challenge: If you can name someone whose first and last name starts with the same letter— like "Walt Whitman"—then the direction reverses and the person who just went has to name the next celebrity.

Note: This game also works with geography—simply use the last letter of the place named as the first letter of the next place. For example, "Kentucky" could lead to "Yemen," which could lead to "Nebraska."

CONVERSATION

When there's not a lot of time to check in with each other, you want to make the conversation count. Make sure everyone's handling the hectic pace of life with these conversation starters about managing stress.

(AGES: 14-100)

- Who do you feel most comfortable talking to about difficult or stressful topics?

- How do you know when you're too stressed? Does it affect your feelings or your outlook on life? How?

- What are some activities you like to do that help you relieve stress?

- Do you notice when family or friends seem stressed out? What shows you that they're feeling stressed? Are there ways you change your interactions with them to help manage their feelings?

- What can other people do to help you feel calmer when you're stressed? In what ways do people's interactions with you make it worse?

SET ASIDE SUNDAYS (OR ANOTHER DAY)

How do families who seem to be constantly scattered in every direction ever manage to get together for a meal? "Schedule it!" says Loren, a Florida mom of an elementary school–aged son and a teen who's preparing to leave for college. "No exceptions unless someone is out of town." In her home, the weeknights are jam-packed with the boys' sports commitments, so the scheduled family dinnertime is every Sunday evening.

We've heard of similar approaches from a number of families, all with the same rule: If dinner is on the family calendar, you can't skip it. While the rule may mean that family members have to say no to the occasional invitation or outing, it also means that there's at least one moment during the week when everyone can take a deep breath and just relax at home together. Loren and her husband, Art, say that with up to six days a week sacrificed to the boys' practices and games, this weekly ritual has allowed them important time to learn things about their kids that they might not otherwise have a chance to discover.

For a Sunday dinner, you may have more time to cook than on a harried weeknight. We recommend taking advantage of the opportunity and making extra portions so you can easily make another weeknight dinner out of leftovers when there's simply no time to cook anything.

FOOD

This menu pairs one of Loren's kids' favorites—meatloaf—with a hearty mac and cheese recipe and a freezer-friendly roasted vegetable dish. By serving meatloaf "burgers" on toasted buns another night, leftover mac and cheese with a side of fruit on a different evening, and popping extras of the squash into the freezer for emergencies, you can extend this one Sunday dinner to help get dinner on the table four separate times!

MEATLOAF
SERVES 6-8

This meatloaf recipe is adapted from one provided to us by cookbook author Ramona Hamblin, author of *just cook here's how*. Leftover slices are great warmed up in a skillet and served as "burgers" or as sandwiches on toasted bread!

INGREDIENTS

2 pounds ground beef

1 medium onion, diced

2 ribs celery, diced

2 medium carrots, peeled and shredded

1 cup seasoned bread crumbs

1 large egg

1 cup tomato sauce

1 teaspoon salt

1/2 teaspoon pepper

1/2 cup ketchup

INSTRUCTIONS

Preheat the oven to 375 degrees F.

Put all ingredients except the ketchup into a bowl and knead until mixed.

Form into a loaf and transfer to a baking dish.

Drizzle the ketchup over the top.

Bake for 60–80 minutes, or until a meat thermometer reads 160 degrees F.

ROASTED SQUASH AND APPLE MASH
SERVES 6-8

This homey side dish roasts in the oven while you prepare the rest of the meal and only needs a quick mash before taking its place on the dinner table. If you're not comfortable peeling and chopping your own squash, look for pre-cut butternut squash in the produce section of your grocery store.

INGREDIENTS

8 cups butternut squash, peeled and cubed

2 medium apples, peeled, cored, and quartered*

1 medium onion, peeled and quartered

2 tablespoons olive oil

1 teaspoon salt

1/4 teaspoon black pepper

2 tablespoons unsalted butter

1/2 teaspoon ground nutmeg

*MacIntosh apples work particularly well for this recipe, but any apple that will cook down soft and blend easily is a good choice.

INSTRUCTIONS

Preheat oven to 400 degrees F.

Combine the squash, apples, and onion on a large baking sheet. Drizzle with the olive oil and season with salt and pepper. Toss to coat evenly, then spread out in a single layer.

Roast the mixture for 30–40 minutes, until the squash is fork tender.

Transfer the mixture to a large serving bowl, add the butter and nutmeg, and mash with a potato masher or immersion blender until it reaches the desired consistency.

MACARONI AND CHEESE

`SERVES 6-8`

This stovetop macaroni and cheese recipe gets a boost from the addition of chopped spinach. Broccoli and cauliflower would also be excellent vegetable mix-ins. We've adapted this recipe from one shared with us by Ramona Hamblin.

INGREDIENTS

1 pound elbow macaroni

1 pound frozen chopped spinach, thawed and squeezed dry

4 tablespoons unsalted butter

1/4 cup flour

4 cups milk

2 teaspoons Dijon mustard

1 1/2 teaspoons salt

1/4 teaspoon black pepper

8 ounces extra-sharp cheddar cheese, shredded

8 ounces fontina cheese, diced

INSTRUCTIONS

Cook the pasta according to package directions. Drain, mix in the spinach, and set aside.

Melt the butter in a large skillet. Whisk in flour and cook for 2 minutes.

Slowly add milk while whisking.

Bring milk mixture to a boil, then reduce the heat until it thickens. Whisk often to avoid burning.

Add the mustard and cheese. Remove from the heat and stir until the sauce is thick and creamy and the cheeses are fully melted.

Pour the sauce over the pasta and spinach. Stir to coat thoroughly and serve.

FUN

Loren and Art enjoy using weekly Sunday dinners to learn more about their kids. A fast-paced game of Two-Minute Question Round is a fun way to uncover little details about each other that you might not know!

HOW TO PLAY

The goal of this game is to answer as many simple "or" questions in two minutes as possible. One person starts as the "interviewer" and chooses someone else to answer questions. (It can be helpful to have a list of questions at the ready, but some families find it more fun when the interviewer is challenged to come up with the questions on the spot.) The interviewer sets a timer and begins asking questions and getting answers as quickly as possible. A third person at the table, if possible, keeps track of how many answers are given before the timer goes off!

CONVERSATION

Use your weekly family time for more than just a check-in with these conversation starters about your family's hopes and dreams.

(AGES 8-13, 14-100)

- If you could make money doing whatever you love to do, what would you do for a living?
- When you graduate from school or retire from your job one day, what do you hope people will say about you?
- How do you want to change the world in the next year?
- Where do you think you'll live in twenty years?
- If you woke up tomorrow and could do one thing that you can't do right now, what would it be?

A list of possible questions to get you started:

Which do you prefer . . . ?

Dogs or cats?
Sneakers or sandals?
Coffee or tea?
Juice or milk?
Chocolate or vanilla?
Earth or space?
Summer or winter?
Movies or TV?
Listen or speak?

Read or hear?
Watch or do?
Football or baseball?
Plays or musicals?
Inside or outside?
Art museum or science museum?
Draw or write?
Run or walk?
Paris or London?

New York or L.A.?
Vacation or staycation?
Socks or no socks?
Zoo or aquarium?
Car or truck?
Plane or train?
Beach or mountains?
Sweet or salty?

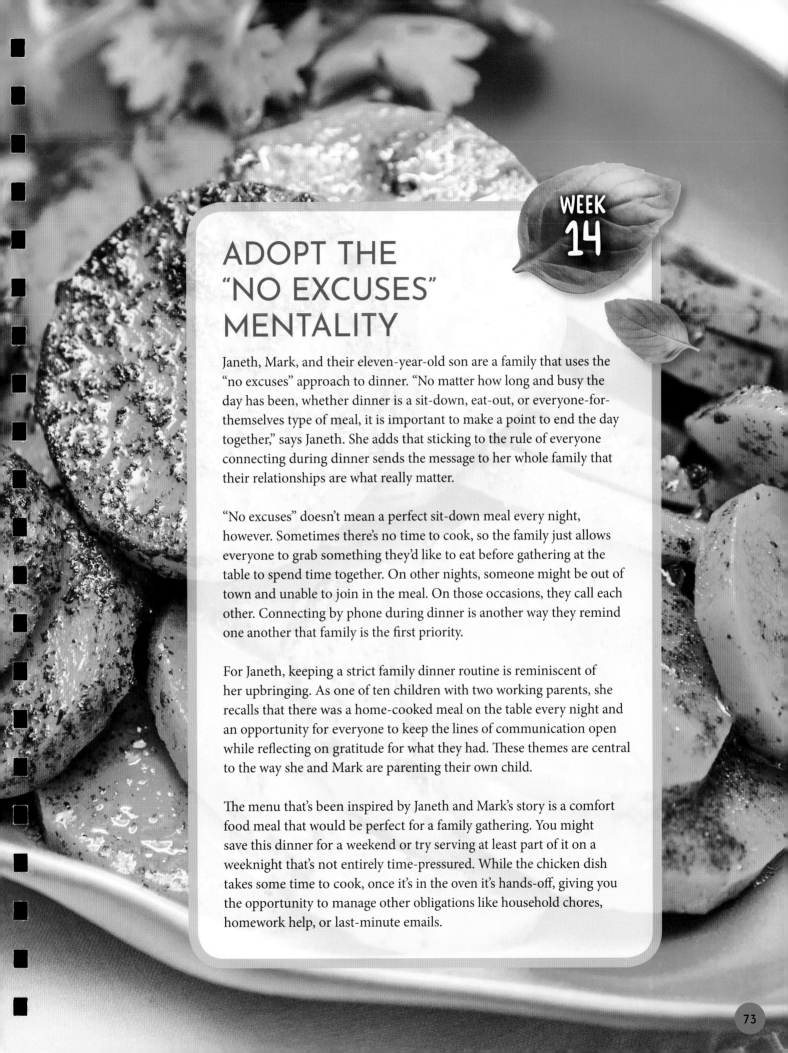

ADOPT THE "NO EXCUSES" MENTALITY

Janeth, Mark, and their eleven-year-old son are a family that uses the "no excuses" approach to dinner. "No matter how long and busy the day has been, whether dinner is a sit-down, eat-out, or everyone-for-themselves type of meal, it is important to make a point to end the day together," says Janeth. She adds that sticking to the rule of everyone connecting during dinner sends the message to her whole family that their relationships are what really matter.

"No excuses" doesn't mean a perfect sit-down meal every night, however. Sometimes there's no time to cook, so the family just allows everyone to grab something they'd like to eat before gathering at the table to spend time together. On other nights, someone might be out of town and unable to join in the meal. On those occasions, they call each other. Connecting by phone during dinner is another way they remind one another that family is the first priority.

For Janeth, keeping a strict family dinner routine is reminiscent of her upbringing. As one of ten children with two working parents, she recalls that there was a home-cooked meal on the table every night and an opportunity for everyone to keep the lines of communication open while reflecting on gratitude for what they had. These themes are central to the way she and Mark are parenting their own child.

The menu that's been inspired by Janeth and Mark's story is a comfort food meal that would be perfect for a family gathering. You might save this dinner for a weekend or try serving at least part of it on a weeknight that's not entirely time-pressured. While the chicken dish takes some time to cook, once it's in the oven it's hands-off, giving you the opportunity to manage other obligations like household chores, homework help, or last-minute emails.

FOOD
This smothered chicken dish can be served simply over rice or potatoes if you'd like, but if you have more time, make your meal extra special with sides of cornbread stuffing and cinnamon dusted carrots.

SMOTHERED CHICKEN WITH APPLE CIDER GRAVY
SERVES 6-8

This chicken dish takes a little time to cook, but most of it is inactive time—meaning that while dinner's doing its thing in the oven, you can spend time with your family.

INGREDIENTS

8 pieces bone-in, skin-on chicken (breasts, drumsticks, or thighs)

1 teaspoon salt

1/2 teaspoon black pepper

4 tablespoons unsalted butter

1 large onion, sliced

2 ribs celery, sliced

3 tablespoons all-purpose flour

6 sprigs fresh thyme, or 2 teaspoons dried thyme

2 cups apple cider

INSTRUCTIONS

Preheat the oven to 375 degrees F and season the chicken pieces with the salt and pepper.

Melt the butter in a Dutch oven over medium-high heat. Add the chicken pieces, skin-side down, and cook until golden brown. You may need to work in batches to keep from overcrowding the pan. Flip the browned chicken pieces over and cook for 2–3 minutes on the other side.

Remove the browned chicken pieces and set aside.

Reduce the heat to medium-low and add the onions and celery to the pan. Cook, stirring often, until the vegetables start to soften.

Sprinkle vegetables with flour, stir well, and cook for 2 minutes.

Add the thyme and apple cider, stirring well to make sure nothing is stuck to the bottom.

Return the chicken to the Dutch oven and cover.

Put the covered Dutch oven into the preheated oven and cook for 45 minutes, until the chicken is very tender and the gravy has thickened. If you used fresh thyme, remove the stems before serving.

CORNBREAD STUFFING
SERVES 8

This stuffing is best when the cornbread has had a chance to dry out, so we recommend letting it sit on the counter for about two days before crumbling.

INGREDIENTS

4 cups finely chopped celery

2 medium onions, diced

1 stick unsalted butter

2 8-inch pans of prepared cornbread, dried out and crumbled

1 14-ounce package herb-seasoned stuffing

2 teaspoons dried rubbed sage

2 teaspoons Italian seasoning

2 large eggs, beaten

28 ounces vegetable broth

INSTRUCTIONS

Preheat oven to 350 degrees F.

Sauté celery and onion in butter until tender.

Combine cornbread, stuffing mix, sage, and Italian seasoning in a large bowl.

Add celery mixture, egg, and broth. Mix thoroughly.

Place all in a 9 by 13–inch baking or casserole dish. Bake for 25 minutes until lightly browned and crusty on top.

CINNAMON CARROTS
SERVES 4-6

These simple carrots get a flavor boost from a little black pepper.

INGREDIENTS

4 tablespoons olive oil

6 medium carrots, peeled and cut diagonally into 1/2 inch pieces

1/2 teaspoon salt

1/2 teaspoon cinnamon (or more to taste)

1/2 teaspoon freshly ground black pepper (or more to taste)

1/2 cup water

INSTRUCTIONS

Heat the olive oil in a deep skillet over medium-high heat. Add the carrots and cook, stirring occasionally, for 3–4 minutes or until the carrots are light golden brown.

Add salt, cinnamon, and pepper to the skillet. Stir to combine.

Add the water, cover the skillet, and simmer for 10–15 minutes, until the carrots are fork tender. Shake the skillet occasionally to avoid any sticking.

Remove the cover from the skillet and serve.

FUN Play a game of 20 Questions dedicated to honoring family memories.

HOW TO PLAY

Someone thinks of a special family memory. The others at the table take turns asking up to twenty yes or no questions to try to guess the memory. The family member who guesses correctly gets to choose the next memory.

CONVERSATION

Making memories at the dinner table is the kind of thing that tends to happen naturally, but you can always nudge things along with these questions.

(AGES 8-13, 14-100)

- Are there certain foods we eat that bring up memories for you? What are they?
- Besides the food, what do you most enjoy about eating with the family?
- What is your most memorable family dinner moment? Why do you remember that moment in particular?
- If you could plan a special family meal for everyone, what would it be like? What would you serve, who would be there, and what would we talk about or do together?
- If someone asked you to share a special food that reminds you of your family, what food would you choose and why?

FIND YOUR FALLBACK MEAL

We've all been there. You get home at the end of a long day, the family is hungry and tired, and you realize you haven't had a chance to get to the grocery store. Before you call for takeout again, consider the idea of a "fallback" dinner—something you can easily make from items that you keep on hand for emergencies.

Beth, a mom of five sons, always has three dozen eggs in her refrigerator so she can quickly make scrambled eggs or omelets if she needs a fallback dinner. Stephanie and Bill, who both work long hours and have an active preteen, keep a pre-cooked rotisserie chicken on hand. Other suggestions we've gotten from families include frozen lasagnas, canned soup with grilled cheese sandwiches, pancakes and quesadillas with fruit. As you come up with a fallback, choose something that's fast, easy, and an established crowd pleaser.

FOOD

This menu includes a healthy, quick pasta recipe that relies entirely on pantry staples and can be made in less time than it would take for pizza delivery to arrive. We're adding a cucumber salad in the hope that you might find a cucumber hanging around in the crisper. If you have feta or any other cheese, you can toss that in too. The pita crisps are a good way to use up a stray pita pocket or two, but you can always substitute whatever bread you have on hand—or leave it off the menu altogether. Like any good fallback meal, ours is meant to be a guideline to help you use what you've got, not a set of rules you have to follow.

PASTA WITH TOMATOES AND CHICKPEAS

`SERVES 6-8`

This budget-friendly recipe was shared with us by the Vermont WIC Program and appears in their "Eat Well" cookbook. In a pinch, you could use canned tomatoes in place of the fresh, but we love the bright flavor fresh tomatoes provide.

INGREDIENTS

1 pound ripe, fresh tomatoes, finely chopped

1 clove of garlic, minced

Salt and pepper

1 teaspoon balsamic vinegar

1 tablespoon chopped fresh basil, or 2 teaspoons dried basil

2 tablespoons olive oil

1 15-ounce can chickpeas, drained and rinsed

1 pound whole-wheat pasta

1/4 cup grated Parmesan cheese

INSTRUCTIONS

Combine tomatoes, garlic, salt, pepper, balsamic vinegar, basil, and olive oil in a medium bowl. Let sit for 15 minutes.

Stir in chickpeas.

Meanwhile, bring a large pot of water to a rolling boil. Add a generous amount of salt and the pasta. Cook *al dente* until the pasta is firm to the bite. Drain.

Toss pasta with chickpea sauce, sprinkle the cheese on, and serve.

CUCUMBER AND FETA SALAD

`SERVES 6`

This cucumber salad is light and refreshing, with saltiness from feta cheese and a sour punch of red wine vinegar.

INGREDIENTS

3 cucumbers, peeled and sliced

1/2 cup olive oil

3 cloves of garlic, crushed

12 ounces feta cheese

Salt and pepper

Dried oregano

Red wine vinegar

INSTRUCTIONS

Rub the crushed garlic cloves around the inside of a salad bowl, then drop them in the bottom and add the olive oil. Let the oil and garlic marinate together for 20–30 minutes.

Remove the garlic pieces from the bowl. Add the cucumber slices to the olive oil and toss to coat. Season with salt and pepper and add vinegar, one tablespoon at a time, stirring and tasting as you go.

Once the cucumbers are seasoned to your liking, crumble in the feta cheese, sprinkle with oregano, toss, and serve.

HERBED PITA CRISPS
SERVES 6-8

Dress up ordinary pita bread with flavorful olive oil, then toast it in the oven to give it a crunch.

INGREDIENTS

4 pita breads, cut into roughly 1 inch wedges

1/2 cup olive oil

1 teaspoon coarse salt

1 teaspoon dried basil

1/2 teaspoon dried oregano

1/4 teaspoon crushed red pepper flakes

INSTRUCTIONS

Preheat oven to 425 degrees F.

In a small bowl, stir together the olive oil, salt, basil, oregano, and pepper flakes.

Arrange pita wedges on a rimmed baking sheet. Brush with the olive oil mixture.

Bake the pita wedges for 15–20 minutes until golden brown and lightly crisp.

FUN
On a night so busy you need a fallback meal, it's always good to have a reliable fallback game too. The Alphabet Game is a simple, fun game that's engaging for everyone at the table, but not too high-energy for the end of a long day.

HOW TO PLAY

As a group, choose a category such as animals, countries, singers, or "people our family knows." One family member starts the game by naming a person/thing from that category that starts with the letter *A*. Then the next person names a person/thing that starts with the letter *B*, the next person finds something for the letter *C*, and so on.

CONVERSATION

At the close of a hectic day, it can be more fun to look ahead and use a little imagination than to reflect back on the busy day you've just finished. Get everyone's minds off their long to-do lists with a conversation about the future.

(AGES 8-13, 14-100)

- If you could invent one thing to make the future a better place, what would it be?
- What would the world be like if we could all live forever?
- If you could travel to the future and see what happens in your life, would you? Why or why not?
- What is one world problem you hope to see solved in the next twenty years?
- What is one cool technology you hope to see in the future?

GRAB AND GO

With a full-time job, overscheduled kids, and a spouse with a disability, Sarah is always looking for a way to balance her desire to have regular family dinners with her many responsibilities. This is especially true during football season, when her kids' calendars are crammed with games, practices, and team events.

Whenever possible, Sarah likes to have the whole family eat at home together so that her spouse can be included in the meal. Therefore, packing a picnic isn't the ideal solution on football nights. However, there's limited time for both cooking and eating, so a make-ahead meal is perfect—as long as reheating time is kept to a minimum!

Sarah doesn't mind spending some extra time on Sundays pulling together meals for the week. A no-heat make-ahead pasta salad is a great compromise that meets all of her needs. The kids can help with the rest of the menu items and set the table, and in no time everyone will be enjoying each other's company over a home-cooked meal.

FOOD

This Nutty Orzo Salad can be made up to two days in advance, so it's ready when you are. Just pull the orzo salad out of the refrigerator, then quickly mix up some olive oil with herbs and garlic to make a bread dip. Then set out honey and sliced nuts to top Greek yogurt for a tasty dessert that can even be taken on the run.

NUTTY ORZO SALAD
SERVES 6

Two different kinds of nuts pack this meatless pasta salad with protein. If you make it in advance, the orzo may absorb some of the oil. Be prepared to drizzle the salad with some extra olive oil and give it a good toss before serving.

INGREDIENTS

1 pound orzo pasta

2 lemons

2-3 cloves of garlic, minced

1/2-3/4 cup olive oil

1 cup slivered almonds

1/2 cup pine nuts

1 pound fresh baby spinach, roughly chopped

1/2 cup grated Parmesan cheese

1 cup oil-packed sun-dried tomatoes, drained and roughly chopped

Salt and pepper to taste

INSTRUCTIONS

Cook the orzo according to package directions. Drain.

Grate the zest of both lemons directly into the hot orzo and add the garlic. Toss well. The heat of the orzo will help distribute the lemon and garlic flavor throughout the pasta.

Pour the almonds and pine nuts into a dry skillet and toast over medium heat. Cook for 5–8 minutes, stirring frequently, until the nuts are lightly toasted and fragrant. Be careful not to burn them!

Add the nuts and chopped spinach to the orzo. Toss well.

Juice the lemons and add the juice to the pasta. Gradually add the olive oil, a few tablespoons at a time, stirring well until the orzo mixture is well moistened.

Add the cheese and sun-dried tomatoes, then season with salt and pepper. Mix well, taste, adjust seasonings, and serve.

OLIVE OIL DIP
SERVES 4-6

This quick olive oil dip dresses up ordinary bread. We like this particular flavor combination, but you can really use any fresh or dried herbs you have on hand. For a special treat, consider a dollop of ricotta cheese in the center of the dish.

INGREDIENTS

1/3 cup extra-virgin olive oil

1 clove of garlic, crushed

1/2 teaspoon dried oregano

1/2 teaspoon dried, crushed rosemary

1 teaspoon grated lemon zest

Ricotta cheese (optional)

INSTRUCTIONS

Combine all ingredients in a small saucepan over medium heat.

Allow the oil to warm for about 5–7 minutes until fragrant. Don't let the garlic start to sizzle.

Turn off the heat and transfer the warm olive oil dip to a small dish.

If using ricotta cheese, place a generous dollop in the middle of the olive oil dip. Spoon some olive oil over the top.

Serve with crusty bread for dipping.

YOGURT WITH HONEY AND NUTS

SERVES 4

Yogurt with nuts and honey is a classic Greek combination. A pinch of cinnamon brings out the sweetness.

INGREDIENTS

4 cups Greek yogurt

8 tablespoons honey

1/2 teaspoon ground cinnamon

4 tablespoons pistachios, coarsely chopped

INSTRUCTIONS

Divide the yogurt evenly among four dishes.

Top each dish with two tablespoons of honey, a sprinkle of cinnamon, and a tablespoon of pistachios.

FUN
Make dinner feel like a party with a kid-friendly version of the well-known party game Never Have I Ever!

HOW TO PLAY

Each person puts up ten fingers. Going around the table, take turns making "Never Have I Ever . . ." statements. Anyone who has had that experience puts down one finger. The person with the most fingers left up at the end of the round wins!

Sample statements:

"Never Have I Ever . . ."

. . . broken a bone

. . . been sent to the principal's office

. . . copied from someone else's paper or let someone else copy from mine

. . . eaten liver

. . . fallen off the jungle gym

. . . forgotten my homework

. . . been in a musical

. . . played an instrument

. . . borrowed something without asking first

. . . had an overdue library book

. . . forgotten to wear underwear

. . . worn the same socks two days in a row

CONVERSATION

It takes leadership skills to get dinner planned, organized, and executed in a brief amount of time. Pass along some of your wisdom with these conversation starters about leadership.

(AGES 14-100)

- What qualities do you think make someone a good leader?

- Who is a leader that you look up to as a role model, either from history or from your own life? What makes them stand out?

- What is one way you've exhibited leadership in the past week?

- Do you find it easy or difficult to take the lead in most situations? Why?

- Do you think there is more than one way to show leadership? Can you think of an example of someone who demonstrates leadership in an unconventional way?

REVIVE THE HABIT

Busy schedules aren't just a challenge for families with kids at home. Michaeleen and Tracy were committed to family dinners when their children were growing up, but after the kids left home, they discovered that it was increasingly easy to let dinnertime slide. With a newly empty nest, both found themselves staying later at work and taking on more evening commitments. And when they did get home in time to eat together, they were more likely to eat quickly at the kitchen counter than they were to cook a meal and sit down to eat it as they would have when the kids were still at home.

Gradually, their connection started to suffer, and they knew they had to make some changes. They started by trying to reclaim a sit-down dinner together whenever possible. "We take more time with each other if we're actually at the table," Michaeleen said. They also rekindled their old habit of planning meals at the start of the week and reverted to easy family favorites that had made dinner manageable during the kids' childhoods: casseroles, slow cooker meals, and quick skillet dinners with fast-cooking proteins like ground beef.

To stay accountable, Michaeleen and Tracy adopted a new habit of sharing dinner ideas, photos, and advice with their grown children. They exchange texts and photos of meals with their son and his new wife, along with articles and tips to help each household stay on track with mealtime routines.

To enjoy a dinner experience that's geared towards child-free families, try a no-fuss twist on a classic beef stroganoff. With the food taken care of, you can move on to our tips and conversation starters developed especially to help couples focus on connecting with one another over a meal.

FOOD

Beef stroganoff gets a practical and budget-friendly makeover by substituting ground beef with more expensive steak or long-cooking stew beef. Serve it over egg noodles with frozen peas and savory roasted tomatoes.

GROUND BEEF STROGANOFF
SERVES 4-6

This easy and budget-friendly recipe comes from Bevan Wallace and originally appeared on her blog, "Real Life Delicious" (reallifedelicious.com).

INGREDIENTS

1 pound wide egg noodles

1 pound ground beef

1/4 teaspoon paprika

Salt and pepper to taste

1 onion, chopped

8 ounces fresh mushrooms, sliced

1-2 cloves of garlic, chopped

1 cup beef or chicken stock

1/2 cup sour cream

2 tablespoons sherry or apple cider vinegar

INSTRUCTIONS

Bring a large pot of salted water to a boil and cook noodles according to package directions. Drain and set aside.

In a large skillet or Dutch oven, brown the meat with the salt, pepper, and paprika until cooked through. Drain the extra fat from the pan if necessary.

Add the onions and garlic. Cook until softened and translucent.

Add the mushrooms. Cook for another 3–5 minutes.

Stir in the stock, sherry or vinegar, and about 2 tablespoons of the sour cream.

Cook for another 5 minutes and season to taste. Add more sour cream if desired for a creamier texture.

Serve over noodles.

PEAS WITH HERB BUTTER
SERVES 4

Give plain frozen peas a makeover with a flavorful herb butter.

INGREDIENTS

1 package (10-12 ounces) frozen peas

3 tablespoons unsalted butter

2 teaspoons finely chopped fresh chives

1 teaspoon finely chopped fresh mint or parsley

Salt and pepper

INSTRUCTIONS

In a wide skillet, melt the butter over medium heat.

Add the peas. Cover and cook for 3–5 minutes, shaking the skillet occasionally.

When the peas are warmed through, add the fresh herbs and stir. Season with salt and pepper to taste.

ROASTED TOMATOES

SERVES 2-4

A sweet and savory seasoning mix creates an almost caramel-like sauce on the tomatoes. You can also substitute four to six plum tomatoes, halved lengthwise, for the grape tomatoes in this recipe.

INGREDIENTS

1 pint grape tomatoes

2 tablespoons brown sugar

1 tablespoon coarsely chopped fresh rosemary

2 cloves of garlic, chopped

3/4 teaspoon coarse salt

1/4 teaspoon crushed red pepper flakes

3 tablespoons olive oil

INSTRUCTIONS

Preheat oven to 400 degrees F.

Pour the tomatoes into an 8- or 9-inch baking dish. Add the seasonings (brown sugar through red pepper flakes) and stir to coat. Drizzle with the olive oil.

Roast the tomatoes for 20–25 minutes, until their skins have started to burst and the brown sugar has melted into a sauce.

FUN
For a couples-only connection, transform your everyday dinner into a restaurant-quality date night.

HOW TO PLAY

Think of the things that make a restaurant meal special, besides someone else cooking the food! What type of lighting sets the mood? How about music, flowers, or candles? You don't have to go all out—a tablecloth, some candles, and a chalkboard "menu" are easy touches that will instantly communicate "date night."

You may feel silly dressing up at home, but this is a grown-up version of make-believe—get dressed like you would for a night out! When you're dressed up and have a nicely set table, you and your partner are almost guaranteed to behave a little differently than you would on a typical night at home. That extra effort is likely to translate to a deeper connection and more thoughtful conversation. Just remember that your in-home "restaurant" is just like any romantic date night venue: tech-free! No TV or phones while you're "dating."

For an extra special touch, consider having a take-out dessert from a special favorite restaurant ready to end the night on a sweet note.

CONVERSATION

Sometimes the comfortable silence familiar to most couples can get a bit too comfortable. Break the silence and get the conversation flowing again with these better alternatives to the old standby of "How was your day?"

(AGES: 14-100)

- What was the most interesting thing you did today?
- If you could change one thing about your day, what would it be?
- I know you've been working on _____. How is that going?
- Have you had the opportunity to learn anything new lately?
- What's something you wish we could do together?
- Where should we take our next trip? Let's choose a place that neither of us have been to before, but have always wanted to visit.

REHEAT
AND EAT

Dinner can't always be the first priority when you walk in the door after a busy day. For many families, there are other competing demands for attention: homework help, housework, playtime with children you haven't seen during the day, or the beginning of a "second shift" of carpooling and organizing evening activities.

With so much to accomplish in the limited evening hours, it's no wonder families sometimes feel as if the time required to chop and sauté gets squeezed out of the schedule. For nights when you're at home but harried, a make-ahead meal is a smart solution to dinnertime with minimal hassle. Whoever gets home first can pop it in the oven to reheat, and the hustle and bustle of a busy family can continue until the timer dings and dinner's ready to eat.

FOOD
This make-ahead casserole has two separate parts—a filling and a topping—that should be combined just before heating to avoid sinking. We recommend serving it with a super-fast citrus salad and an easy recipe for a dressed-up package of frozen corn, but on the busiest evenings you can always just slice an avocado and set out a bowl of grape tomatoes, and dinner is done!

TAMALE POT PiE
SERVES 6-8

To make this ahead of time, you can cook the filling up to three days in advance and keep in the refrigerator. The cornbread crust mixture can be made up to twenty-four hours in advance (be sure to store that in the refrigerator too). If you're assembling both items straight from the fridge, you may need to adjust the baking time by a few minutes to be sure everything gets properly heated through.

INGREDIENTS

Filling

1 1/2 pounds ground beef or turkey

1 cup diced onion

4 cloves of garlic, minced

2 cups diced red bell pepper

2 tablespoons olive oil

2 cups cooked dark kidney beans or black beans

1 1/4 cups tomato puree

1 teaspoon salt

1/4 teaspoon crushed red pepper flakes

2 teaspoons ground cumin

2 teaspoons dried oregano

Crust

1 cup yellow cornmeal

1 cup all-purpose flour

2 teaspoons baking powder

1/4 teaspoon salt

1 tablespoon honey

1/2 cup vegetable oil

2 large eggs, beaten

1 cup milk

INSTRUCTIONS

In a large skillet, prepare the filling by sautéeing the meat, onions, garlic, and bell pepper in oil over medium-high heat until the meat is browned and the vegetables are softened, about 7 minutes.

Add the beans, tomato puree, and seasonings. Stir to combine.

Allow the filling to bubble around the edges and cook, stirring occasionally, for about 5 minutes to let the flavors combine.

Transfer the filling to an 8 by 8–inch oven-safe dish.

Preheat your oven to 400 degrees F.

Prepare the crust by whisking together the cornmeal, flour, baking powder, and salt in a large bowl.

Combine the honey, oil, eggs, and milk and add to the dry ingredients. Stir thoroughly until all of the ingredients are just moistened.

Spread the cornbread batter evenly over the filling in the casserole dish.

Bake, uncovered, for 35–45 minutes until a toothpick inserted in the center of the crust comes out free of batter.

SKILLET CORN WITH TOMATOES

SERVES 4-6

Take frozen corn to the next level with this easy makeover.

INGREDIENTS

4 tablespoons unsalted butter

3 green onions, minced

1 16-ounce package frozen corn kernels

1 cup grape tomatoes, halved

1/2 teaspoon salt

Juice of 1 lime

INSTRUCTIONS

Melt the butter in a large skillet over medium heat. Add the green onions and sauté for 2 minutes until fragrant and slightly softened.

Add the corn and tomatoes to the skillet. Season with salt and cook for 5–7 minutes, stirring occasionally. The corn should be heated through and the tomatoes should be warmed and slightly softened.

Remove from the heat and add the lime juice, a squeeze at a time, tasting until it reaches the right level of lime. Adjust the salt level as needed and serve.

CITRUS SALAD WITH RED ONION

SERVES 6

Fruit salad takes on a savory flavor twist in this fresh, bright side dish.

INGREDIENTS

1 ruby red grapefruit, peeled and segmented

1 navel orange, peeled and segmented

1/2 cup thinly sliced red onion

2 tablespoons chopped fresh oregano or 1/2 cup arugula

1/2 teaspoon salt

1/4 teaspoon black pepper

1/3 cup olive oil

1/4 cup pine nuts to garnish, optional

INSTRUCTIONS

Segment the fruit over a bowl to catch all the juices.

Arrange the segments of grapefruit and orange on a plate. Scatter the red onions over the fruit.

Add the oregano or arugula, salt, and pepper to the citrus juices. Whisk in the olive oil.

Drizzle the dressing over the fruit and onions. Allow the salad to sit for at least 5 minutes before serving.

FUN

Test your family's food knowledge with a round of Ingredient Race.

HOW TO PLAY

Pick one of the ingredients from your meal and put it on the counter or in the center of the table. Give everyone a piece of paper and a pencil and take two minutes to write down as many dinners that use that ingredient as possible. Whoever comes up with the most dinners wins!

CONVERSATION

Speaking of writing down as many correct answers as you can . . . we often tell parents not to bring up potentially touchy subjects at the dinner table. But depending on the circumstances and what works well for your family, you might be able to talk about common dilemmas without adding tension to the meal—and it can be important to do so every once in a while.

Sometimes kids are more receptive to sensitive topics when parents open up and share their own mistakes. One example might be sharing a story about a time when someone asked you to cheat, and talking about how you handled the situation (and importantly, what you learned). Being honest about your own experiences may help kids feel more secure in answering questions like these.

(AGES 14-100)

- Have you ever witnessed anyone cheating (at school, at a game, or anywhere else)? How did you handle it?

- If you knew that kids in your class had cheated on a big test but they didn't get caught, would you tell the teacher? Why or why not?

- Why do you think people are tempted to cheat?

- People tend to think of "cheating" as copying someone else's answers on a test or getting the answers ahead of time. Do you think there are other ways to cheat at school?

- Besides school, can you think of other ways people commonly "cheat," such as sharing passwords to streaming services? What do you think about those practices?

SLOW DOWN AND ENJOY

"Busy" doesn't always mean too busy to sit down to dinner. For some families, the challenge is slowing down enough to enjoy the meal once they've gathered at the table. With homework, email, evening meetings, and activities, you may feel like dinner is just a quick "pit stop" in between all the other items on the to-do list.

Michelle and John of Ontario, Canada, count themselves as part of the "dine and dash" crowd. Michelle admits that while they have managed to make regular dinners with their thirteen year old son a priority, she finds it hard to stay at the table for long and can't relax and enjoy the meal because she's frequently distracted by all the things that still need to be accomplished before the end of the day. The couple's son also tends to rush through eating so he can finish homework or capitalize on some free time.

John and Michelle realized that the value they wanted from family dinners—a sense of connection and a chance to feel caught up on one another's lives—was getting lost in the rush to eat, clean up, and move on. They started intentionally adding time to the meal and using preselected conversation starters and activity ideas to keep everyone focused on the dinner table. Slowly, they began to relax and enjoy mealtimes more. Now the family uses the "Rose, Thorn, and Bud" format for sharing stories from their days, and it's become such an important part of dinner at their house that even their son's friends will ask to get it started when they join the family for meals.

FOOD

A favorite meal for this family includes steak and Caesar salad, so we're sharing weeknight friendly versions of both, along with a creamy corn casserole that can be made ahead of time and reheated if you're short on cooking time.

TANO'S STEAK TIPS

SERVES 6

Our Executive Director, Lynn Barendsen, provided this recipe, which is her son Tano's favorite dinner.

INGREDIENTS

1 tablespoon chopped fresh rosemary

1 tablespoon chopped fresh sage

1 tablespoon chopped fresh thyme leaves

2 tablespoons kosher salt

2 tablespoons freshly ground black pepper

2 pounds steak tips, about 1 inch thick

2 tablespoons olive oil

INSTRUCTIONS

In a small bowl, mix all herbs, salt, and pepper until combined.

Pat steak tips dry and coat with the rub.

Brush gently with olive oil.

Place on a preheated grill (or in a cast-iron skillet) and cook for about 5 minutes per side of 1 inch thick steak tips for medium-rare steak. For thicker meat, add a minute or two. For thinner meat, decrease the time. For rarer or more well-done meat, adjust the time accordingly.

DRESS-IT-IN-A-BOWL CAESAR SALAD

SERVES 4-6

Our friend April Hamilton provided this recipe for an anchovy-free Caesar dressing that's done in seconds. She often adds grilled chicken to make this salad a complete meal on its own. The original recipe was published in her book, *Counter Intelligence: The Best of April's Kitchen.*

INGREDIENTS

1 head romaine lettuce

1 lemon

1 teaspoon Dijon mustard

Salt and pepper to taste

5 tablespoons extra virgin olive oil, divided

1/2 cup freshly grated Parmesan cheese, divided

1 baguette, torn into bite-sized pieces

3 cloves of garlic, smashed

INSTRUCTIONS

Preheat oven to 350 degrees F.

Wash and dry the lettuce. Keep chilled until ready to serve.

Mix the lemon, mustard, salt, and pepper in a large salad bowl. Gradually whisk in 3 tablespoons olive oil, then add about 2 tablespoons Parmesan.

Tear the lettuce and add it to the bowl. Toss the salad, then top with remaining Parmesan.

To make the croutons, place the baguette pieces in a large bowl and drizzle with about 2 tablespoons olive oil.

Smash 3 cloves of garlic and toss with bread.

Spread out on a baking sheet and bake 10 minutes. Carefully toss and turn the croutons. Continue baking for 5–10 minutes until croutons are crunchy and golden.

Add the croutons to the salad and serve.

FRESH CORN SPOONBREAD
SERVES 6

This creamy side dish can be made up to forty-eight hours in advance, then baked just before you're ready to serve.

INGREDIENTS

1 cup milk

1 tablespoon unsalted butter

1/2 cup yellow cornmeal

1/2 teaspoon salt

1/4 teaspoon black pepper

1 1/2 cups corn kernels, fresh or frozen

2/3 cup chopped green onions

1 cup plain, whole-milk yogurt

1 teaspoon baking powder

2 large eggs, beaten

INSTRUCTIONS

Preheat oven to 400 degrees F.

Butter an 8-inch square baking dish and set aside.

In a medium saucepan over high heat, combine the milk, butter, cornmeal, salt, and pepper. Allow the mixture to come to a boil and cook, whisking constantly until it's thick, about 3–5 minutes.

Transfer the cornmeal mixture to a large mixing bowl. Stir in the corn kernels, green onions, yogurt, and baking powder.

Add the beaten eggs and mix thoroughly.

Pour the batter into the prepared baking dish and bake for 40–50 minutes, until the spoonbread is golden brown and puffed and a toothpick inserted in the center comes out mostly clean. Let the spoonbread cool slightly before serving.

FUN

Rose, Thorn, and Bud is a popular dinner game that's even been used in the White House to get family dinner off to a positive start!

HOW TO PLAY

Go around the table and ask each person to share the rose (the best or most special part of their day), and the thorn (the most difficult part of their day). In our favorite version of the game, you can also add a bud (something to look forward to).

This can be a great way to get around the dreaded one-word answers when you ask, "How was your day?" It helps everyone think about sharing their day in a new way.

After your kids are used to sharing their "rose" and "thorn," get those creative juices flowing by asking them to come up with a different analogy for the best and most difficult parts of the day (peak and pit, high and low, you name it!).

CONVERSATION

Michelle is an addiction counselor specializing in technology addictions, so it's important for her and John to be sure their teenage son understands why they feel placing limits on his technology access is a healthy choice. Bring the topic to your dinner table with these conversation starters about balancing technology use.

(AGES 14-100)

- How are face-to-face conversations, phone calls, and text conversations all different from one another? Which do you prefer and why?

- Are there certain types of conversations that you think are better conducted in person versus via phone or text? Explain.

- Can you think of any reasons why it might sometimes be a good idea to take a break from screen time?

- What are your favorite things to do without computers, phones, or TV?

- Do you think that the same technology limits should be applied to parents and kids of all ages? Why or why not?

REINVENT LEFTOVERS

Making dinner happen on a tight timeline is much easier with a meal plan, but it's even easier if that plan includes smart ways to use leftovers for another dinner or two throughout the week. There's a reason so many of us have memories of baked chicken, meatloaf, and casseroles from our childhood family dinners—they're the type of meals that would easily lend themselves to a second act later in the week, giving busy parents a little time away from the kitchen.

The idea of leftovers for dinner has gotten a bit of a bad rap over the years, but many families are returning to this smart strategy, with a fresher twist to keep the "Ugh, this again?" complaints at bay. Bill and Stephanie from Rhode Island are among the parents we've met who try to incorporate one evening's leftovers into a whole new dish later in the week. With two hectic work schedules and a preteen athlete who frequently has practices, games, and weekend tournaments, dinnertime sometimes gets pushed late in the evening. They often find themselves trying to trade responsibilities to keep the family schedule moving forward, with one parent rushing to complete necessary errands and start a meal after work while the other leaves the office to catch a few minutes of the day's practice or game and handles carpooling. When the goal is often to just make sure everyone has eaten before 9:00 p.m., they prefer to spend their precious time sitting down together instead of cooking elaborate dinners, so they often take shortcuts like using leftovers of a roast chicken (either homemade or store-bought) to create a healthy meal in minutes.

FOOD

This chicken torta recipe is great for quickly repurposing leftovers into something fresh and fun, and since it's more about assembly than actual cooking, every member of the family can pitch in to make the prep time even faster. Put the corn on the grill before you start making the sandwiches and the avocado salad, and everything should be ready in a snap.

CHICKEN TORTAS
SERVES 6-8

This recipe is slightly adapted from one provided by Arizona WIC. It's not only fast and easy, but budget-friendly as well.

INGREDIENTS

1 15-ounce can pinto beans, drained and rinsed

4 cups cooked, shredded chicken

2 cups shredded romaine lettuce

1/2 cup thinly sliced radishes

1 white onion, thinly sliced

4 French bread rolls

1 cup salsa

Shredded Monterey Jack cheese

INSTRUCTIONS

Place beans in a small saucepan. Cook over medium heat until warm.

Lightly mash beans with a fork. Set aside.

Cut each French roll in half lengthwise.

Divide chicken, beans, lettuce, radishes, and onion evenly into four servings.

Place one serving of ingredients on bottom half of each roll. Top with salsa and sprinkle with cheese.

Place other half of the roll on top.

Serve immediately.

GRILLED CORN
SERVES 4

Grilling whole ears of corn is a fast and flavorful way to prepare a well-known family dinner side dish. Here we're recommending a finishing step that's inspired by elotes (Mexican street corn), but you can opt for just a drizzle of plain melted butter if you prefer.

INGREDIENTS

4 ears corn, husked

4 tablespoons unsalted butter, melted

1/4 cup grated Parmesan cheese or cotija cheese

1/2 teaspoon coarse salt

1 lime, zested

INSTRUCTIONS

Heat a grill or grill pan to medium. Brush with vegetable oil to be sure the corn won't stick.

Grill the corn for about 10 minutes, turning frequently. The ears should get slightly charred but not blackened.

In a small bowl, combine the butter, cheese, salt, and the zest of the lime.

Remove the ears of corn from the grill. Brush them with the butter mixture.

Cut the lime into wedges and serve with the corn.

AVOCADO AND TOMATO SALAD

SERVES 4-6

It doesn't get much faster than this simple avocado salad, which pairs well with almost any grilled dish.

INGREDIENTS

2 avocados, peeled and sliced

3 plum tomatoes, chopped

1/2 cup thinly sliced red onion

1 teaspoon salt

1/2 teaspoon black pepper

2 tablespoons olive oil

Juice of 1 lime

INSTRUCTIONS

Combine the avocados, tomatoes, and onion in a medium bowl.

Sprinkle with salt and pepper. Add the lime juice and olive oil and mix well.

FUN

Parents of a certain generation might remember a game called "Six Degrees of Kevin Bacon." Test the knowledge of media-savvy kids with your own version of the Six Degrees game, Kevin Bacon not required.

HOW TO PLAY

Choose a family member to take the Six Degrees challenge. Give that person the name of two celebrities. That person has to try to name movies or TV shows that will link the two in six movies or fewer. For example, you might name "Johnny Depp and Jonathan Rhys Meyers." Answers might include:

Johnny Depp was in Pirates of the Caribbean with Keira Knightley.

Keira Knightley was in Bend it Like Beckham with Jonathan Rhys Meyers.

That's only two moves! After winning the challenge, that person has the opportunity to choose another player and challenge them with two new celebrities.

CONVERSATION

Bill and Stephanie have a busy preteen athlete who's also an avid sports fan. The whole family enjoys taking in games together. Sportsmanship is an important topic for them, and it's good for any family that wants to talk about playing fairly and winning and losing graciously.

(AGES 8-13, 14-100)

- Do you think you're a competitive person? In what way?

- Whether in sports or in any competitive activity, what are some ways that you can show "sportsmanship?" What does "sportsmanship" mean to you?

- Is it important to you to receive trophies or awards to recognize your contributions to a team or a group? Why or why not?

- Are there times when losing at something feels easier than at other times? When is it easier to lose? When is it harder?

- Does the way that a professional athlete reacts to a big win or a big loss affect the way you view them?

EMBRACE THE SPLIT SHIFT

Kristin works three nights a week on the twelve-hour overnight shift. Her husband works five days a week. Her two teenagers have busy lives of their own. Family dinner still happens in their house, but it's almost never the whole family sitting down together. Instead, they approach mealtimes like they approach their work schedules: as a split shift. "This is the norm," Kristin says.

Instead of a single family dinner, Kristin's family has two each night. One mealtime might be Kristin and one teen eating early before they're off to work and evening activities. Another might be Kristin's husband eating with the other child after they both get home from long days. The arrangements vary day-to-day, but rarely do all four manage a sit-down. Still, dinner is a priority that's managed creatively with two mealtimes every night—and despite what you might think, it's not really twice as much work.

If you're a "split shift" dinner family, what you serve can be just as important as when you serve it. Try to rely on meals that heat and hold well, and won't become less appetizing as the evening wears on (just think of how that pork chop will look and taste after a few turns in the microwave!). If you plan dinners that allow each person to do a little assembly work, it gives everyone the opportunity to eat something that feels freshly made no matter what time they eventually sit down to dinner.

FOOD

This soup recipe is perfect for "split shift" dinners since it can be made ahead, holds well in the refrigerator or freezer, can take plenty of reheating without losing its appeal, and can even be kept warm in a slow cooker if you prefer. We're pairing it with cranberry turkey sandwiches—just make the fixings for the sandwiches available and your family members can do the rest. Individual mug cakes that take just a few minutes in the microwave are a fun way to provide a warm, comforting dessert that's ready whenever you are, and they're easy enough for even elementary school–aged kids to make (with a little adult guidance).

BUTTERNUT SQUASH AND PEAR SOUP

SERVES 6-8

You can adjust the texture of this soup to suit your family's preferences. If you like it thicker, use less broth. If you prefer it thinner, use more.

INGREDIENTS

4 tablespoons unsalted butter

1 cup diced onion

6 cups peeled, cubed butternut squash

2 medium pears, peeled and diced

1 1/2 tablespoons chopped fresh rosemary

8 cups chicken stock

1/3 cup heavy cream (optional)

Salt and pepper to taste

INSTRUCTIONS

Heat the butter in a large pot over medium heat.

Sauté the onions in the butter until soft and translucent, about 5–8 minutes.

Add the squash, pears, and rosemary. Cook, stirring occasionally, for 5 minutes.

Add the broth, cover, and bring to a boil. Reduce the heat and simmer until the squash is very tender, about 20 minutes.

Puree the soup using an immersion blender, or by transferring in batches to a regular blender, until smooth.

Add the cream and season to taste.

CRANBERRY TURKEY SANDWICHES

SERVES 4

Let every family member assemble his or her own sandwich so everyone has a fresh (and customized) meal.

INGREDIENTS

4 crusty sandwich rolls

1/2 cup soft garlic-herb cheese, such as cream cheese or Boursin

1/2 cup whole-berry cranberry sauce

1 cup arugula or baby spinach

1 pound deli sliced smoked turkey

INSTRUCTIONS

Cut the sandwich rolls in half. Spread the top half of each with 2 tablespoons of the garlic-herb cheese.

Onto the bottom roll, layer on 4 ounces of turkey per sandwich and a handful of arugula. Top with 2 tablespoons of cranberry sauce.

Add the top roll to each sandwich and serve.

BANANA CHOCOLATE CHIP MUG CAKES

MAKES 1 INDIVIDUAL MUG CAKE

Mug cakes are a fun way to provide a warm, comforting dessert to each member of the family on demand. Even young grade-school children can make their own cakes with just a little adult help.

INGREDIENTS

1/2 ripe banana

1 large egg

1 tablespoon milk

1/2 teaspoon vanilla

3 tablespoons pure maple syrup

1 tablespoon unsalted butter, softened

1/2 teaspoon baking powder

3 tablespoons all-purpose flour

2 tablespoons chocolate chips

INSTRUCTIONS

In a standard-sized household mug, beat together the mashed banana and egg with a fork. Add the milk, vanilla, maple syrup, and softened butter. Stir well.

Stir in the baking powder and flour, mixing just until the batter is well combined.

Microwave for 1 minute, then stir again. Add the chocolate chips and put the mug back into the microwave.

Microwave for an additional 2 minutes, until the cake is set. Be careful—mug cakes can be hot when they first come out! We recommend letting the cake sit for a minute or two to cool before digging in.

FUN

Let everyone join in the fun by creating a collaborative food poem. Leave a whiteboard or notepad handy so each person can contribute when they sit down to eat.

HOW TO PLAY

When it's time to eat, each person takes a bite of food and writes down the first word that comes to mind. You could have everyone choose just one word or a word for each item on the plate. As each person adds their own words, you'll build a spontaneous poem about your dinner!

CONVERSATION

Encourage your family to get a little creative as they talk about their days. Use these conversation prompts to reinvent "How was your day?" for more interesting and engaging answers.

(AGES 8-13, 14-100)

- If you had to write a newspaper article about your day, what would the headline be?

- If you had to repeat one moment from today, every day for the rest of your life, which moment would you choose and why?

- If today were a color, what color would it be?

- Describe your day using only movie titles.

- In a movie about today, what would the theme song be?

PLAN THE "CAN'T FAIL" DINNER

When you're constantly racing the clock to get a healthy dinner on the table, one of the best things to do is to learn a few "can't fail" dinner recipes. A "can't fail" dinner is something you feel good about making, can be pulled together quickly, and is an established crowd-pleaser, so you know there will be no whining once it's served.

Ideally, a "can't fail" dinner is the type of thing you can easily decide to make whenever you're stuck for ideas, and it should involve only a handful of ingredients and not a lot of fussy prep work. The Family Dinner Project team member Bri frequently makes one of her mom's "can't fail" dinners—a chicken and pasta recipe that was adapted from a restaurant dish Bri's sister enjoyed when they were kids. It was listed on the menu as "Pasta Poulet," a play on "Pasta Chicken," and the easy homemade version has been one of the family's "can't fail" meals for almost thirty years.

FOOD

This whole meal can be made in twenty minutes! Bri's mom always served this dish with a tossed salad, but Bri's kids are crazy about broccoli, so we're recommending an easy broccoli dish with lemon butter as the perfect side for your "can't fail" pasta dinner. If you're feeling ambitious—or if you've got willing helpers—you can mix up a batch of popcorn balls and let them set while you eat.

PASTA POULET
SERVES 6-8

In a pinch, you can use pasta water instead of the broth in this recipe, but the flavor won't be quite as well developed.

INGREDIENTS

1 pound angel hair pasta

2 tablespoons olive oil

4 cloves of garlic

1 pound boneless, skinless chicken breast, cut into bite-sized cubes

1 tablespoon dried basil

2 teaspoons dried oregano

1 teaspoon salt

1/2 teaspoon black pepper

1 1/2 cups chicken broth

4 medium tomatoes, diced

4-6 green onions, diced

INSTRUCTIONS

Cook the pasta according to package directions.

While the pasta is cooking, warm the olive oil in a skillet over medium heat. Add the garlic and sauté for about 30 seconds, just until fragrant.

Add the chicken to the skillet and cook, stirring frequently, until lightly browned.

Season with the basil, oregano, salt, and pepper.

Add the chicken broth, stir to combine, and simmer for 5–7 minutes.

Add the tomatoes and green onions and cook for an additional 2–3 minutes, just until the tomatoes are softened.

Toss the chicken mixture with the cooked, drained pasta. Serve with Parmesan cheese as desired.

LEMON BUTTER BROCCOLI
SERVES 4-6

Give plain steamed broccoli a boost with lemony butter.

INGREDIENTS

1 pound broccoli, trimmed and cut into florets

4 tablespoons unsalted butter

1 teaspoon salt

1 lemon, zested and juiced

INSTRUCTIONS

Put the broccoli into a deep skillet. Add about a half-inch of water in the bottom, cover, and set over high heat.

When the water begins to boil, turn the heat to low. Allow the broccoli to steam for about 4–5 minutes, until bright green and pierceable with a fork but firm.

Drain the broccoli and return to the dry skillet. Add the butter, salt, 1 teaspoon lemon zest, and the juice of half the lemon to the skillet.

Put the lid back onto the pan and let the broccoli sit for another minute or so, just until the heat of the pan has melted the butter.

Stir before serving.

HARVEST POPCORN BALLS
MAKES 12 POPCORN BALLS

Adding dried fruit and pumpkin seeds to popcorn balls gives them great texture and adds a unique twist to a classic dessert.

INGREDIENTS

1/4 cup unsalted butter

2 cups miniature marshmallows

1/2 teaspoon ground cinnamon

8 cups plain, unsalted popped popcorn

2/3 cup roasted, salted pumpkin seeds

1 cup dried cranberries or cherries

INSTRUCTIONS

Combine the butter and marshmallows in a small saucepan. Cook and stir until melted.

Add the cinnamon to the marshmallow mixture, stir, and allow to cook for 1 additional minute.

In a large bowl, combine the popcorn, pumpkin seeds, and cranberries or cherries.

Pour the marshmallow mixture over the popcorn mix and stir carefully, until everything is evenly coated.

Using slightly wet hands to prevent sticking, form the mixture into balls about the size of a baseball, pressing firmly to compact the ingredients so they'll hold their shape. There should be about twelve popcorn balls.

Set the popcorn balls on a sheet pan to dry for 30 minutes.

FUN
Engage your kids' critical thinking skills with a fun guessing game called Who Did You See?

HOW TO PLAY

The game starts with one person pretending that they ran into someone the whole family knows. They say "Today I ran into someone in the supermarket (at work, downtown, at the dentist's office, etc.)."

The rest of the family then asks yes or no questions to help them guess who it was. The first person to guess correctly wins and takes the next turn.

CONVERSATION

We share so much at family dinner—not just food, fun, and conversation, but our values, expectations, attention, and time. Tonight's conversation is dedicated to developing ideas about sharing with young kids.

(AGES 2-7)

- Do you like to share? What types of things do you like to share?
- Are there times when it's okay not to share?
- What are some things you can share with others that aren't objects?
- How does it make you feel when somebody shares with you?
- Who is one person you would love to share a special thing with? What would you share with them if you could share anything?

PART III
IT'S TOO MUCH WORK!

One parent we know said, "It's not that I don't have time for dinner. It's just that sometimes I get everyone home at the end of a long day and think, 'Ugh . . . do I have to do anything else?'" Cooking and cleanup can feel like a monumental task, especially if you've still got a to-do list of additional things to take care of before bed.

Adding to the challenge of getting dinner on the table is the fact that not everyone has the same skill level when it comes to meal preparation. A lack of confidence in the kitchen can make planning and cooking feel more difficult. On the other side of the coin, if one person in the household is a competent cook and others aren't, too much responsibility can end up on the shoulders of a single family member. These ideas for sharing the workload, mastering simple recipes, and teaching the rest of the family lifelong skills can help ease the dinnertime burden.

ROTATE RESPONSIBILITIES

There's no question that family dinner takes some work, but there's no rule that says all the work has to fall to one person. The concept that "many hands make light work" applies to dinner as well—and not just to the cooking, but to the planning, shopping, and cleanup.

Jacqui and Josh have developed a smart and consistent rotation of responsibilities that keeps their three kids engaged in every stage of family dinner, so no one person has to be overwhelmed by the workload. In their household, there are three "helper positions" that rotate among the kids each week. One child is on prep duty, meaning that they set the table every night, pour drinks, and so forth. Another child might have planning duty, which involves helping to choose meals and side dishes for the whole family, as well as going to the grocery store with a parent to select fruits, vegetables, and other items for the week. And the third child is on the clean-up crew, clearing dishes, throwing out trash, and helping to stow leftovers.

This teamwork approach to dinner can also include cooking. One of our team members has a slot on her family chore chart for "Kitchen Helper of the Week." Whichever child is named for that week can be called upon at any time to come help prep and cook meals for the family. Some jobs, like making jars of overnight oats to stash in the refrigerator for family breakfasts, are things the kids can do all by themselves. Other jobs, like chopping vegetables and sautéing onions, are best done with adult supervision, but over time the kids are able to take more ownership.

FOOD

Two-ingredient salmon, a simple pasta side dish, and roasted asparagus are all low-cook items that are perfect for helping hands of all ages. This salmon recipe is so easy, in fact, that many older kids will be able to make it all on their own.

SALMON WITH PESTO
SERVES 4-6

Baking the salmon in the oven means this dish is entirely hands-off, making it a great one for young helpers to master since they won't have to stand over a hot skillet.

INGREDIENTS

2 pounds salmon filets

1 cup prepared pesto

Salt and pepper to taste

INSTRUCTIONS

Preheat oven to 400 degrees F. Line a rimmed baking sheet with foil or parchment paper.

Season the salmon lightly with salt and pepper. Using a silicone spatula or the back of a spoon, spread the pesto evenly over the salmon pieces.

Bake for about 15 minutes or until the salmon flakes easily with a fork.

PASTA WITH OIL AND GARLIC
SERVES 6-8

This recipe for a staple side dish was originally provided to us by Ramona Hamblin. You can use any pasta shape you like, but we recommend farfalle as a fun presentation for kids to enjoy.

INGREDIENTS

1 pound farfalle

1/2 cup extra-virgin olive oil

5 cloves of garlic, minced

1/4 teaspoon crushed red pepper flakes (optional)

1/2 cup fresh parsley, chopped

1 teaspoon salt

1 cup freshly grated Parmesan cheese

INSTRUCTIONS

Cook pasta according to package directions.

Gently heat oil in a large pan. Sauté garlic and crushed pepper (if using) for 2–3 minutes.

Remove from heat. Stir in parsley, salt, and pepper.

Top with Parmesan cheese and serve.

ROASTED ASPARAGUS WITH SHAVED PARMESAN

`SERVES 4`

Roasting asparagus gives it a slightly nutty flavor that you can't get from boiling or steaming. The addition of big pieces of shaved Parmesan cheese on top can be irresistible to young chefs!

INGREDIENTS

1 bunch asparagus, washed and trimmed

1 tablespoon olive oil

Salt and pepper to taste

Juice of 1/2 a lemon

1/2 cup shaved Parmesan cheese

INSTRUCTIONS

Preheat oven to 450 degrees F.

Spread asparagus in roasting pan. Sprinkle olive oil over the top and coat evenly by hand. Sprinkle with salt and pepper.

Roast for 10 minutes.

Remove from oven. Squeeze lemon juice over asparagus and stir gently to mix.

Sprinkle with freshly shaved Parmesan.

FUN
Work on getting kids involved in the grocery shopping with a fun scavenger hunt activity!

HOW TO PLAY

Next time you're at the grocery store with a young helper, send them on this scavenger hunt. Our list includes challenges such as "Find a cheese that came from a foreign country" and "Find one item in the produce section that came from the state where you live." If you're feeling creative, add some new challenges to the list. You might include some ideas that relate to your menu for the week, like "Find a green vegetable that goes with mac and cheese" or "Find two out of five ingredients that we'll use when we make spaghetti."

You can make your own scavenger hunt, or you can find one on our website at thefamilydinnerproject.org/fun/grocery-scavenger-hunt/

CONVERSATION

When you model responsibility and trust kids to take on age-appropriate tasks, it helps them to develop into mature adults. These conversation starters are another way to help kids develop a growing sense of themselves as responsible people.

(AGES 2-7, 8-13)

- What's something you're responsible for right now that makes you feel proud?
- What do you hope to be responsible for as you get older?
- Have you ever been responsible for doing something, but you didn't follow through? What happened?
- How can you show grown-ups that you are responsible?
- Do you feel like you have enough responsibilities in our family or not enough?

LEAN ON A DINNER VILLAGE

Sometimes the help you need to get dinner on the table might come from outside your home. When difficult circumstances like illness or absence take a toll on the family, planning and cooking regular meals may be one of the first things that falls to the wayside. That's when finding a "dinner village"–a group of people who can help with meals and who can later count on your support in return—can be a meaningful and important way to continue a family dinner routine despite major life challenges.

Sana and her family discovered the importance of a dinner village when her mother-in-law was terminally ill. Sana and her husband, along with her brother- and sister-in-law, moved in with her in-laws in Minnesota to help out. During that difficult time, they all came to appreciate both the closeness that was fostered by the living arrangement and the ease of making family dinners with so many adults on hand to help. "Each evening was a celebration of togetherness and gratitude for our blessings," Sana recalls, but she adds that there was a practical element to the living situation, which she and her husband began to miss once everyone had moved back home.

Recognizing how much easier meals were when they all shared the workload, Sana and her sister-in-law have now created a dinner rotation strategy that works for everyone. They take turns hosting the whole family at their houses throughout the week and share the cooking responsibilities between them. Maintaining the shared responsibility for mealtimes has helped keep the whole family close despite living in separate homes.

FOOD

Sana's family enjoys trying new healthy recipes and with young nieces and nephews around, there's always a need for easy dishes with kid appeal. The whole dinner village can get involved in a menu like this one. The hosting family can make the chicken dish while guests can bring the ribbon salad and the makings for fruit sundaes. After the meal is over, even the littlest diners can help assemble dessert.

SKILLET CHICKEN WITH GOAT CHEESE SAUCE

SERVES 4

This fast chicken dish gets finished with crumbled goat cheese, which melts to create a creamy and slightly tangy sauce. You might want some crusty bread handy to mop up the leftovers!

INGREDIENTS

3 tablespoons olive oil, divided

4 boneless, skinless chicken breasts

4 cloves of garlic, minced

1 28-ounce can crushed tomatoes

Salt and pepper to taste

8 ounces goat cheese

1/2 cup thinly sliced fresh basil

INSTRUCTIONS

Heat 2 tablespoons of the olive oil in a deep skillet over medium heat.

Season the chicken breasts with salt and pepper. Add them to the skillet and cook for 4–5 minutes on each side until golden brown. Remove the browned chicken from the skillet and set aside.

Add another tablespoon of oil to the skillet. Sauté the garlic for 30 seconds to a minute until fragrant, scraping up any browned bits from the chicken with a spatula or wooden spoon.

Pour the crushed tomatoes into the pan. Season with a pinch of salt and pepper and stir. Cover and simmer for 5 minutes.

Remove the lid from the pan and add the chicken and any accumulated juices back into the pan, nestling the chicken down into the sauce. Simmer, uncovered, for 5 minutes.

Crumble the goat cheese over the chicken and cover the pan. Let it cook for an additional 2 minutes or so to start melting the goat cheese.

Remove from heat, stir, and top with fresh basil.

RIBBON SALAD

SERVES 4-6

This recipe is easy to customize by tossing different combinations of vegetables in separate bowls. You can change things up by using almost any vegetable that can be prepared with a peeler.

INGREDIENTS

1/2 pound carrots

1/2 pound asparagus

1 sweet bell pepper

1/2 cup fresh parsley leaves

1 clove of garlic, peeled

1/2 teaspoon kosher salt

2 tablespoons fresh lemon juice

1/3 cup extra-virgin olive oil

INSTRUCTIONS

Use a vegetable peeler to shave the carrots, asparagus, and bell pepper into long strips. Combine in a large bowl.

In a food processor, blender, or chopper, combine the parsley, garlic, salt, and lemon juice. Blend, adding the olive oil slowly. Add salt to taste.

Toss the vegetables with the dressing.

FRUIT SUNDAES
SERVES 4-6

Sundaes are fun, but not every day is an ice cream occasion! Use fruit as the base for your dessert to change things up a little.

INGREDIENTS

4 cups assorted sliced fruit (e.g., bananas, berries, diced apples, peaches)

1/2 cup chopped nuts (optional)

1 cup whipped cream*

Chocolate and caramel sundae syrups

Sprinkles or mini-marshmallows (optional)

*Our whipped cream recipe (and dance-party whipping method!) are shared on page 58!

INSTRUCTIONS

Divide the sliced fruit among individual serving dishes.

Top with chopped nuts, whipped cream, sundae syrup of your choice, and any other toppings you like.

FUN
Help kids make connections to their family history with a brain-teasing game of Which One?

HOW TO PLAY

Whoever is asking the questions thinks of two people (e.g., Nana and Grammy, Mom and Dad) and asks the rest of the table questions to which only one of the two people is the right answer. (Which one got married when she was 19? Which one met her husband in California? Which one has seven brothers and sisters?)

CONVERSATION

For Sana and her family, one of the benefits of their "dinner village" is having the opportunity to discuss tricky social issues with the extended family on a regular basis and get advice from one another. One common challenge that's relevant to adults and kids alike is deciding how much is appropriate to share on social media. Broach the subject with your family using these conversation starters.

(AGES 14-100)

- Some people use the term "digital decorum" to describe the way they think others should behave online. What does "digital decorum" mean to you? Can you give examples?

- Another term often used is "digital citizen." What does it mean to be a "digital citizen?" How can you contribute in a positive way to your digital community?

- What do you wish your parents/kids understood about your social media use?

- Have you ever seen a social media post from a friend or family member that made you uncomfortable? Did you talk to that person about your discomfort? Why or why not?

- If you were asked to give a younger person three rules for using social media sensibly, what rules would you give them?

- Have you ever posted something and then regretted it? What did you do about it? What did you learn?

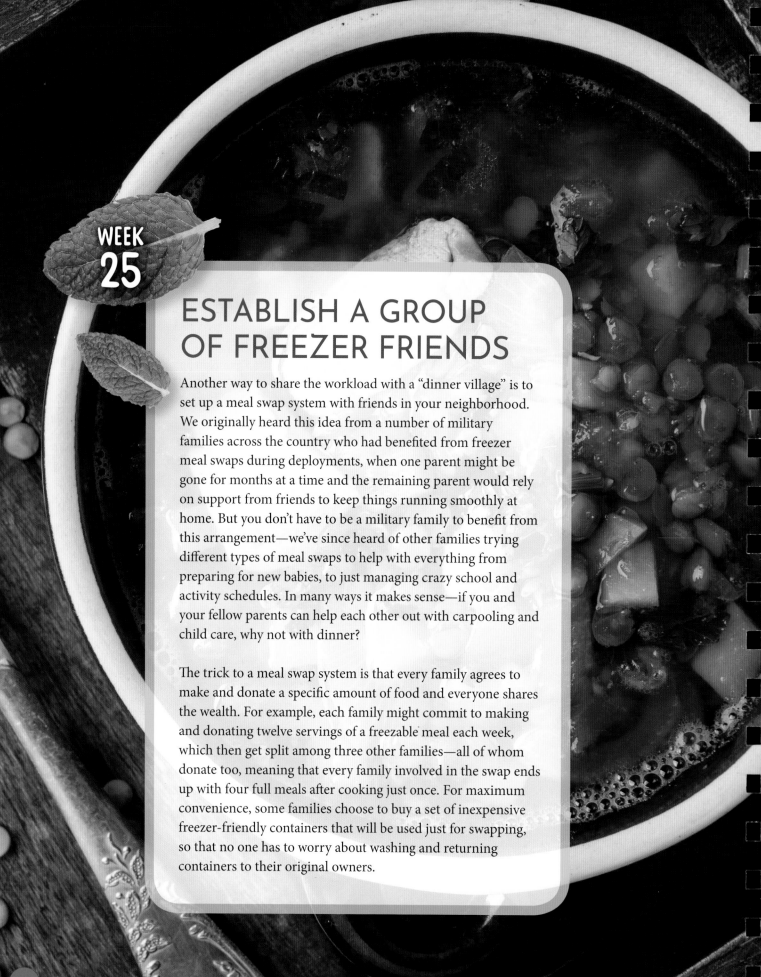

ESTABLISH A GROUP OF FREEZER FRIENDS

Another way to share the workload with a "dinner village" is to set up a meal swap system with friends in your neighborhood. We originally heard this idea from a number of military families across the country who had benefited from freezer meal swaps during deployments, when one parent might be gone for months at a time and the remaining parent would rely on support from friends to keep things running smoothly at home. But you don't have to be a military family to benefit from this arrangement—we've since heard of other families trying different types of meal swaps to help with everything from preparing for new babies, to just managing crazy school and activity schedules. In many ways it makes sense—if you and your fellow parents can help each other out with carpooling and child care, why not with dinner?

The trick to a meal swap system is that every family agrees to make and donate a specific amount of food and everyone shares the wealth. For example, each family might commit to making and donating twelve servings of a freezable meal each week, which then get split among three other families—all of whom donate too, meaning that every family involved in the swap ends up with four full meals after cooking just once. For maximum convenience, some families choose to buy a set of inexpensive freezer-friendly containers that will be used just for swapping, so that no one has to worry about washing and returning containers to their original owners.

FOOD This freezer-friendly menu would work perfectly as a way to get a "fallback dinner" stocked for a busy night or for a meal swap with friends. If you do choose to freeze and eat later, we recommend defrosting the soup and the muffins in the refrigerator overnight before reheating.

CHICKEN AND LENTIL SOUP
SERVES 6

This hearty chicken and lentil soup originated on team member Bri's blog, "Red, Round or Green." It keeps in the freezer for up to three months.

INGREDIENTS

3 tablespoons olive oil

1 large onion, diced

2 ribs celery, diced

3 cloves of garlic, minced

2 red bell peppers, diced

4 medium carrots, peeled and thinly sliced

1/4 teaspoon crushed red pepper flakes

1 teaspoon dried thyme

2 teaspoons dried basil

1 1/2 teaspoons salt

4 cups chicken stock

1 cup dried lentils, rinsed

1 28-ounce can diced tomatoes with juice

1 cup pumpkin puree

3 cups diced or shredded cooked chicken*

If you don't have cooked chicken on hand, you can add 2 uncooked, diced boneless skinless chicken breasts to the soup with the lentils and liquid and proceed as directed.

INSTRUCTIONS

In a large pot over medium heat, warm the olive oil and sauté the garlic, onions, celery, and bell peppers until softened, about 5–7 minutes.

Add the carrots, red pepper flakes, thyme, basil, and salt. Stir.

Add the chicken stock and lentils. Cover and bring to a boil. Reduce the heat to a simmer and cook for about 15 minutes.

Add the tomatoes and pumpkin puree. Stir well and continue to simmer, uncovered, for an additional 15–20 minutes until the lentils are very tender.

Stir in the cooked chicken. Taste and adjust seasonings as desired. Continue to cook until the chicken is just warmed through.

ZUCCHINI MUFFINS

MAKES ABOUT 2 DOZEN MUFFINS

This recipe from the Barendsen-Rossi family is a family favorite. The unusual addition of olive oil makes these zucchini muffins extra moist. To freeze, wrap well and place in an airtight container for up to a month.

INGREDIENTS

3 large eggs

2 cups granulated sugar

2 cups grated zucchini

1 cup olive oil

1 tablespoon vanilla extract

2 teaspoons ground cinnamon

1 teaspoon salt

2 teaspoons baking soda

2 1/2 cups all-purpose flour

INSTRUCTIONS

Preheat oven to 350 degrees F. Line, or grease and flour, tins for two dozen muffins.

Beat together the eggs and sugar until well combined. Stir in the zucchini, oil, and vanilla extract.

Whisk together the dry ingredients (cinnamon, salt, baking soda, and flour) in a medium bowl. Stir into the wet ingredients, mixing just until combined.

Spoon the batter into the prepared muffin cups, filling about 3/4 full.

Bake the muffins for 20–25 minutes until golden brown and a toothpick inserted in the center comes out clean.

FUN

Becoming a part of a meal swap group can certainly be a practical choice that benefits your family, but it's also a great opportunity to model habits of sharing and giving back to others. Extend the lesson with a fun family activity: creating your own Family Giving Pledge.

HOW TO PLAY

At the dinner table, talk about different ways that your family can give back to others and different causes that are important to you. Then brainstorm ideas to fill in the blanks below to create your own Giving Pledge. Turn the pledge into a poster or other visual with the kids' help. Hang it someplace where everyone will see it regularly and remember your family's commitment to kindness.

CONVERSATION

Reinforce the service theme with these conversation starters about giving back and changing the world.

(ALL AGES)

- What can you give to or do for someone that doesn't cost any money?

- What is a strength or a gift you have that you could teach/share with others?

- Think of someone you know who has given back to others. What are some things that person has done for others that you find admirable? In what ways could we learn from their example?

- Does it always take money to make real change in the world? What are some ways people have changed things for the better without any financial cost?

- What is one way people in your community are working to change things for the better? Is there any way you can help?

THE PLEDGE:

We, the _____ family, want to give the world _____ because we care about _____. We can do this by __ _____. Giving _____ makes us _____!

REMEMBER WHY IT'S WORTH IT

Feeling overwhelmed by the work of family dinner can sometimes lead to bigger challenges. It's easy to let the stress of everyday life lead to unhealthy habits, like too much fast food and too few fruits and vegetables.

That was the case for Xiaohong and her children, who got a wake-up call when the family doctor prescribed family dinners at home. The whole family's health was suffering, and one of the children had developed a severe weight problem. As a single parent, Xiaohong had a full plate of responsibilities and was having trouble devoting time and effort to home-cooked meals. "Getting dinner on the table and everyone gathered by 7:00 p.m. is a rarity," she reflected, as the West Virginia mother's time was dedicated to both her work responsibilities and the needs of her children, ages 10, 15, and 18. But once she realized that grabbing quick and easy meals on the go had become a medical issue, she quickly started working with her children to change the family's habits.

Getting everyone involved in choosing healthier versions of take-out favorites, with lots of fresh vegetables and less meat, was a big effort that paid off. Within just a few months, the family's health and eating habits improved, and the youngest child lost a significant amount of weight. Now the whole family schedules sit-down dinners at home three times a week and makes sure to check the calendar so they stay on track.

FOOD

Try our version of one of Xiaohong's family favorites—dumplings—with a restaurant-inspired vegetable side dish that includes a kid-friendly sauce. A simple fruit dessert is a fresh, sweet, and nutritious way to end the meal.

ORIGAMI DUMPLINGS

SERVES 4-6

This recipe is slightly adapted from one originally provided by the Swick-Troekel family and included in Anne Fishel's book, *Home for Dinner: Mixing Food, Fun, and Conversation for a Happier Family and Healthier Kids*. We recommend making the filling a day or two in advance to speed up preparation and make the dumplings easier to handle.

INGREDIENTS

1 package firm tofu, drained

1 tablespoon Chinese five-spice powder

3 tablespoons vegetable oil, divided

2 cloves of garlic, minced

1 tablespoon minced fresh ginger

1 cup each of finely chopped green cabbage, carrots, mushrooms, and zucchini

1 package dumpling (wonton) wrappers

Soy sauce, for dipping

INSTRUCTIONS

Cut the drained tofu into small cubes and toss with Chinese five spice.

Coat a large skillet with a generous layer of oil. Fry the tofu, stirring often so it doesn't stick. It may crumble some, but that doesn't matter! Once it has browned slightly, remove it.

Add a little more oil to the skillet. Fry the garlic and ginger until the garlic is very lightly browned. Then add the carrots and cook for 2 minutes before adding the cabbage. After another 2 minutes, add the mushrooms. A minute later, add the zucchini. Continue cooking until all of the vegetables are softened and easy to eat.

Turn off the heat, add the tofu back to the filling, and mix well.

Set up your filling station with stacks of wrappers, teaspoons, a plate, and a dish of water. To fill the dumplings, spoon a small amount of filling into the center of a wrapper. Use your finger to brush water along the edges of the wrapper to glue them together. Fold the dumplings in any shape you prefer (simple triangles are easiest) and pinch to seal well.

Spray a vegetable steamer well with oil or cooking spray. Place the vegetable steamer, in a large pot with a lid. Place dumplings on the steamer and boil water below the level of the dumplings. Leave the lid on the pot. Pour a little water over the dumplings once or twice during the next 5 minutes. The dumpling skins should contract and look shiny when they're finished.

Remove carefully and serve with soy sauce.

INDO-CHINESE CAULIFLOWER WITH BARBECUE SAUCE

SERVES 4

This is an at-home version of a dish that's often listed on restaurant menus as Gobi Manchurian. Make sure to serve it right away or the cauliflower will get soggy.

INGREDIENTS

1 1/2 cups prepared barbecue sauce

Vegetable oil

3 cloves of garlic, minced

1 head cauliflower, trimmed and cut into florets

1 cup cornstarch

INSTRUCTIONS

Place a small saucepan over medium heat. Add the barbecue sauce, two tablespoons of oil, and minced garlic. Stir and cook until the mixture starts to thicken, then remove from the heat and set aside.

Pour an inch of oil into the bottom of a deep, heavy skillet or large pot. Set over medium high heat.

While the oil heats, toss the cauliflower florets in cornstarch.

Test the heat of the oil by sprinkling a pinch of cornstarch into the oil. If it sizzles and begins to send up small bubbles, the oil is ready.

Carefully add the cauliflower florets to the oil, making sure not to overcrowd the pan. You may have to work in batches. Fry until golden brown, then remove from the oil with a slotted spoon and transfer to the sauce.

Once all the cauliflower has been browned and transferred to the sauce, stir to coat well and serve.

MANGO AND BANANA "NiCE" CREAM
SERVES 4

Not ice cream but "nice" cream, this frozen dessert takes just seconds to make in a blender or food processor.

INGREDIENTS

1 cup frozen mango cubes

3 frozen bananas, broken into chunks

INSTRUCTIONS

Put the mango cubes and banana chunks into a blender or food processor.

Blend on high speed for 2–3 minutes, until creamy like soft-serve ice cream.

Serve immediately.

FUN
Speaking of fruits and vegetables, try this fun guessing game—it's not really about healthy eating, but we call it the Fruit and Vegetable Game anyway. Having fun together at the table is a healthy habit too!

HOW TO PLAY

One family member (the leader of the round) thinks of a person known by everyone at the table. Others then ask the leader metaphorical questions to try to guess the person. For example: "If the person were a vegetable, what vegetable would she be?" "If he were a fruit/animal/color, which one would he be?" The idea is to stick to figurative rather than literal thinking. Whoever guesses the person first gets to be the leader of the next round.

CONVERSATION

Changing your family's habits entirely is a big undertaking that requires a strong commitment to setting and achieving goals.

Talk about goal-setting at your dinner table with these conversation starters.

(AGES 8-13, 14-100)

- Where do you hope to see yourself in five years? What are some steps you can start taking right now to help you get there?

- What is one thing you've always wanted to do, but haven't done yet? What has prevented you from doing it?

- Finish this sentence: "One day, I will be known for _____."

- Who is a person you admire for not giving up on their dreams? What can you learn from their example?

- Have you ever worked hard to achieve a goal and been successful? What are some things you did that could be applied to other goals in life?

TRY THEME NIGHTS

We regularly ask families what helps them with meal planning, and they frequently say that assigning themes to each night of the week is a huge help. This tip works so well that our team often uses it when creating our daily "Dinner Tonight" posts. When you have a theme to work with, it can help focus your efforts so that instead of feeling overwhelmed by all the possibilities or completely blank and uninspired, you can easily generate a few solid ideas that form the building blocks for a week of great family meals.

Popular ideas for theme nights include "Meatless Monday" (a national campaign), "Taco Tuesday," "Wild Wednesday" (try a new recipe!) or "Wake Up Wednesday" (breakfast for dinner), "Thrifty Thursday" (low-cost recipes), and "Favorites Friday" (let family members take turns choosing a favorite dish). You can choose whatever themes work for you and make them as simple or complex as you'd like. Some families simply decide that every Wednesday they'll serve pasta, for example, or that Saturday nights are pizza nights.

Once you've got your themes decided, remember that they exist to help you generate ideas, not to be limiting. For example, on your next "Taco Tuesday" you could try thinking outside the tortilla by serving this taco-spiced turkey burger and bean dip.

FOOD

These turkey burgers are a fun twist on tacos and can be made spicy or mild, depending on your family's tastes. Serve sliced vegetables and tortilla chips with an easy layered black bean dip for a creative side dish and finish the meal with a fun and flavorful fresh melon dessert.

TURKEY TACO BURGERS
SERVES 4

This fun twist on burger night can be customized to suit every eater. If pepper jack is too spicy, use a mild cheese, such as American. Add hot sauce or salsa if it's not spicy enough! Pile on the avocado or leave it off, add tomatoes and lettuce (or don't), or try mixing things up with toppings like black olives, pickled jalapeños, or sour cream.

INGREDIENTS

3/4 teaspoon chili powder

1/2 teaspoon garlic powder

1/2 teaspoon salt, plus a little more for the avocado

1/4 teaspoon cumin

1 pound ground turkey

4 deli-cut slices pepper jack cheese

1 ripe avocado

1/2 teaspoon lemon juice

4 kaiser or bulkie rolls

Romaine lettuce leaves

Sliced tomato

INSTRUCTIONS

Preheat a grill to medium heat.

In a medium bowl, mix together the chili powder, garlic powder, salt, and cumin. Add the turkey and mix well, until thoroughly combined.

Shape the turkey mixture into four patties. Grill the patties for 5–7 minutes per side until cooked completely through.

Add a slice of cheese to each patty 2 minutes before removing from the grill. Allow the cheese to melt while the burgers finish cooking.

Mash the avocado in a small bowl. Add a sprinkle of salt and lemon juice. Stir well.

Spread the avocado mixture on the buns. Add a burger patty to each and top with lettuce and tomato.

LAYERED BLACK BEAN DiP
SERVES 6-8

This dip recipe was provided by the Onondaga Cornell Cooperative Extension and is an easy, budget-friendly addition to any menu. Scoop it with chips or crisp raw vegetables.

INGREDIENTS

1 15-ounce can black beans, drained and rinsed

1/4 teaspoon onion powder

1/4 teaspoon dried oregano

1/8 teaspoon garlic powder

1/8 teaspoon cayenne pepper

1/2 cup chunky style salsa

1/2 cup sour cream

1/4 cup chopped green onions

1/2 cup shredded cheddar cheese

INSTRUCTIONS

Mash beans and mix with onion powder, dried oregano, garlic powder, and cayenne pepper. Spread in a shallow bowl or pie plate.

Top with salsa, sour cream, green onions, and grated cheese.

HONEYDEW WITH MINT AND GINGER
SERVES 8

If you're not a fan of honeydew or can't get a good ripe one, substitute cantaloupe in this recipe.

INGREDIENTS

1/4 cup sugar

1/2 cup water

1 1-inch piece ginger, peeled and sliced into medallions

1 honeydew melon, peeled and cut into bite-sized pieces

2 tablespoons chopped fresh mint

INSTRUCTIONS

Combine the sugar, water, and ginger in a small saucepan. Bring to a boil and stir until the sugar dissolves. Turn off heat and let the ginger steep in the hot syrup for 10 minutes. Remove the ginger and let the syrup cool.

Pour the cooled syrup over the honeydew and sprinkle the melon with mint.

FUN
Relax and get to know one another a little better with a round of Smash or Pass, a forced choice game.

HOW TO PLAY

In this game of choices, everyone agrees on a category, like celebrities, animals, or vacation spots. Person A chooses two things that fit that category ("Leopard or zebra?") The next person at the table chooses one item to "smash," or reject, and another to "pass" to the next round. They then suggest a replacement for the "smashed" item ("I'm smashing zebra and passing leopard. Leopard or elephant?"). Keep going around the table and find out which suggestion gets "passed" the longest!

CONVERSATION

Family dinner can be a good opportunity to bring up serious topics in a relaxed and open way. Take some time to open up a discussion about human rights and equality at your dinner table with these family-friendly conversations starters.

(AGES 8-13, 14-100)

What does "fairness" mean to you?

- Have you ever stood up for something you believed in, even if other people thought you were wrong? What did you do? Was it hard to stand up for your beliefs?

- Do you think there are certain types of people in your community or in the world who have more opportunities or authority than others? Can you give examples?

- How have you seen human rights change during your lifetime? Do you think there can or should be further changes? In what ways?

- Can you give an example of ways you've seen people in our community talk about or take action on the topic of human rights?

LET THE LITTLE HELPERS IN

The concept of family dinner as a lot of work takes on new meaning when there are toddlers at the table! As any parent who has dined with little ones will tell you, the younger the dining companions, the more work it takes just to get through a meal together. Cutting food, wiping spills, fetching drinks, and keeping young children engaged enough to stay at the table can all make dinner feel like an Olympic sport.

Brynna and Albert live in Los Angeles with their two young boys. They've learned all about managing the dinner workload as they've raised a kindergartener and two-year-old on family meals. From the very beginning, they've relied on letting the children take an active, hands-on role in mealtime in order to help the evenings go more smoothly. For their two-year-old, jobs like choosing one of the family dinners for the week or selecting different ingredients at the grocery store help him to take part in dinner preparations and feel ownership over what's being served. That's a big help in winning over the potentially fussy palates of young children. The five-year-old is now big enough to take a more active role in the kitchen and can prep simple ingredients alongside his parents. While in some ways, having young children help in the kitchen can make the work go more slowly and might contribute to the mess, in other ways, Brynna and Albert have found that dinner is much easier when they allow their son to help. Like many young children, he's more eager to pitch in with all aspects of dinnertime, like table-setting and cleanup, when he's given responsibility for helping to cook the meal. He's also more open to trying new foods and eating what's served when he's prepared it himself.

FOOD

Keeping the menu simple and low-cook is important when you're planning to actively invite kids to help. This spread of open-faced Caprese sandwiches, antipasto kebabs, and banana boats is the ultimate "kid cook" meal. Young children can cut soft mozzarella cheese with dull knives, pick basil leaves, layer sandwich ingredients, thread items onto lollipop sticks for the antipasto kebabs, and create their own banana boat masterpieces for dessert.

OPEN-FACED CAPRESE SANDWICHES
SERVES 4

Teen family dinner advocate Laura Jones created this recipe, which is perfect for helping hands!

INGREDIENTS

2 tablespoons olive oil, divided

1 clove of garlic, minced

8 slices (about 1/2 inch thick) crusty Italian bread

3 medium ripe tomatoes, sliced

1 pound fresh mozzarella cheese, sliced thinly

16 fresh basil leaves

2 tablespoons balsamic vinegar

Salt and pepper to taste

INSTRUCTIONS

Prepare a grill for medium heat. Combine 1 tablespoon oil and the garlic. Brush onto one side of bread.

Lay bread oiled-side down on grill and cook until slightly toasted, about 2 minutes.

Turn bread over and lay tomato slices on bread to fit, overlapping if needed. Set cheese slices on top of tomatoes. Cover grill and cook until cheese starts to melt, about 4 minutes.

Transfer sandwiches to a platter. Put 2 basil leaves over each sandwich and drizzle with remaining 1 tablespoon oil and the vinegar. Sprinkle with salt and pepper.

ANTIPASTO KEBABS
SERVES 6-8

You can really put anything you like on your kebabs, but we're suggesting a selection of classic antipasto ingredients to get the ideas flowing. Feel free to use toothpicks or skewers if adults are making and eating the kebabs, but lollipop sticks (available at craft stores and online) are the safe alternative for small hands.

INGREDIENTS

1/2 cup pitted olives

1 cup roasted red peppers, cut into 1-inch chunks

1/2 cup baby spinach leaves

1/2 cup marinated artichoke hearts, drained and halved

Thin slices or cubes of salami or pepperoni (optional)

Cubes of provolone cheese (optional)

Lollipop sticks

Olive oil

Salt and pepper to taste

INSTRUCTIONS

Thread ingredients onto your lollipop sticks in alternating patterns. Try as many different combinations as you can dream up.

If desired, drizzle with a little olive oil, salt, and pepper before serving.

BANANA BOATS

MAKES 1 BANANA BOAT

This recipe, provided by TFDP team member Anne, was originally created for cooking in the embers of a campfire. For the at-home version, we're using the oven.

INGREDIENTS

1 banana

4 squares (1/2 ounce each) chocolate

3 marshmallows

Aluminum foil

INSTRUCTIONS

Preheat oven to 350 degrees F.

Slice each banana down the middle, keeping the skin on. Place alternating pieces of chocolate and marshmallows in the cavity.

Wrap the stuffed banana tightly in aluminum foil.

Place your wrapped bananas in the oven. A baking sheet underneath is a smart idea to catch any drips. Bake for 10–15 minutes until the insides are melted and gooey.

FUN

Get the giggles going with a supremely silly game of Cat and Cow.

HOW TO PLAY

One person at the table is the "leader." The leader says either "Cat" or "Cow." When the leader says "Cat," the others meow. When the leader says "Cow," the others moo. Keep saying "Cat" and "Cow," faster and faster, switching back and forth and making the pattern more and more random until somebody "moos" when they should have "meowed" or "meows" when they should have "mooed!"

CONVERSATION

Young children are still learning social-emotional skills and sometimes need guidance from us on developing good relationships with others. Encourage the message that it's cool to be kind with these conversation starters.

(AGES 2-7)

- What's one kind thing you've done for someone else this week? How did it make you feel to do it?

- Tell me the nicest thing someone else has done for you lately.

- What does it mean to show kindness to someone? Can you give examples of things that are kind? What about things that are not kind to do to others?

- Is it sometimes hard to be kind? When does it feel harder to behave kindly?

- What sorts of things can people do for you to make you feel happy? What's one thing you can do tomorrow to make someone else feel happy?

USE MULTIPURPOSE INGREDIENTS

Amy and Tom have three athletic kids and a mountain of activities and commitments to coordinate on a daily basis. By the time they manage to get home for dinner, whatever they're going to eat has to be mostly prepared. Otherwise, cooking a meal on top of everything else just feels like too much to deal with. Amy likes to set aside a few minutes on Saturdays and Sundays to get ahead of meal preparation for the week, and she's always looking for easy ideas she can pull together without a lot of time and effort. "It doesn't have to be fancy, as long as we're all sitting down together and making a meal," she says.

This dinner menu is perfect for families like Amy and Tom's, because with a few minutes of prep time, Amy can make a single dressing that she can use twice in the same meal: once for marinating the chicken and again for dressing the bean salad. Both dishes will improve if they sit overnight and if Tom or Amy makes a double batch of the dressing, they can keep extras in the refrigerator for up to two weeks to get a jump-start on more meals.

FOOD

Chicken sandwiches are a crowd-pleasing family dinner solution that requires very little preparation. As long as you remember to mix up the dressing and marinate the chicken, you'll have both the main dish and a good part of your side dishes well on their way to the table in no time. Using frozen mixed vegetables as the basis for a three-bean salad means minimal chopping to do. A simple tomato salad with goat cheese can be thrown together at the last minute while the chicken cooks and you'll have a colorful, healthy meal in minutes.

EASY GRILLED CHICKEN SANDWICHES
SERVES 4

You can add condiments to your chicken sandwiches if you like—mayo, mustard, or whatever you prefer—but they're also tasty just as they are!

INGREDIENTS

1 tablespoon garlic powder

1 tablespoon dried oregano

1 1/2 teaspoons coarse salt

1/2 teaspoon black pepper

1/2 teaspoon crushed red pepper flakes

2 teaspoons honey

6 tablespoons red wine vinegar

6 tablespoons olive oil

1 pound boneless, skinless chicken breast, cut into 4 equal portions

4 kaiser rolls

Sliced tomatoes

Lettuce leaves

INSTRUCTIONS

To make the marinade, whisk the spices, honey, vinegar, and oil in a small bowl until thoroughly combined.

Pour half of the marinade over the chicken and toss to coat. Reserve the rest of the marinade for use on the bean salad.

Cover and refrigerate for a minimum of 2 hours and up to overnight.

Grill the chicken breasts over medium heat for 12–14 minutes until cooked through.

Allow the chicken to rest for 5–10 minutes before making the sandwiches.

Pile a few lettuce leaves, several slices of tomato, and a piece of chicken onto a lightly toasted bun. Add condiments if desired.

SHORTCUT THREE BEAN SALAD
SERVES 4-6

Choosing a frozen vegetable mix that includes two different types of beans (along with whatever other vegetables might be included) means you'll have a major head start on a three bean salad! Use the reserved half of the marinade from the grilled chicken sandwiches to dress your salad for a fast side dish.

INGREDIENTS

3 tablespoons finely minced onion

1/4 cup finely minced red bell pepper

1 tablespoon Dijon mustard

1 tablespoon honey

6 tablespoons Italian marinade, from grilled chicken sandwich recipe

1 cup thawed frozen vegetable mix, including lima beans and green beans

1 15-ounce can chickpeas, drained and rinsed

INSTRUCTIONS

In a large bowl, combine the onion and peppers with the Dijon mustard, honey, and reserved marinade. Mix well and allow to marinate for 10 minutes.

Add the mixed vegetables and chickpeas to the bowl. Toss to coat. Taste and adjust seasonings as needed.

TOMATO AND GOAT CHEESE SALAD
SERVES 6-8

If you're in a hurry, you can skip the crispy shallots in this salad, but they're a delicious addition if you have the extra minutes.

INGREDIENTS

3 cloves of garlic, crushed

3 tablespoons butter

3 shallots, peeled and sliced

2 pints grape tomatoes, halved

Kosher salt

Pepper

1/2 cup olive oil

Balsamic vinegar

8 ounces goat cheese

1/4 cup fresh parsley leaves, chopped

INSTRUCTIONS

Rub the crushed garlic cloves around the inside of a salad bowl. Drop the cloves in the bottom and cover with the olive oil. Set aside.

Melt the butter in a skillet over medium heat. Add the sliced shallots and sauté, stirring occasionally, until crispy. This can take several minutes. Check frequently to make sure they're not burning.

Once the shallots are golden brown and crisp, remove to a plate and spread out to cool to keep them from getting soggy.

Remove the garlic pieces from the salad bowl and discard. Add the tomatoes, salt, and pepper to the bowl. Toss with the olive oil and drizzle in balsamic vinegar, one tablespoon at a time until the tomatoes are seasoned to your liking.

Stir in the goat cheese and sprinkle the parsley and crispy shallots over the top.

FUN
Work on observation skills, turn-taking, and listening skills with a game of Different Drummers.

HOW TO PLAY

Pick one person to be the leader. The leader begins clapping or tapping a beat on the table. The others around the table begin tapping or clapping along with the leader. The leader can change the beat whenever they choose, and everyone else must follow suit. Then, without warning, the leader stops drumming. The last person to stop drumming is out.

CONVERSATION

You can help kids develop an appreciation for similarities and differences among people with these conversation starters devoted to differences.

(AGES 8-13)

- What are some ways you're different from your friends? What about your parents and siblings?

- Have you ever seen someone treated unkindly or unfairly by others because they looked different, spoke a different language, or came from a different culture? How did it make you feel, and how do you think it made them feel?

- Have you ever learned something surprising about another person who was very different from you? What was it? Did it change the way you thought about that person?

- Are there some types of differences you'd like to learn more about? For example, are there other cultures or beliefs that are interesting to you?

- Have you ever been in a situation where you felt different from the other people around you? What was that like?

TEACH TEENS
TO TAKE CHARGE

As convenience foods become more widely available and schedules get busier, fewer families are cooking at home. Some of the things that get lost are families' knowledge, tips, and traditions around meal-planning, budgeting, and cooking simple meals.

That's where people like Kathy come in. Kathy is a family and consumer sciences teacher in Indiana who always tried to stick to a family dinner routine in her own home. She realized that many of her high school students and their parents were struggling to do the same. While she made sure that they understood the benefits of family dinners and why it was important to eat together, it became clear to her that some of them didn't know how to cook.

Kathy started talking to students and their families about dinner. She found that many of them were stuck on how to help parents lighten their workloads in the kitchen, as well as worrying about spending lots of time, money, and energy preparing healthy foods that not everyone would enjoy. She now teaches her students to prepare easy and healthy items that are presented to the whole school community, including parents, at a tasting event each year. This means families can try new foods in a low-pressure environment, and students can help reduce the family dinner workload by continuing to take responsibility for preparing the favorite items at home. By putting teens in charge of choosing and preparing foods for their families, she's able to make dinnertime easier in many households, and is passing along skills that will keep family dinners going in the future.

FOOD

One of the simple recipes Kathy and her family enjoy is this white chicken chili, which is perfect for beginning cooks as it requires no chopping. Along with the hearty chili, kids can stir together ingredients for chai-spiced hot cocoa to serve with simple pancake-battered apple ring "doughnuts."

WHITE CHICKEN CHILI

SERVES 6

Kathy's chicken chili recipe is an easy throw-together meal perfect for busy nights. Over time, you could make your own adjustments to the recipe. Testing different types of beans, using a variety of seasonings and adding fresh vegetables are all simple swaps that could make Kathy's recipe your own.

INGREDIENTS

4 boneless, skinless chicken breasts

1 package taco seasoning*

1/2 cup water

1/2 jar salsa

2 (15-ounce) cans tomatoes with green chilies

2 (15-ounce) cans navy beans, drained and rinsed

1 (15-ounce) can black beans, drained and rinsed

4-6 cups chicken broth

1 4-ounce can green chilies

Garlic powder to taste

Onion powder to taste

Cumin to taste

Salt and pepper to taste

*If you prefer homemade, our recipe for homemade taco seasoning is included on page 206. Three tablespoons of our seasoning blend is roughly equal to a commercially prepared seasoning packet.

INSTRUCTIONS

Place chicken breasts in a large pot with the taco seasoning, water, salsa, and one can of tomatoes with chilies. Bring to a boil, reduce to a simmer, and cook until the chicken is cooked through, about 20 minutes.

Remove the chicken from the liquid, shred with two forks, and set aside.

Bring the liquid in the pot back to a boil and allow it to reduce for 5–10 minutes. Add the remaining ingredients (second can of tomatoes, navy beans, black beans, chicken broth, green chilies, and seasonings), season with salt and pepper, and cook for 30–40 minutes.

Taste and adjust seasonings as desired. For a slightly thicker chili, remove some of the beans and mash them before adding back to the pot.

Stir in the chicken and serve.

EASY APPLE "DOUGHNUTS"

SERVES 4

These "doughnuts" have a surprise inside: rings of fresh apple!

INGREDIENTS

1/2 cup all-purpose flour

1/2 teaspoon baking powder

1/4 teaspoon baking soda

1/4 teaspoon ground nutmeg

1 large egg

1/2 teaspoon vanilla extract

6 tablespoons apple cider

2 tablespoons unsalted butter

2 medium apples, peeled, cored, and cut crosswise into 1/4-inch thick rings

1/2 cup granulated sugar

1 teaspoon ground cinnamon

INSTRUCTIONS

In a medium bowl, whisk together the flour, baking powder, baking soda, and nutmeg.

Add the egg and vanilla and mix together.

Add the apple cider and whisk slowly until a smooth batter forms.

Melt the butter in a skillet over medium-high heat.

Dip the apple slices into the batter to coat them. Let excess batter drip off.

When the butter in the skillet starts to bubble, add the apple slices in a single layer. You may have to work in batches.

Let the apple slices cook for about 2 minutes on the first side, just until golden brown and set. Flip and cook for another 1–2 minutes on the second side until golden brown.

Remove the apple "doughnuts" from the pan and set on paper towels.

In a shallow dish, mix together the cinnamon and sugar. Toss the apple "doughnuts" in the cinnamon sugar and serve.

CHAI-SPICED HOT COCOA

MAKES ABOUT 16 CUPS OF HOT COCOA

This chai-spiced cocoa mix is a unique take on a family favorite! You can store the mix in an airtight container in the pantry for up to a month, or in the refrigerator or freezer for up to six months. It's also good for gifting to others.

INGREDIENTS

2/3 cup unsweetened cocoa powder

3/4 cup confectioner's sugar

1 teaspoon ground cinnamon

1/2 teaspoon ground cardamom

1/2 teaspoon ground nutmeg

1/4 teaspoon ground cloves

4 ounces bittersweet chocolate, grated

Milk

INSTRUCTIONS

Mix all dry ingredients in a large bowl until thoroughly combined.

To make hot cocoa, stir 1–2 tablespoons of the mix into a cup of hot milk.

Store mix in an airtight container in a cool place.

FUN
Play a round of Guess the Title, a twist on traditional guessing games.

HOW TO PLAY

Each person lists a bunch of items, tangible or abstract, and the rest of the family has to guess what the title of the list might be. For example: sleeping late, sand in my sheets, no TV, outdoor shower, losing my sunglasses, riding waves. The title is "My Beach Vacation."

CONVERSATION

Part of teaching your teens to take on more responsibility includes making sure they understand their personal responsibilities not just at dinnertime, but in the way they behave elsewhere. It's important for all of us to take responsibility for behaviors like not spreading gossip, treating people respectfully, and doing the right thing even when others aren't. Reinforce these concepts with conversation starters about behaving responsibly.

(AGES 14-100)

- What is each person's responsibility for checking whether something is valid or not before sharing it with others? Do you always check to find out whether or not something is true when you hear it?

- Has a friend ever asked you to keep a secret that you felt uncomfortable keeping? What did you do? Are there times when it's important to break a friend's confidence?

- Have you ever been pressured to "go along with the crowd" when you knew that it was the wrong decision? How did you handle it? Would you do anything differently next time?

- Have you ever made a judgment about someone that later turned out to be wrong? What caused you to judge them that way in the first place and what changed your opinion?

- Are there times when it's better not to be honest than to tell the truth, or do you think that total honesty is the best policy? Can you give an example?

KEEP THE SHOPPING LIST SHORT

Kristi and Tom have two busy girls and a very full family life. Between all their commitments at home and in their community, the amount of time and energy they can devote to family dinners is often scant. But since both Kristi and her husband were raised in households that prioritized eating together, they believe that family dinner is non-negotiable. Sometimes when the schedule is really hectic, they rely on nearby grandparents to provide a family meal experience for their daughters, while on other nights, they're determined to make dinner happen in their own home. That's where their "twenty-one dinners rotation" comes in.

Besides being pressed for time, Kristi also wants to keep a close eye on the family budget. She keeps a list of twenty-one (or so) easy, low-budget meals that require a short shopping list and minimal fuss. Those ideas form the basis of everything the family eats when they sit down together, freeing up the adults to engage with one another and their kids.

This menu was inspired by Kristi's low-effort, low-budget requirements. With just a few readily available and generally inexpensive ingredients that are used in each dish throughout the meal, this family dinner menu is flavorful and low-stress. The chicken dish does take some time to cook, but much of it is hands-off time, meaning that you can take care of other priorities while dinner is in the oven.

FOOD

Baking chicken and rice in the same pot makes both dinner and clean-up easier. Since you'll be buying oranges anyway, use some of them to brighten up a spinach salad. For dessert, combine two of the greatest apple dips—nut butter and caramel—in one delicious dish.

ORANGE THYME BAKED CHICKEN AND RICE

SERVES 6-8

If you're pressed for time during the week, you can make this one-pot chicken and rice dish over the weekend and reheat single servings on a hectic evening. It holds up well to leftover use.

INGREDIENTS

2 tablespoons unsalted butter

1 tablespoon olive oil

8 bone-in, skin-on chicken thighs

2 teaspoons salt, divided

1/2 teaspoon black pepper, divided

12 sprigs fresh thyme

1 large onion, sliced

3 cloves of garlic, minced

Juice and zest of 1 navel orange

2 cups long-grain brown rice

4 cups chicken stock

1 bay leaf

INSTRUCTIONS

Preheat oven to 375 degrees F.

In a large Dutch oven over medium-high heat, melt the butter and olive oil together. Season the skin side of the chicken thighs with 1 teaspoon of salt and 1/4 teaspoon of pepper. Working in batches to keep from overcrowding the pan, place the chicken thighs into the hot oil and butter, skin-side down. Cook for 4–5 minutes until the skins are very golden brown and crisp. Turn the chicken pieces over and cook for another minute on the other side. Remove the chicken pieces to a plate and repeat with the remaining chicken.

Standing back from the pot, carefully toss 8 of the whole thyme sprigs into the hot drippings. Fry the thyme for 1 minute, then remove the stems from the oil with tongs and discard.

Add the sliced onions and garlic to the pot and cook, stirring, for 3–5 minutes until soft and beginning to brown. Add the orange juice to the pot and stir, scraping any browned bits off the bottom.

Pour the rice into the pan and stir to coat the grains of rice in the liquid and distribute the onions and garlic throughout the rice. Add the chicken stock to the pot. Season with the remaining salt and pepper. Add the bay leaf and stir well.

Nestle the chicken thighs on top of the rice mixture and pour in any juices that were left on the plate. Cover the Dutch oven tightly and bring to a boil. As soon as the liquid is boiling, transfer the covered dish to the oven. Bake for 1 hour, until the liquid is absorbed and the rice is fully cooked.

Remove the lid from the pot and sprinkle the hot chicken and rice with the zest of the orange and the leaves from the remaining 4 sprigs of thyme.

SPINACH SALAD WITH APPLES AND ORANGES
SERVES 6-8

A simple spinach salad seems fancy enough for company with the addition of lots of fresh fruit and a fresh herb dressing.

INGREDIENTS

8 cups loosely packed baby spinach leaves

1/2 cup thinly sliced red onion

2 navel oranges

1 cup diced apple*

1 tablespoon red wine vinegar

1 tablespoon fresh thyme leaves

1/4 cup olive oil

1 teaspoon salt

*A crisp, tart variety like Granny Smith works well here.

INSTRUCTIONS

Peel and segment one of the oranges and set the segments aside.

In a large bowl, combine zest and juice of the second orange. Add the thyme leaves, salt, and red wine vinegar. Whisk to combine, then slowly add the olive oil to make a dressing.

Add the diced apples to the vinaigrette and toss to coat.

Add the spinach leaves and onion to the bowl. Toss well until the salad is evenly coated with the dressing.

Arrange the orange segments on top and serve.

APPLE SLICES WITH PEANUT BUTTER CARAMEL DIP
SERVES 6-8

If allergies are a concern, you can use a different nut butter in this dip, or omit the nut butter entirely and double the amount of butter you use in the caramel.

INGREDIENTS

1 cup granulated sugar

2 tablespoons water

2 tablespoons unsalted butter

1/2 cup heavy cream

1/4 cup unsweetened, salted peanut butter

4 apples, sliced

INSTRUCTIONS

In a heavy-bottomed medium saucepan, combine the sugar and water over medium heat. Do not stir—when making caramel, stirring can cause the sugar to crystallize, which won't make a smooth dip.

Watch the sugar mixture carefully. As it cooks, the sugar should melt and become translucent, then start to turn golden. Swirl the pan around frequently to make sure the sugar cooks evenly.

When the mixture is amber-colored all the way through, remove from heat. Add the butter and cream. At this point, the pan will likely bubble up violently. Don't worry!

Stir the mixture together until the bubbling subsides. Return the pan to the stove and add the peanut butter.

Cook over medium heat for an additional 5 minutes, stirring occasionally until a smooth caramel coats the back of a spoon. It will thicken more as it cools.

Let the sauce cool until it's just slightly warm and still pourable. Serve with the apple slices.

FUN Test your music knowledge with the Song Game!

HOW TO PLAY

The first player chooses a word or a category (e.g., love). Each person at the table then has to come up with a song that uses that word in the lyrics and then sing at least a verse of it. So, for the "love" example, one person could sing part of "Love Stinks . . . yeah yeah" or "Crazy Love" or "Love Is All You Need." After everyone's done, the next person chooses a new word (or category) and the hits keep on coming!

CONVERSATION

Keep the entertainment going with conversation starters about movies and music.

(AGES 8-13, 14-100)

- If you could have a character from a movie as a best friend, who would it be?
- If you could jump into any scene from a movie, what scene would you choose and why?
- What is the greatest song ever written?
- What band do you think is the most underrated? Why?
- Would you rather be a rock star or a movie star?

135

PART IV
WE'RE TOO DISTRACTED!

"But can't I just finish watching this?"

It's a familiar refrain from nine-year-old Patrick, who loves family dinner—but hates when it interrupts his favorite TV shows. After a long day of school, sports, and music lessons, he's ready to unwind with some screen time. His parents and older brother, however, are hoping to hurry up and get everyone to the table so they can eat and get on with their various to-do lists: homework, work obligations, and volunteer commitments. When they do sit down, they know it's going to be a challenge to stay focused on the conversation instead of thinking of all the other things they need to get done after dinner.

The same scene plays out in countless homes every night, and it can be hard to resist the lure of distractions—even when we know we should be enjoying dinner together instead. Read on for plenty of creative ideas from families who have managed to strike the right balance between dinner time and distractions.

BINGE ON BOOKS

Sometimes a creative solution is the best way to keep everyone together and engaged in mealtimes. Narelle's kids were more interested in technology and other distractions than eating and interacting at mealtimes. When she tried to re-focus their attention on dinner, battles would ensue. Complicating matters, Narelle and her kids were at home in Australia, while her husband was living in New Zealand for work until the whole family could join him. In an effort to gain everyone's attention and build family cohesion in preparation for the big move, Narelle started bringing a book to the table for a shared family read-aloud. With a book to focus on, meals became more peaceful and the conversation started to flow more naturally.

You don't actually need to read at the table to harness the power of books at your meals, though that certainly works well for some families. Many popular books include scenes related to food; you could make a recipe based on a favorite storybook, like green eggs and ham from Dr. Seuss or spaghetti and meatballs from *Cloudy with a Chance of Meatballs*. You can also promote reading and literacy skills by playing a variety of word games at the table, like the one featured here!

FOOD

Our simple tomato sauce and basic meatball recipes pair perfectly with pasta and a copy of *Strega Nona* or *Cloudy with a Chance of Meatballs*. They're also freezer-friendly, so if you're inspired to make a big batch, you'll have another dinner ready to go on a busy evening. Serve with a green salad and a dressing recipe that you can vary as you like.

BASIC MEATBALLS

MAKES APPROXIMATELY 24 MEATBALLS

This gluten-free meatball recipe is one of the most popular recipes from TFDP team member Bri's blog, "Red, Round, or Green." She doubles the recipe whenever she makes it and keeps a supply of meatballs in the freezer for busy weeks.

INGREDIENTS

1 small onion

3 cloves of garlic

4 large eggs

1 teaspoon salt

1 teaspoon dried oregano

1/4 teaspoon crushed red pepper flakes

1/4 teaspoon black pepper

1/2 cup rolled oats

1/4 cup freshly grated Parmesan cheese

1 pound ground beef

1 pound ground pork

2 tablespoons olive oil

INSTRUCTIONS

Preheat the oven to 400 degrees F.

Using a Microplane, grate the onion and garlic directly into a large mixing bowl. This will not only break them down very finely to mix thoroughly with the meat, but will also ensure that all the juices of the onion get into the bowl. As an alternative, blitz the onion and garlic in a food processor until very finely chopped, almost pureed.

Add the eggs to the grated onion and garlic. Beat thoroughly.

Season with the salt, oregano, red pepper flakes, and black pepper. Stir to combine.

Add the oats and Parmesan cheese. Mix until it's the consistency of very wet sand.

Add the ground beef and pork to the bowl. Using a large fork or your hands, thoroughly combine all the ingredients until the mixture is well homogenized. Set aside.

Pour the olive oil into the center of a rimmed baking sheet and tilt to coat the pan completely with the oil.

Form the meat mixture into balls about 1 1/2 ounces each (the size of ping-pong balls) and place on the oiled baking sheet about 1/2 inch apart.

Bake for 20–25 minutes, until the meatballs are browned on top and set on the bottoms.

SPAGHETTI WITH SIMPLE TOMATO SAUCE

SERVES 4-6

Everybody needs a good spaghetti recipe. This sauce can easily be doubled and popped into the freezer, so you have a fallback meal for another night!

INGREDIENTS

1 pound spaghetti

2 tablespoons olive oil

1 medium onion, diced

3 cloves of garlic, minced

1 28-ounce can diced tomatoes

1 tablespoon dried oregano

1 tablespoon dried basil

1 tablespoon parsley

Salt and pepper to taste

INSTRUCTIONS

Prepare spaghetti according to package directions.

While the pasta is cooking, heat olive oil in a pan over low heat.

Add onion and sauté until clear.

Add garlic and cook until fragrant—do not let garlic start to brown.

Add tomatoes and stir.

Add herbs and salt and pepper to taste.

Simmer for about 10 minutes to blend the flavors.

For a smooth sauce, mash with a potato masher or put the sauce through a blender. Otherwise, just serve the sauce as is!

GREEN SALAD WITH INFINITELY VARIABLE VINAIGRETTE

SERVES 4-6

This is not so much a recipe as it is a method. What your family likes in a salad dressing might be different from another person's preferences, so we like to think of this Infinitely Variable Vinaigrette as a template everyone can use to find their own perfect blend.

INGREDIENTS

6 cups loosely packed salad greens

2 tablespoons vinegar, lemon juice, or lime juice

1/2 cup olive oil

1 tablespoon finely chopped fresh herbs, or 1 teaspoon dried herbs

Salt and pepper

Sugar, brown sugar, or honey (optional)

1 tablespoon Dijon mustard (optional)

INSTRUCTIONS

As a general rule of thumb, use 3 parts oil to 1 part acid, such as vinegar or citrus. Flavor ideas include:

Olive oil, red wine vinegar, mustard, thyme.

Olive oil, lemon juice, oregano, pinch of paprika, honey.

Canola oil, lime juice, chili powder, honey, garlic.

Olive oil, white wine vinegar, chives, mustard.

Olive oil, balsamic vinegar, mustard, honey, garlic.

Place your dressing ingredients in a jar with a tight-fitting screw-on lid.

Shake, shake, shake until everything is well combined. This is a great activity for young chefs! Add salt to taste. If things taste too tart, add a little sugar or honey.

Toss dressing with greens. Start with just a little, then add more as needed. Serve immediately.

FUN
Move from reading a story together to creating a story together with a round of Story Starters!

HOW TO PLAY

Write several words on slips of paper and put them in a box. Have each person at the table choose a word from the box. These words are now your "Story Starters." Everyone at the table helps to make up a story using all the words that were chosen!

Tip: Sometimes kids, especially young ones, will get "stuck" and have a hard time moving the story forward. It can be helpful to prompt them by asking "And then what happened?" or using a story-specific bridge like, "And then the dog said . . ."

CONVERSATION

Make storytelling the centerpiece of your family dinner with these conversation starters about reading and telling stories.

(ALL AGES)

- What is your favorite childhood storybook? What makes that book so special to you?

- If you could rewrite the ending to any story, what story would you choose and how would you change the ending?

- Do you prefer to read or to write? To listen to stories or to tell them?

- If you were to write a book, what would it be about?

- If today were a chapter in a book, what would you title it? What do you hope tomorrow's chapter title might be?

GIVE EVERYONE
A TURN

For many families, conversation difficulties stem from trouble with turn-taking, because one person monopolizes most of the dinner discussion. It can be hard work trying to direct the conversation so that everyone has the floor.

When their children were growing up, Susan and Rich instituted a tradition at the dinner table to help ensure that every family member had a turn to speak. Eating by candlelight, they would begin dinner by passing one of the candles around the table as each person shared a detail about the day or a reason to feel grateful. The tradition of speaking while holding the candle helped ensure that everyone had an opportunity to share and reinforced lessons of not interrupting. Susan and Rich are now grandparents, but their whole family still remembers fondly the tradition of passing the candle at dinner.

Whether it's passing a candle, using another object (some families have a "talking stick" or small stuffed toy), or simply going around in age order or order of seating, having a strategy to make sure all family members get a turn to have their say is important in establishing a mealtime environment that's welcoming to all. Try the table activity below for a twist on Susan and Rich's turn-taking fun.

FOOD

Keep everyone at the table engaged not just in the conversation but in the food as well with our interactive menu of Do-It-Yourself Salad and fondue.

DO-IT-YOURSELF SALAD BAR

SERVES 4-6

Besides being a great interactive meal idea, Do-It-Yourself Salad is a fantastic way to clean out your refrigerator. You can add anything you like to your salad bar and use up all the bits and pieces you don't want to waste!

INGREDIENTS

8 cups loosely packed leafy salad greens

8-12 ounces leftover cooked chicken, ham, turkey, or fish

4 ounces cheese of your choice

1 medium apple, diced

1 bunch grapes

1/2 small cucumber, sliced

1 pint grape tomatoes

2 medium carrots, sliced

2 hard-boiled eggs, quartered (optional)

1/2 cup almonds, walnuts, sunflower seeds, or pumpkin seeds

Salad dressing of your choice*

*Our recipe for homemade vinaigrette is on page 140.

INSTRUCTIONS

Pile greens into a large bowl or platter.

Cut meats into bite-sized pieces. Cube or shred cheeses. Arrange in small bowls or on a plate.

Prepare the other vegetables and fruits as needed—dice apples, slice cucumbers, slice carrots, cut grapes and tomatoes in half—and place in small bowls or arrange in piles on a platter.

Cut hard boiled eggs in quarters and place in a small bowl.

Place nuts or seeds in a small bowl.

Set out your family's favorite salad dressings and let everyone make their own salads.

CHEESY BASIL GARLIC BREAD

SERVES 12-16

This garlic bread recipe makes enough for a big crowd, so if you're not expecting guests, you can wrap one half of the bread securely and freeze for another night. Wrap and freeze the extra loaf after assembly but before baking.

INGREDIENTS

1 long loaf French or Italian bread

12 tablespoons unsalted butter, softened

4 cloves of garlic

1 1/2 teaspoons salt

1 cup loosely packed fresh basil leaves

1/4 cup freshly grated Parmesan cheese

1 cup shredded mozzarella cheese

INSTRUCTIONS

Preheat oven to 375 degrees F. Cut bread in half lengthwise and set aside.

In a food processor, combine butter, garlic, and salt. Blend until creamy.

Add basil and cheeses to the food processor and pulse just until evenly combined.

Generously spread the butter mixture on the cut sides of the bread. Place the bread, butter side up, on a large rimmed baking sheet.

Bake for 15 minutes until the bread is crunchy and the butter mixture is melted and bubbly.

Cut each half into slices and serve hot.

CHOCOLATE FONDUE WITH FRUIT
SERVES 4

Chocolate fondue sounds fancy, but it's so simple even young kids can make it themselves with a microwave and a little parental supervision.

INGREDIENTS

1 cup semisweet, milk, or dark chocolate chips

3-6 tablespoons heavy cream

Fresh strawberries and banana chunks

INSTRUCTIONS

Combine chocolate chips and 3 tablespoons of cream in a heatproof measuring cup or dish.

Microwave on high for 30 seconds at a time, stirring between intervals, until the mixture is smooth and dippable. If it seems too stiff, stir in additional cream one tablespoon at a time until the desired consistency is reached.

Dip fruit into the warm chocolate mixture.

FUN
Susan and Rich passed a candle to encourage everyone to share their gratitude at the table. Another way to show gratitude is to turn giving thanks into an alphabet game.

HOW TO PLAY

Go around the table and have each family member share something for which he or she is grateful, but in alphabetical order. So maybe you're thankful for animals, your son is grateful for bananas, and so on until everyone is feeling gratitude from A to Z!

CONVERSATION

Keep the gratitude flowing with additional conversation starters about being thankful and how to show it.

(ALL AGES)

- How do you feel when others thank you?

- What are some ways to show that you're grateful for something, besides saying thank you?

- Share three things you feel thankful for right now.

- Do you notice when others forget to thank you for things? How does that make you feel?

- What are some ways you might help another person to develop a more grateful attitude?

TRY THE UNCONVENTIONAL APPROACH

Personality has a lot to do with how different family members might engage at mealtimes. While some kids have plenty to say, or can at least be encouraged to start sharing with just a good question or two, others are naturally more shy or reluctant to talk.

New York parent Denise found that despite her best efforts, her "very quiet" fifteen-year-old daughter, Grace, didn't always say much when Denise initiated conversation. But with a busy work schedule and lengthy commute, the family of two usually couldn't even sit down together until almost 8:00 p.m. With Grace's evenings taken up by mounting homework demands, trying to connect with her daughter over dinner felt more urgent to Denise than ever. So Denise decided to fill their time together with a shared activity that would get them focused on something other than questions about the day. To introduce some fun and to relieve some of the pressure Grace might be feeling about talking, they began what they now call the "never-ending UNO game." The classic card game stays on the dinner table and is resumed every night while they eat. With the pressure to hold a conversation diminished by focusing on an activity, they both started to relax and feel more open to talking.

Over time, Denise started asking questions that were specifically designed to be outlandish, so that her daughter would naturally react. "Did anyone fart at school today?" she might ask, or "Did anyone trip over their shoelaces? Fall off a chair? Burst into giggles until they couldn't stop?" Before long, Grace's responses had evolved from laughing and saying "Yes" or "No" to sharing stories: "No, but you know what did happen? . . ."

Try this family dinner patterned after Denise's strategies and see what develops at your table.

FOOD

Denise and her daughter enjoy vegetarian meals and like most busy families, the faster, the better! Let kids help build these baked quesadillas for an easy, family-friendly vegetarian meal, and have fun working together to make guacamole for dipping. Bean and corn salad is a healthy and delicious side dish to add a protein punch.

BAKED VEGGIE QUESADILLAS
SERVES 4-6

This recipe is slightly adapted from one shared with us by our friends at the Recipe for Success Foundation. You can make it your own by changing the types of vegetables and cheeses you try in your quesadillas.

INGREDIENTS

1 tablespoon olive oil

1 cup corn kernels, thawed from frozen

1 cup diced bell pepper

1 cup diced tomatoes

6 whole-wheat tortillas

1 1/2 cups Monterey Jack cheese

1 green onion, finely chopped

1 cup sour cream

2 tablespoons chopped fresh cilantro

Salt and pepper to taste.

INSTRUCTIONS

Add olive oil to a sauté pan over medium heat. Add the corn, bell pepper, and tomatoes. Sauté until they are just soft.

Remove from heat and set aside.

Preheat oven to 400 degrees F. Lay three of the tortillas on a sheet pan.

Evenly spread the cheese onto the tortillas.

Sprinkle the sautéed veggies and chopped green onion over all three tortillas. Cover each tortilla with the remaining three tortillas.

Place sheet pan in oven. Bake 5 minutes until tortillas are crisp and the cheese is melted.

Mix the cilantro and sour cream in a small bowl. Add salt and pepper to taste and serve with the quesadillas.

GUACAMOLE
SERVES 4-6

At our Community Dinner events, one of our favorite activities is teaching families how to make guacamole together. We encourage every family to taste as they go, so they can create the guacamole they prefer.

INGREDIENTS

2 ripe avocados

2 cloves of garlic, minced

2 limes

1 teaspoon salt

2 plum tomatoes, chopped

1/4 cup finely diced red onion

INSTRUCTIONS

Pit the avocados and scoop the flesh into a medium bowl.

Using a fork, mash the avocado until it's smooth but still has some texture. Add the juice of one lime and stir.

Gradually add garlic, salt, and additional lime juice, tasting as you go, until you're happy with the taste of your guacamole. Stir in the tomatoes and onion, taste again, and adjust seasonings as needed.

BEAN AND CORN SALAD

SERVES 4-6

This salad can be made ahead of time, as the flavors will only get better as it sits.

INGREDIENTS

4 cups corn kernels, fresh or thawed from frozen

8 ounces Monterey Jack cheese, diced

1 small red onion, diced

1 red bell pepper, chopped

1 15-ounce can black beans, drained and rinsed

2 tablespoons balsamic vinegar

1/4 cup olive oil

1 teaspoon pepper

2 teaspoons garlic salt

1/2 bunch (about 1/4 cup) fresh cilantro, chopped (optional)

INSTRUCTIONS

Combine corn, cheese, onion, bell pepper, and black beans in a large bowl.

Season with vinegar, olive oil, garlic salt, and pepper. Taste and adjust as needed.

Sprinkle with chopped cilantro, stir, and serve.

FUN
What game will get your family talking? Sometimes the simplest ideas are the most fun. Follow Denise's example and think of favorite games that are table friendly.

HOW TO PLAY

Bring favorite games to the table and play while you eat, or bring dinner to a comfortable game playing spot. Good suggestions for a variety of ages include card games like UNO, Crazy Eights, Sleeping Queens, War, Go Fish, or Exploding Kittens; travel-sized board games; or trivia card sets such as Trivial Pursuit, Professor Noggin, or BrainQuest.

CONVERSATION

Dinner conversations can be fun! Shake things up with less talkative family members by introducing some silliness to the experience.

- What was the funniest or strangest thing that happened today?
- What's your favorite silly face to make? Silly sound? Demonstrate!
- If you joined the circus, what would your circus act be?
- If people count sheep to get to sleep, what do sheep count?
- If you had a pet dragon, what would you name it? What would you do together?

(AGES 2-7)

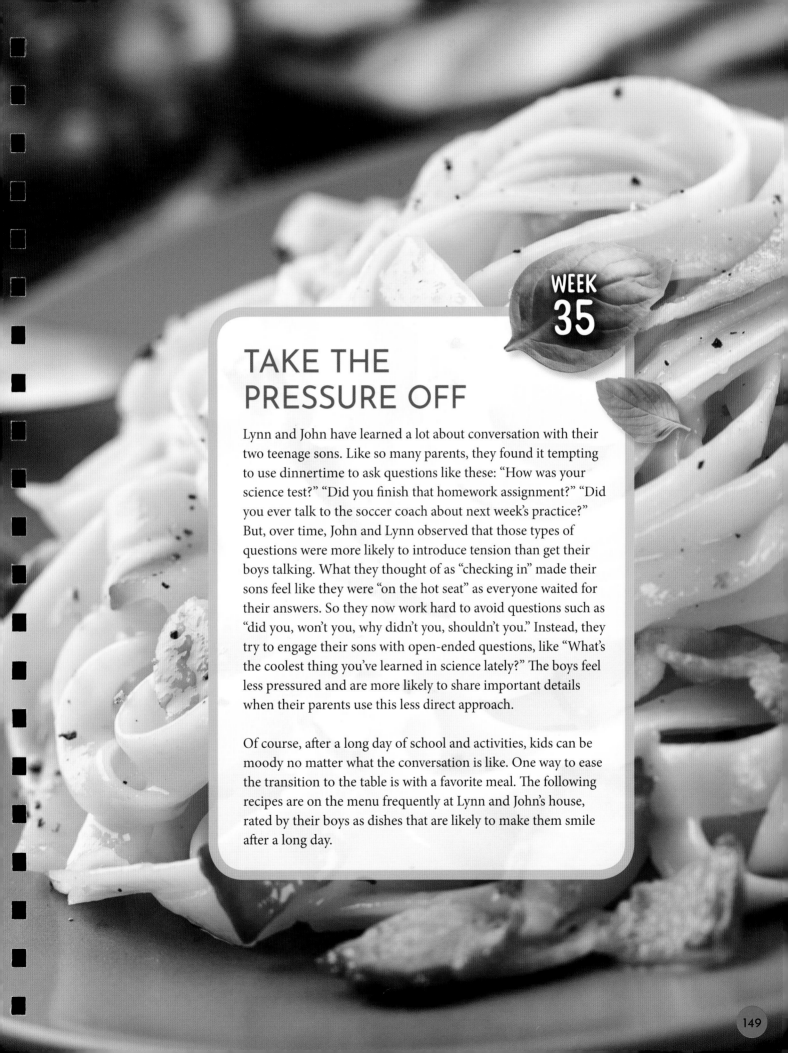

TAKE THE PRESSURE OFF

Lynn and John have learned a lot about conversation with their two teenage sons. Like so many parents, they found it tempting to use dinnertime to ask questions like these: "How was your science test?" "Did you finish that homework assignment?" "Did you ever talk to the soccer coach about next week's practice?" But, over time, John and Lynn observed that those types of questions were more likely to introduce tension than get their boys talking. What they thought of as "checking in" made their sons feel like they were "on the hot seat" as everyone waited for their answers. So they now work hard to avoid questions such as "did you, won't you, why didn't you, shouldn't you." Instead, they try to engage their sons with open-ended questions, like "What's the coolest thing you've learned in science lately?" The boys feel less pressured and are more likely to share important details when their parents use this less direct approach.

Of course, after a long day of school and activities, kids can be moody no matter what the conversation is like. One way to ease the transition to the table is with a favorite meal. The following recipes are on the menu frequently at Lynn and John's house, rated by their boys as dishes that are likely to make them smile after a long day.

FOOD

A menu of rich pasta with pancetta gets balanced out by vibrant sautéed spinach and classic fruity dessert. You could also serve the pasta dish here with a big salad with a bright, acidic dressing, which Lynn and John often do on busy nights.

LUCA'S PANCETTA PASTA

SERVES 4-6

Lynn and John's son, Luca, loves this rich pasta dish. They keep the pancetta in the freezer to make it easier to dice.

INGREDIENTS

1 pound linguine

4 thick slices pancetta, diced

2 tablespoons olive oil, divided

3 cloves of garlic, minced

Juice of ½ lemon, or more to taste

1/2 cup chopped fresh parsley

Pinch of crushed red pepper flakes

Grated Parmesan cheese

INSTRUCTIONS

Cook pasta in boiling salted water. Stop cooking 1–2 minutes before the pasta reaches al dente—it will finish cooking with the rest of the ingredients.

Drain the pasta, reserving 1 cup of the starchy pasta water.

Heat 1 tablespoon of olive oil in a large skillet over medium heat. Add pancetta and sauté until golden brown and crisp.

Remove pancetta from the pan with a slotted spoon and reserve.

Add garlic to the pan and sauté for 30 seconds to 1 minute until fragrant but not browned.

Return the pancetta to the pan. Add the pasta and remaining tablespoon of olive oil. Toss to coat.

Add the reserved pasta water and lemon juice. Mix well. Cook for an additional minute or two until pasta is cooked through.

Add the chopped parsley and red pepper flakes as desired. Mix well and serve with grated Parmesan at the table.

SAUTÉED SPINACH

SERVES 4-6

Make sure to start this recipe with a nice big pan! Two pounds of fresh spinach takes up a lot of space, but in just a minute or two it will wilt down to the perfect amount for your family.

INGREDIENTS

2 tablespoons olive oil

3 cloves of garlic, chopped

2 pounds fresh baby spinach leaves

1 teaspoon salt

1/2 teaspoon black pepper

INSTRUCTIONS

Heat olive oil in a large, deep skillet over medium heat.

Add the garlic and cook for 30 seconds until fragrant but not browned.

Add the spinach to the skillet and toss. Cook for 3–5 minutes, stirring occasionally, until the spinach is wilted.

Season with salt and pepper, stir well, and serve immediately.

PEACH MELBA

SERVES 4-6

This classic dessert is a favorite of Lynn's. She says her family lived in a farmhouse with plenty of peach trees when she was a child, so her mother developed this recipe as a way of dealing with the summer overload of fruit.

INGREDIENTS

10 ounces fresh or frozen raspberries

1/4 cup water

1/4 cup sugar

1/4 teaspoon cream of tartar

Vanilla ice cream

Sliced peaches (about 1/2 peach per person)

INSTRUCTIONS

Press the raspberries through a fine mesh sieve over a small saucepan. Add water to the puree in the saucepan.

Stir the sugar and cream of tartar into the raspberry puree in the saucepan.

Heat to boiling, stirring occasionally.

Boil for 3 minutes, stirring constantly.

Allow the sauce to cool before using. It will thicken slightly.

Scoop ice cream into bowls and top with peach slices. Pour raspberry sauce over the ice cream and peaches and enjoy.

FUN

"Two Truths and a Tall Tale" is a family favorite game for Lynn, John, and their sons. It's a good way to get everyone to tell stories about their day without having to ask questions that put a child in the hot seat. John is known as the "master" of this game, constantly spinning more and more inventive stories until even those who know him best have a hard time deciding which are the tall tales!

HOW TO PLAY

Ask everyone at the table to tell three things that happened during the day: two true things and one thing that's made up. The rest of the table will guess which is the tall tale. Sometimes this game is easier if everyone gets a chance to write down their three things before sharing.

CONVERSATION

Get past transactional conversations with your teens by flipping the script entirely: Let them share their views on parenting with these parent-and-child conversation starters.

(AGES 14-100)

- Do you think it's more fun to be the parent or the child? Why?

- What's one thing about your life as a teen that you wish your parents understood better?

- Do you think you have the right amount of freedom? Not enough? Too much?

- If you could improve our household rules, what changes would you suggest?

- Do you think most of the teens you know are trustworthy? Why or why not? Do you think parents' trust of their teens (or lack of trust) has an impact on behavior?

INTRODUCE SOME FLEXIBILITY

Sometimes the best way to keep kids—especially teens—engaged in family dinner is to allow a little bit of flexibility and independence without totally breaking your family commitment to spending time together at the table. Debra, whose kids are now grown, recalls how one of her sons in particular pushed back against required family dinners when he was a teen. At that point in time, the Michigan family tried to gather as often as possible for dinner together, but had a non-negotiable, once-per-week meal scheduled on Friday evenings. Preferring to go out with friends than to stay home with family, Debra's son rebelled.

Her solution was to introduce flexibility without compromising the family's rules: Each child in the family was issued five "get out of dinner free" passes. Throughout the course of a year, they could use their passes to skip the required weekly dinner. While we expected the story might end with Debra's son using all five right away, the opposite happened. Knowing that he could miss dinner if he chose to, he instead decided to save his passes for good reasons—and ended up almost never using them. In fact, as he grew older, he confessed to his parents that with maturity came a different outlook. He had realized that there were times when his friends were trying to encourage him to join them in certain risky behaviors. Rather than use his passes to skip dinner and join in, he'd used the family's weekly dinner as a welcome excuse to avoid a difficult situation. "Our strictness about these 'stupid dinners' gave him a great out," Debra recalls.

Now starting families of their own, Debra's children are continuing the weekly family dinners in their households, and she and her husband enjoy joining in when they're able to visit. Try our version of the family's favorite garlic chicken, along with a potato recipe that's simple enough to be a side dish staple.

FOOD

Debra and her family originally shared a slow-cooking recipe for garlic chicken with us, but we've adapted their recipe to make it a little faster and easier so you can serve it any night of the week. Finish your meal with a sweet, tangy, and delicious way to dress up a store-bought cake.

40 CLOVE GARLIC CHICKEN

SERVES 6-8

Debra's family enjoys a recipe for 40 Clove Garlic Chicken that originated with Jane Brody's "Good Food Book," but we've adapted their favorite here to shorten the cooking time and streamline preparation. If the idea of counting out forty individual cloves of garlic seems daunting, feel free to just use two whole heads of garlic. It will be plenty!

INGREDIENTS

6 tablespoons olive oil, divided

8 boneless, skinless chicken thighs

40 cloves garlic, peeled but left whole

1 cup diced onion

1/2 cup diced celery

1 teaspoon dried tarragon

Salt and pepper to taste

1/2 cup dry vermouth, white wine, or white grape juice mixed with a tablespoon of white wine vinegar

2 1/2 cups chicken stock, divided

INSTRUCTIONS

Heat 2 tablespoons of olive oil in a large Dutch oven over medium-high heat. (If you don't have a Dutch oven, a large pot works as well.)

Sprinkle the chicken with salt and pepper on both sides. Sauté the chicken pieces in the olive oil until golden brown, turning once. Remove the chicken to a bowl and set aside.

Add two more tablespoons of olive oil to the pan and add the garlic cloves. Turn the heat to medium and cook the garlic, stirring frequently until deep golden brown all over.

Add 1 1/2 cups of chicken stock to the pan, bring to a boil, and cook uncovered for 15 minutes, until the garlic is softened and the stock has reduced by half. Add the garlic and stock to the bowl with the chicken and return the pan to the heat.

Put the remaining 2 tablespoons of oil into the pot and sauté the onion and celery until translucent, about 3–5 minutes. Add the tarragon and a pinch of salt and pepper.

Pour in the vermouth, wine, or grape juice and cook, stirring occasionally, until most of the liquid has evaporated.

Add the chicken, garlic, and juices back into the pan. Pour in the last cup of chicken stock and bring to a boil, then reduce to a simmer and cook for another 10–15 minutes, until the chicken is very tender and the garlic is soft and almost falling apart.

Serve chicken with garlic.

SIMPLE ROASTED POTATOES

SERVES 4

These roasted potatoes are likely to become a staple in your family dinner repertoire. They're easy, versatile, and delicious.

INGREDIENTS

5 medium Yukon Gold potatoes, scrubbed and cut into 1/4-inch wedges

2-3 tablespoons olive oil

Kosher salt and pepper to taste

INSTRUCTIONS

Preheat oven to 450 degrees F.

Rub potato wedges all over with olive oil and spread in roasting pan.

Sprinkle with kosher salt and pepper to taste.

Roast for 35–45 minutes or until brown and crispy.

ANGEL FOOD CAKE WITH LIME DRIZZLE
SERVES 8-12

Give yourself a break and buy a store-bought angel food cake for dessert! Make it special with a quick lime drizzle and add whipped cream if you like.

INGREDIENTS

1/4 cup fresh lime juice

1 teaspoon lime zest

1/4 cup granulated sugar

1/4 cup water

1 store-bought angel food cake

3 cups chopped fruit, such as mangoes and berries

INSTRUCTIONS

Combine the lime juice, lime zest, sugar, and water in a small saucepan. Bring to a boil and cook until the sugar dissolves.

Transfer to a bowl and refrigerate until cooled.

Serve slices of cake topped with fruit and a few spoonfuls of the lime syrup.

FUN

Challenge your family and friends with a brain-teasing game of Fictionary!

HOW TO PLAY

This game is great if you have a dictionary or smartphone handy. The Picker chooses an obscure or strange word from the dictionary and announces it to the table, spelling it but not giving its definition. Make sure no one at the table knows the word! Then every player writes down a made-up definition for the word, initials it, and hands it to the Picker. The Picker writes down the real definition to the word and puts it in the pile as well. The Picker reads all the definitions aloud and everyone votes for the phrase they believe is the correct definition. The person who wrote the definition that gets the most votes gets a point. If no one guesses the correct definition, the Picker gets a point.

CONVERSATION

It's normal for kids—especially teens—to want to assert their independence and prioritize their desires and needs over those of the family. Get them thinking and talking about individual wants versus the good of others with these conversation starters.

(AGES 14-100)

- Are there ways in which you sometimes change your behavior or expectations to be a good friend or family member?

- Have you ever given up something that really mattered to you in order to make someone else happy? Do you regret your choice?

- Can you think of a time when you've acted selfishly? How about a time when you've acted selflessly? Which was more difficult?

- Have you ever been in a situation where you had to make a decision between doing what would benefit you the most, and doing something that would benefit others? Describe what that was like.

- We're often taught to think of others' needs, but are there times when it's okay or even necessary to put yourself first? Can you give examples?

DITCH DIGITAL DISTRACTIONS

Like many parents, Sheri and Ben were frustrated by packed calendars and the difficulty of fitting in dinner, but they were also concerned about the distraction of everyone's phones when they did manage to sit down together. Sheri, Ben, and their two school-aged kids were all feeling the lure of technology. Despite eating together, they found themselves wanting to bring devices to the table, check just one more message, send one more text, or play one more game.

Their phones were eating into the precious time they had together and making it hard to connect as a family, so Sheri and Ben decided they all needed a clear reminder that the dinner table wasn't a place where technology was welcome. Sheri, a designer, came up with a custom-built phone crate that started as a centerpiece on their family table but quickly became a thriving small business as friends and family asked for crates of their own. "It really does remind us to put our phones in the crate so we're not distracted during dinner!" Sheri says of her simple yet effective idea.

Now the family focuses on maximizing their free time to make dinner together possible. One night a week, the kids have no scheduled activities, so Ben and Sheri have made that night distraction-free family dinner night. The kids now particularly look forward to Tuesdays with their parents, because Tuesdays mean a guaranteed time when everyone will put away their phones and spend time at the table together.

FOOD

In addition to working on limiting distractions, Sheri and Ben are trying to encourage their kids to try new foods. These easy fish tacos are just the type of dish they might offer their daughters so they might eat more seafood. Serve with a creative homemade salsa and fruity dessert to help kick off your own distraction-free dinner.

FISH TACOS

SERVES 6

This recipe came from the USDA and the Centers for Disease Control and Prevention. Feel free to experiment with toppings and different salsas to create new flavor combinations!

INGREDIENTS

1/2 cup sour cream

1/4 cup mayonnaise

1/2 cup chopped cilantro

1 package taco seasoning, divided*

1 pound cod or other white fish filets, cut into 1-inch pieces

2 tablespoons olive oil, divided

2 tablespoons lemon juice

12 6-inch corn tortillas, warmed

2 cups shredded red or green cabbage

2 cups diced tomato

Lime wedges

Salsa, hot sauce, or taco sauce for garnish

*The Family Dinner Project's taco seasoning recipe is included on page 206 of this book. Three tablespoons of our seasoning mix would be roughly equivalent to one package of commercially produced seasoning.

INSTRUCTIONS

In a small bowl, combine sour cream, mayonnaise, cilantro, and 2 tablespoons seasoning mix.

In a medium bowl, combine fish, 1 tablespoon of olive oil, lemon juice, and remaining seasoning mix.

Warm the remaining olive oil in a skillet over medium heat and add the fish. Cook, stirring constantly, over medium-high heat for 4–5 minutes or until fish flakes easily when tested with a fork.

Fill warm tortillas with fish.

Top with cabbage, tomato, sour cream mixture, lime wedges, and salsa, hot sauce, or taco sauce of your choice.

PINEAPPLE AND MANGO SALSA
SERVES 6-8

This refreshing and fruity salsa pairs well with fish and chicken or is equally good on tortilla chips.

INGREDIENTS

1 cup diced mango

1 cup canned crushed pineapple, drained

1/2 cup diced red onion

1/2 cup diced red bell pepper

1 small jalapeño, diced (optional)

3 tablespoons chopped cilantro

Juice of 1 lime

Salt and pepper to taste

INSTRUCTIONS

Stir together mango, pineapple, onion, bell pepper, and jalapeño in a small bowl. Let them marinate together for 10 minutes.

Add cilantro and lime juice. Season with salt and pepper, taste and adjust seasonings as needed.

STRAWBERRY FOOL
SERVES 4

A "fool" is a dessert of whipped cream and fruit. Jam makes it easy to customize to your taste. For added crunch, top your fool with crumbled cookies or toasted nuts.

INGREDIENTS

1/2 cup strawberry jam

1 1/4 cups heavy cream

1 tablespoon granulated sugar

1 cup fresh strawberries

INSTRUCTIONS

In a large bowl, beat the heavy cream with the sugar until stiff peaks form.

In a small bowl, whisk the jam until smooth. Fold into the whipped cream.

Spoon into serving dishes and garnish with fresh strawberries.

FUN

If, like Ben and Sheri, you can only manage one or two distraction-free family nights per week, why not try to build an extra-fun tradition into your evenings like going Upside Down and Backwards?

HOW TO PLAY

Start a breakfast or dinner tradition around the theme of upside down and backwards! Pull out all the stops and have breakfast for dinner: Dress in your favorite pajamas and eat pancakes, cereal, or eggs. Bring stuffed animals to the table. Or try dinner for breakfast! Cold pizza anyone? Or, if you're feeling really crazy, an occasional dessert before dinner (say, an ice cream appetizer?) never hurt anyone. You can also think of other activities that might go along with an upside down tradition, like reading bedtime stories at breakfast or having dinner in bed. It's your family's tradition, so get as kooky as you want!

CONVERSATION

With digital distractions stowed away for dinner, you might want to reinforce why you've chosen a device-free mealtime. Try exploring the topic with these conversation starters about interacting with others.

(AGES 8–13, 14–100)

- What are some things you can do in a conversation to show the other person that you're truly interested in listening to them?

- How are face-to-face conversations, phone calls, texts, and online chats different from one another? Which do you prefer and why?

- What are some things that others do in conversations to help you feel comfortable in opening up and talking honestly with them? What are some things that others do to make you feel less comfortable speaking honestly?

- Are there certain things that you feel like you can say online that you wouldn't say to someone's face? Why do you think that is?

- Besides talking, what are some ways that you can feel connected to someone else?

BE MINDFUL WHEN YOU'RE TOGETHER

With two kids at home, two grown kids who are starting families of their own, and a foundation to run on top of everything else, Lori and Wayne Earl have plenty of reasons to be distracted from family dinner. They also have some very good reasons to cherish the time together.

Lori and Wayne are the mother and father of Esther Earl, a well-known "Nerdfighter" and the inspiration for John Green's character Hazel in the novel *A Fault in Our Stars*. Esther died of thyroid cancer in 2010 at the age of sixteen. Her family has started the This Star Won't Go Out Foundation in her honor.

Like most families, Lori, Wayne, and their kids find it hard to prioritize meals together, but Lori says they emphasize gratitude for any kind of community during a meal, even if it's just eating with one other person. To keep their bonds strong, they try to take each child still living at home out weekly for a special meal one-on-one where they can have uninterrupted time with a parent. They use holidays and special occasion meals when everyone can gather as a way to rekindle old family dinner traditions like going around the table to answer a specific question.

The family ate dinner together regularly when all the children were young and now that they're mostly grown, Lori and Wayne are conscious of not allowing distractions to impede the limited time they have together. While they say they still "long for those family dinners," now that everyone has transitioned into living their own lives, they focus on being mindful and grateful for what they have when they're together. Of a recent meal at their daughter's new home, Lori says, "It was so ordinary and yet extraordinary! We shared a delicious meal and sat around the table and talked. It was community."

FOOD
The family's favorite dishes are largely inspired by having lived internationally. Lori was raised abroad and she and Wayne lived in a few different countries with their children over the years. The whole family has a soft spot for this African Curry recipe and Rice Cream Pie.

AFRICAN CURRY
SERVES 4-6

Lori's childhood in Ghana is the origin of this family favorite. Lori says it's best served over rice, generously topped with a variety of fruits and nuts.

INGREDIENTS

1 tablespoon vegetable oil

1 onion, chopped

2 cloves of garlic, minced

3 tablespoons curry powder

1/2 teaspoon cayenne pepper

6 ounces tomato paste

6 cups chicken broth

14 ounces coconut milk

1 1/2 pounds boneless, skinless chicken breast, cut into bite-sized cubes

1 teaspoon salt

2 tablespoons cornstarch

1/2 cup water

2 tablespoons lemon juice

Coconut rice (recipe follows)

Optional toppings: raisins, coconut flakes, mandarin orange segments, chopped peppers, and tomatoes

INSTRUCTIONS

Heat the oil in a large pot over medium heat. Sauté the onion and garlic until translucent.

Add the curry powder and cayenne pepper. Cook, stirring for 2–3 minutes.

Stir in the tomato paste and allow to cook for another 2–3 minutes, watching carefully to make sure it doesn't stick. (Turn the heat down as needed.)

Add the broth and coconut milk. Stir well and bring to a boil.

Turn the heat down and allow the soup to simmer for 20 minutes.

Add in the chicken pieces and salt. Cook for 15 minutes, until the chicken is cooked through.

In a small bowl or jar, mix the cornstarch and water until fully incorporated with no lumps. Stir the cornstarch slurry into the curry. Raise the heat and allow to cook for 5 minutes or until thickened.

Add the lemon juice and stir well.

Serve over cooked rice with toppings as desired.

COCONUT RICE
SERVES 4-6

You can certainly serve your curry over plain white rice, but if you'd like to add a little interest, try cooking the rice in coconut milk.

INGREDIENTS

1 1/2 cups Basmati rice

2 cups water

1 cup unsweetened coconut milk

1 teaspoon salt

INSTRUCTIONS

Combine all ingredients in a medium saucepan. Cover with a tight-fitting lid and bring to a boil.

Reduce the heat to a simmer and allow the rice to cook for about 20 minutes, until the liquid is absorbed and the rice is cooked through.

Remove from heat. Allow the rice to stand for an additional 5 minutes. Fluff with a fork before serving.

RICE CREAM PIE

SERVES 8

This is a favorite special occasion dessert in Lori and Wayne's family. If peanut butter is a no-go in your household, you can substitute another nut or seed butter, or use a traditional marshmallow-and-butter Rice Krispies treat recipe as the basis for your crust.

INGREDIENTS

1 quart ice cream, flavor of your choice

1/2 cup light corn syrup

1/2 cup peanut butter

3 cups Rice Krispies-style cereal

Ice cream toppings, as desired

INSTRUCTIONS

Allow your ice cream to soften at room temperature for 20–30 minutes.

While the ice cream is softening, mix the corn syrup and peanut butter thoroughly.

Add the Rice Krispies cereal to the peanut butter mixture and stir until fully combined.

Press the mixture into a pie plate and freeze for 5–10 minutes to set.

Scoop the softened ice cream into the prepared crust and smooth to fill the crust evenly.

Freeze until firm. Serve with your favorite ice cream toppings!

FUN
Inspired by their daughter Esther's message of spreading love throughout the world, Lori and Wayne recommend this fun origami project as a way to add warmth to the dinner table.

HOW TO PLAY

Make dinnertime fun, creative, and meaningful by writing messages of love or inspiration on origami stars. Place them at different people's plates and read aloud to each other, trying to guess who sent each note!

You can find a template for origami stars on our website at <hyplink>https://thefamilydinnerproject.org/fun/dinner-games/ages-14-100-dinner-games/origami-love-notes/</hyplink>.

CONVERSATION

Carry the theme of spreading love through your dinner with these conversation starters about the power of love in our lives and in the world.

(AGES 8-13, 14-100)

- How does it affect you when someone shows their love for you?

- How does it make you feel to show someone else that you love them?

- Is it easier to say "I love you" to some people, and harder to say it to others? Why?

- Have you ever had to do something difficult in order to show your love for someone? Tell us about it.

- What's one thing you can do today to spread love in the world? What about this week or this month?

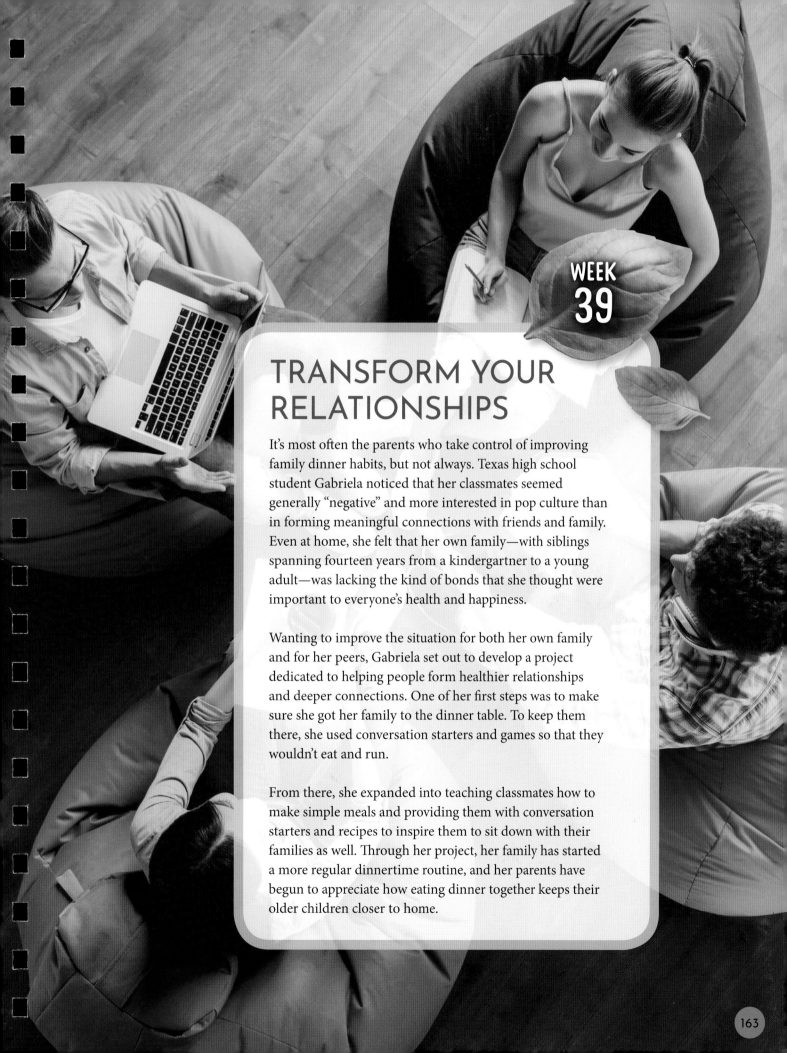

TRANSFORM YOUR RELATIONSHIPS

It's most often the parents who take control of improving family dinner habits, but not always. Texas high school student Gabriela noticed that her classmates seemed generally "negative" and more interested in pop culture than in forming meaningful connections with friends and family. Even at home, she felt that her own family—with siblings spanning fourteen years from a kindergartner to a young adult—was lacking the kind of bonds that she thought were important to everyone's health and happiness.

Wanting to improve the situation for both her own family and for her peers, Gabriela set out to develop a project dedicated to helping people form healthier relationships and deeper connections. One of her first steps was to make sure she got her family to the dinner table. To keep them there, she used conversation starters and games so that they wouldn't eat and run.

From there, she expanded into teaching classmates how to make simple meals and providing them with conversation starters and recipes to inspire them to sit down with their families as well. Through her project, her family has started a more regular dinnertime routine, and her parents have begun to appreciate how eating dinner together keeps their older children closer to home.

FOOD

A favorite dish in Gabriela's household is chili, so we're recommending a special chili recipe from the family of one of our team members. While you don't need much to go with this hearty dish, a unique fruit and cheese quesadilla is a fun addition to the menu.

VITO'S TURKEY CHILI
`SERVES 4-6`

This turkey chili recipe comes from the household of TFDP's executive director Lynn Barendsen. Her husband, John, got this hearty recipe from his own father, who wanted to give his old beef chili a makeover. As with most chili recipes, its flavor improves after a day or two, so it's perfect as a make-ahead meal.

INGREDIENTS

2 tablespoons olive oil

1 large onion, chopped

1 pound ground turkey

4 cloves of garlic, minced

1/2 tablespoon chili powder

1/2 tablespoon ground cumin

1/2 tablespoon dried oregano

1/2 teaspoon hot pepper flakes

1 15-ounce can black beans, drained and rinsed

1 28-ounce can whole tomatoes with juice

1 chipotle chili pepper, chopped (optional)

Salt and pepper to taste

Optional toppings: cheese, avocado, cilantro, sour cream

INSTRUCTIONS

Heat oil in a large pan. Add onion and cook over medium heat for 5 minutes, stirring often.

Add turkey and cook, stirring, until it changes color, about 5 minutes.

Add garlic, spices, and black beans. Stir over low heat for a minute to coat the turkey in the spices.

Add tomatoes and juice, and chipotle if using.

Bring to a boil, breaking tomatoes apart with a wooden spoon.

Cook uncovered over medium to low heat for 30 minutes or until the mixture is thickened.

Taste and adjust spices. Serve hot with toppings if desired.

GRILLED PEACH QUESADILLAS
`SERVES 6 AS A SIDE DISH,` `2-3 AS A MAIN DISH`

These sweet and savory quesadillas are great with chili, but you can also serve them on their own for a light lunch or dinner.

INGREDIENTS

2 medium-sized ripe peaches

2 tablespoons olive oil

6 flour tortillas

3 cups shredded Monterey Jack or Pepper Jack cheese

1/2 cup chopped fresh basil

1/4 cup minced fresh chives

INSTRUCTIONS

Cut the peaches in half and remove the pits.

Place the peaches, cut sides down, on a hot grill. Cook for 3–5 minutes, until they begin to soften and show grill marks.

Let the peaches cool slightly so they're easier to handle, then slice thinly.

Lightly brush one side of each tortilla with oil. Place the tortillas, oil sides down, on the hot grill.

Evenly divide the shredded cheese between the tortillas.

Layer sliced peaches over one half of each tortilla only, leaving the other half covered with just cheese.

Sprinkle the basil and chives evenly over the peaches.

Allow the quesadillas to cook until the cheese is almost fully melted. Carefully fold the cheese only half of each tortilla over the peach and herb filling, pressing down gently to help the quesadillas stick together.

Let the quesadillas cook for one minute more, just until the cheese is completely melted. Remove from the heat, slice each quesadilla in half, and serve.

BERRY AND CHOCOLATE "ICE CREAM" SANDWICHES

MAKES 12 MINI SANDWICHES

These little gems are so easy to assemble, older kids could handle the task all by themselves! This is a great activity for kids to do while you start on dinner, since the sandwiches will need to freeze for about 30 minutes.

INGREDIENTS

1 cup heavy whipping cream

1 tablespoon powdered sugar

3/4 cup raspberries or chopped strawberries

1 ounce bittersweet chocolate, finely chopped

1/2 teaspoon vanilla extract

12 graham cracker sheets, broken in half

INSTRUCTIONS

Using an electric mixer on high speed, whip the cream and powdered sugar together until soft peaks form.

Gently fold the berries, vanilla, and chopped chocolate into the whipped cream.

Top twelve of the cracker halves with the whipped cream mixture (each should take about a heaped tablespoon). Gently top with the remaining cracker halves to make sandwiches.

Wrap each sandwich in foil or plastic wrap and freeze until the filling is firm, at least 30 minutes.

FUN
Follow Gabriela's example and pass the positivity on to others with a Message in a Bottle activity.

HOW TO PLAY

Encourage an imaginative act of kindness by making "Messages in a Bottle." Collect empty bottles (wash well!) and have family members write kind notes to friends and neighbors. Stuff the bottles and leave them anonymously on doorsteps or in mailboxes with a note that says, "Messages from a friend to brighten your day! Fill this bottle for another, then give it away!"

CONVERSATION

An important factor in helping kids learn how to build healthy relationships with others is modeling good relationship habits at home. Reinforce lessons about healthy relationships with these conversation starters.

(AGES 8-13, 14-100)

- What do you think are the ideal characteristics for a life partner or spouse?
- How does someone act when they are "in love?"
- What do you think is the difference between love and romance?
- Do you believe in love at first sight?
- Can you think of some examples from books, TV shows, or movies of healthy and unhealthy relationships?

IF YOU CAN'T
BEAT 'EM, JOIN 'EM

If distractions have really taken over dinnertime, it might work best to sometimes use them to your advantage rather than trying to fight the trend. Single dad Scott found that working with his kids' desire for screen time made them more willing to have dinner as a family.

Trying to capitalize on his limited time with his three sons, Scott wanted to sit down to dinner and enjoy conversation, but the kids wanted to leave the table to watch TV and would zone out rather than talk. As the situation progressed to eating while watching, Scott felt increasingly frustrated—until he hit upon a solution.

He convinced his kids to cook dinner with him for just one night. Together, they made a ratatouille-inspired pasta sauce, then watched the Pixar movie *Ratatouille* while they ate. The shared cooking experience allowed Scott to spark little conversations during the movie, and they talked about the film, the ingredients, and how their version of the dish compared to the on-screen masterpiece. After that evening, the kids became more interested in having dinner as a family. Soon they were all enjoying screen-free dinners together in addition to their movie nights.

We've used Scott's idea as inspiration for a *Ratatouille* dinner, but you could certainly try any number of "Dinner and a Movie" ideas of your own!

FOOD
Veggie-packed ratatouille pasta is a good way to build a rainbow of healthy ingredients on kids' plates. A simple carrot salad and build-your-own crêpes give additional French flair to your family dinner.

RATATOUILLE PASTA
SERVES 6

This pasta sauce uses the classic vegetables found in ratatouille: eggplant, tomatoes, and zucchini. You can modify the recipe to add other vegetables that your family might enjoy.

INGREDIENTS

1 pound penne pasta

1 medium onion, diced

4 cloves of garlic, minced

3 tablespoons olive oil

1 medium eggplant, cut into 1/2-inch cubes

1 zucchini, chopped

1 28-ounce can crushed tomatoes

2 teaspoons dried basil

1 teaspoon dried marjoram

2 teaspoons coarse salt

2 tablespoons red wine vinegar

INSTRUCTIONS

Cook the pasta according to package directions. Drain and set aside.

Heat a large, deep skillet or Dutch oven over medium heat. Sauté the garlic and onion in the olive oil until translucent, about 5 minutes.

Add the eggplant and zucchini and stir well. Cook, stirring frequently for 5–7 minutes, until the vegetables have started to soften.

Season with basil, marjoram, and salt. Add the crushed tomatoes. Simmer for 15 minutes to cook the vegetables down and blend the flavors.

Remove from heat. Add 1 tablespoon of vinegar and stir well. Taste. Adjust the seasonings as necessary. For a sharper flavor, add the second tablespoon of vinegar.

Toss the sauce with the cooked pasta and serve.

FRENCH CARROT SALAD

SERVES 4-6

Fresh carrots and herbs make a refreshing, light salad all on their own. Honey in the dressing helps bring out the natural sweetness of the carrots and gives kid appeal to this dish.

INGREDIENTS

6 medium carrots, peeled and shredded

3 tablespoons minced fresh chives

1/4 cup finely chopped fresh parsley

Juice of 1 lemon

2 tablespoons olive oil

1 tablespoon honey

1 teaspoon coarse salt

1/4 teaspoon black pepper

INSTRUCTIONS

Combine the carrots, chives, and parsley in a medium bowl.

Whisk together the lemon juice, olive oil, honey, salt, and pepper. Pour over the salad, toss, and serve.

BUILD-YOUR-OWN CRÊPES

SERVES 8

Ready-to-eat crêpes can be found in either the freezer section or bakery section of many supermarkets, and they are much faster and easier than making your own! Let everyone fill their own crêpes with an assortment of fresh fruits, chocolate, lemon curd, and cream.

INGREDIENTS

8 ready-to-use crêpes

1 cup chopped fresh berries

2 bananas, thinly sliced

1 cup chocolate hazelnut spread

1 cup prepared lemon curd

1 cup whipped cream

INSTRUCTIONS

Gently warm your crepes according to package directions.

Set out bowls of berries, bananas, chocolate hazelnut spread, lemon curd, and whipped cream.

Let everyone fill their own crêpes with their favorite toppings.

FUN Tonight's dinner experience is a meal and activity all in one.

HOW TO PLAY

Have "Dinner and a Movie" at your house by choosing a family-friendly film to watch together while you eat. Rather than a chance to zone out on screen time, make sure it's a special event by setting the scene with a themed dinner that matches your movie selection, and by interacting with one another while watching. Try these tips to enhance the shared watching and eating experience:

Set "screen breaks" where you intentionally pause the movie. During these times, you can dish up more food, bring plates to the dishwasher, or get dessert ready. You can also use these breaks as an opportunity to talk with one another about what you're watching.

Unleash your inner movie critics by giving thumbs up or thumbs down to different scenes and characters, asking family members who they might cast if they were directing the film or asking kids to narrate a short "Film Critics' Corner" after the movie.

Play "Silent Film" by turning off the sound (no subtitles allowed!) and asking kids to guess what characters are saying, or to help you decode actors' facial expressions and body language.

CONVERSATION

Incorporating screen time into family dinner can be a sensible way to compromise and bring balance to your time together. These conversation starters can help you explore the why and when of shared screen time.

(AGES 2-7, 8-13)

- How do you know when you've had too much screen time? Are there different ways your body and brain feel when you spend a lot of time looking at screens versus how they feel when you don't?

- Have you ever missed out on a fun activity or forgotten to do something important because you were having screen time instead? Tell us about it.

- What are some ways that using technology like TV, computers, and smartphones can help us to make connections with other people?

- How is watching a movie or TV show together different from sitting on the couch next to each other using phones or tablets?

- If you could share a screen-based experience with the whole family, what would you choose and why?

PART V
WE'RE TOO TENSE!

"I hated family dinner growing up. My dad was always yelling, nobody had anything nice to say, and I felt like I was being forced to spend time with these people I didn't even like just because we were supposed to have dinner together."

Comments like these are tough for us to hear. Nobody should have to feel like a hostage at their own dinner table. In fact, if family dinners are really that miserable on a regular basis, it's safe to say that the great benefits that can come with eating dinner together aren't going to come through.

Still, we're only human, and human beings have moods—good, bad, and ugly. So how can you manage those moods while ensuring that the dinner table is a welcoming place for everyone? We've learned a lot from families who have tackled tension at the table and come up with creative solutions to take the negativity off the menu for good.

TAKE TOUGH TOPICS OFF THE TABLE

Keeping the dinner table a relaxing, positive space for all family members can be tricky, especially with teens. Jackie and Mark, who were trying to reunite after a period of separation, discovered that firsthand. Their teen daughters were prone to emotional outbursts and anger at the dinner table. After some serious thought, Jackie realized that much of what was fueling the girls' behavior was embarrassment and discomfort with the topics being discussed.

Mark genuinely wanted to use dinnertime as an opportunity to talk with the girls about grades, dating, and other important aspects of their lives, but the conversations would usually spiral quickly into an argument. Jackie observed that their daughters didn't always want to discuss personal topics in front of the whole family. However, they might be more willing to open up about sensitive subjects like boyfriends or academic struggles privately in a heart-to-heart with one parent.

She and Mark decided to "reboot" their family dinners and totally change the mood of mealtimes. They started by agreeing to take potentially touchy subjects off the table. Then, they focused on creating a positive atmosphere. Once a week, they set the table with nice dishes, glassware, and candles to help set the tone for a relaxing meal. As they've worked on altering the tone of family dinners, the girls have become more willing participants in mealtimes. "I really like not talking about family issues," one daughter reports. "That used to ruin the meal, and I don't like to have my meals ruined."

FOOD
To set the tone for a relaxing family dinner with teens, try this delicious pasta recipe developed by teenage chef Nate. With a little practice, your teens could make this dish themselves!

CHEF NATE'S SAUSAGE FUSILLI
`SERVES 6`

Our friend Nate—teenager and budding chef extraordinaire—makes this pasta dish for his family when he wants something quick and comforting.

INGREDIENTS

1 pound fusilli pasta

2 tablespoons butter

1 tablespoon olive oil

1 clove of garlic, minced

1 pound bulk-style sweet Italian sausage

Dash of fennel seeds

2 lemons, juiced and zested

1 cup white wine, or chicken broth with 1 tablespoon white wine vinegar or lemon juice

Salt and pepper to taste

1/4 teaspoon crushed red pepper flakes

Parmesan cheese

INSTRUCTIONS

Cook the fusilli in boiling water according to package directions.

Combine the olive oil and butter in a large cast iron skillet.

Melt butter over medium heat. Add garlic and sauté until golden brown.

Add the sausage and fennel seeds. Cook until golden brown.

Add the juice and zest of the lemon and stir.

After about 5 minutes, pour in the wine and stir.

Reduce heat, cover, and let reduce by half.

Drain the fusilli and add it into the sausage mixture. Stir until the pasta is well coated.

Season with salt, pepper, and crushed red pepper flakes.

Serve with Parmesan cheese and a lemon wedge.

SAUTÉED ESCAROLE
`SERVES 4-6`

Escarole is a hearty Italian green that's popular in soups and salads. Here it gets quickly sautéed to make an easy side dish. Make sure to thoroughly dry the leaves before cooking. If there's any water on them, they'll splatter when they hit the oil.

INGREDIENTS

Olive oil

1 head escarole, rinsed, thoroughly dried, and torn

Salt and pepper to taste

3 cloves garlic, chopped

1/4 cup almonds, toasted

Parmesan cheese

INSTRUCTIONS

In a large pan, heat 2 tablespoons of olive oil until shimmering. Add just enough of the escarole to cover the bottom of the pan.

Season the escarole with salt and pepper and sauté for about 45 seconds, just until wilted. It's okay if it gets lightly browned; escarole does not tend to turn bitter when cooked.

Remove the wilted escarole to a bowl. Add more olive oil to the pan, heat to shimmering and repeat the process with a fresh batch of escarole. Continue until all the escarole has been wilted and removed to the bowl, making sure to start each batch with fresh olive oil to prevent a scorched oil flavor.

Add a final coating of olive oil to the empty pan and gently cook the garlic, being careful not to let it brown. After a few minutes, when the garlic is very fragrant, return all the cooked escarole to the pan and toss to coat.

Sprinkle the finished escarole with the almonds and top with Parmesan cheese.

PARMESAN PUFFS

MAKES 16 PUFFS

Take a tasty shortcut to homemade bread with these bite-sized puffs made from prepared pizza dough.

INGREDIENTS

6 tablespoons unsalted butter

1 teaspoon garlic powder

1/2 teaspoon salt

1/2 teaspoon dried oregano

1 pound pizza dough

1/2 cup freshly grated Parmesan cheese

INSTRUCTIONS

Preheat oven to 450 degrees F. Lightly grease a 9 by 13–inch baking dish.

In a small saucepan, melt the butter. Stir in the garlic powder, salt, and oregano. Remove from heat.

Divide the pizza dough into sixteen equal pieces (one ounce each, about the size of a walnut). Roll the pieces into balls and place them into the greased dish. It's okay if some of them touch slightly.

Brush the butter mixture over the dough balls, making sure to use it all.

Top the dough balls with the grated Parmesan and bake for 12–15 minutes until golden brown and crusty. Make sure to peek underneath—if the bottoms are pale and very doughy, give the puffs a few more minutes to be sure they're baked through.

FUN Keep the mood light with a challenging and silly rhyming game, Higglety Pigglety.

HOW TO PLAY

One person thinks of a rhyming pair of words, like Funny Bunny. Then the person gives clues that are synonyms for the two words: hilarious furry mammal. Additionally, the person clues everyone in to how many syllables each word is by using the phrases "higglety pigglety" (for three syllable words), "higgy piggy" (for two syllable words), or "hig pig" (for one syllable words). For example, Funny Bunny is a "higgy piggy," but Old Mold is a "hig pig." Everyone tries to guess. Whoever gets it first thinks of the next one.

CONVERSATION

Jackie and Mark's daughters prefer mealtimes that aren't too serious—as demonstrated by the family "burp jar," where everyone deposits a quarter if they're caught burping at the table. Your family might enjoy these humor-inspired conversation starters.

(AGES 8-10, 14-100)

- What's the funniest thing that you've seen lately?
- Have you heard any good jokes recently? Tell one!
- What's the funniest movie or TV show you've ever seen? What makes it so funny?
- Who do you know that can always make you laugh?
- They say "laughter is the best medicine." Do you think that's true? Why or why not?

INVITE A COMPROMISE

Not all tension at the table shows up as arguing or yelling. Sometimes it can lead to withdrawal instead, with some family members wanting to avoid dinner. That's what was happening with Aditi and Hasit's teenage son, Dev. He would either eat very quickly and leave the table as soon as possible, or he'd ask to take his dinner to his room.

The family of five—including a teen daughter and elderly grandmother—had always enjoyed meals together, but as Dev got older, he was becoming uncomfortable with his father's insistence on using dinnertime as an opportunity to talk about serious topics like politics, world events, and difficult family issues. Rather than start an argument at the table, the young man preferred to avoid discomfort and conflict by removing himself from the situation.

Aditi sat down with her son and explained that having him at the dinner table provided his parents with a good opportunity to get insight into his well-being. His appetite, demeanor, and quick departure from the table all helped her to see that there might be something going on in his life that was affecting his moods and mental health.

Dev, on the other hand, wanted his parents to understand that sometimes their choice of dinner conversation topics made him feel moody or defensive. He proposed a solution: His parents could bring up the weighty topics that they ordinarily discussed at dinner during other times of day when there was an opportunity for conversation, such as in the car. In return, he'd do his best to join the family at the dinner table and to stay there. Understanding that his parents viewed dinnertime as a window into his well-being made him much more willing to look for a solution that would satisfy them all rather than shutting down.

FOOD

Aditi, Hasit, and their family enjoy a wide variety of foods from many cultures. While Aditi does most of the cooking in the household, she and her husband value help from all members of the family and like to encourage the kids to lend a hand in the kitchen whenever possible. These easy recipes for a homemade Indian meal are perfect for building emerging cooking skills and getting everyone involved in dinner preparations.

TANDOORI CHICKEN
SERVES 4-6

Our friend Paromita shared this recipe for her dad's special Tandoori Chicken.

INGREDIENTS

1/2 cup plain yogurt

2 tablespoons vegetable oil

2 tablespoons tandoori masala spice blend*

1 tablespoon grated fresh ginger

3 cloves of garlic, minced

1/4 teaspoon salt

Pinch of cayenne pepper (optional)

6 boneless skinless chicken thighs

Naan bread or rice (optional)

Lemon juice (optional)

Slices of onion or bell pepper (optional)

*If you can't find tandoori masala spice blend in your grocery store, look for the more widely available garam masala instead. To make garam masala into tandoori masala, mix 1 tablespoon of garam masala with 1 tablespoon ground cumin, 2 teaspoons paprika, and 1/2 teaspoon turmeric.

INSTRUCTIONS

Mix the yogurt, oil, ginger, garlic, and spices thoroughly in a large bowl.

Cut the chicken thighs in half and add the chicken to the marinade. Toss to coat thoroughly.

Refrigerate for a minimum of 1 hour and up to 8 hours.

Preheat oven to 375 degrees F. Arrange the chicken pieces on a baking sheet.

Bake for 10 minutes, flip, then bake for an additional 10 minutes, or until fully cooked through.

Serve warm with naan bread or rice. Garnish with freshly squeezed lemon juice and slices of onion or bell pepper, if desired.

SPICY CHICKPEAS
SERVES 4

Paromita's mom taught her how to make this Bengali comfort food dish, which they enjoy serving over rice or scooped up in naan bread.

INGREDIENTS

2 tablespoons canola oil

1 medium onion, diced

3 cloves of garlic, minced

2 teaspoons finely grated fresh ginger

1 1/2 teaspoons garam masala

2 teaspoons ground cumin

1/2 teaspoon turmeric

1 15-ounce can chickpeas, drained and rinsed

1/2 cup water

1 cup canned diced tomatoes, with juice

1 teaspoon sugar

1/2 teaspoon salt

Cilantro for garnish (optional)

INSTRUCTIONS

Heat the canola oil in a large skillet over medium heat.

Add the onion, garlic, ginger, garam masala, cumin, and turmeric. Cook, stirring frequently, until the onions are softened, about 5 minutes.

Add the chickpeas, water, diced tomatoes, sugar, and salt. Raise the heat to high and cook, stirring once every minute until the sauce begins to dry out.

Serve warm with parantha bread, naan bread, or tortillas. Cilantro leaves make a nice optional garnish.

CUCUMBER RAITA
SERVES 6

Raita is a cooling condiment that can be made ahead of time. Leaving it in the refrigerator for a day or two helps the flavors to blend. Drizzle it over your chickpeas or use for dipping the chicken.

INGREDIENTS

1 cup plain whole milk yogurt

2/3 cup finely diced cucumber

1 green onion, finely diced

1 tablespoon lemon juice

1 teaspoon salt

1/2 teaspoon ground cumin

INSTRUCTIONS

Stir together all ingredients in a small bowl.

Taste and adjust salt and cumin as needed. The cumin should not be overpowering.

Let the raita sit for at least 15 minutes before serving.

FUN

The Salad Bowl Game is a perfect blend of fun and meaningful conversation that's likely to keep everyone engaged.

HOW TO PLAY

Before dinner, each family member writes down the names of five people they admire on five separate pieces of paper. These people can be fictional characters, historical figures, people you know personally, or people you have never met. Mix up all the pieces of paper in a bowl and place this bowl on the table during dinner. Each family member takes a turn drawing a name from the bowl and describes this person to the rest of the family. The only rule is that the "describer" cannot say the person's name or any part of the name. Once the person is identified, try to guess who put this name in the bowl. Talk about why the person plucked from the salad bowl is admirable.

CONVERSATION

Politics and world events might feel too heavy for dinner conversation to Aditi's teenage son, but the family can still have meaningful conversations. These questions bring the conversation down from world news to what's right in your own backyard.

(AGES 8-13, 14-100)

- What does "home" mean to you?
- If you've lived in more than one place: When someone asks where you come from, how do you answer? For example, is it where you live currently, where you grew up, or the part of the world where your ancestors lived?
- What would make you want to leave a place that you call home?
- How important are surroundings in creating a feeling of being home? What about the people who are there with you?
- If you could change one thing about your home, physically or otherwise, what would it be?

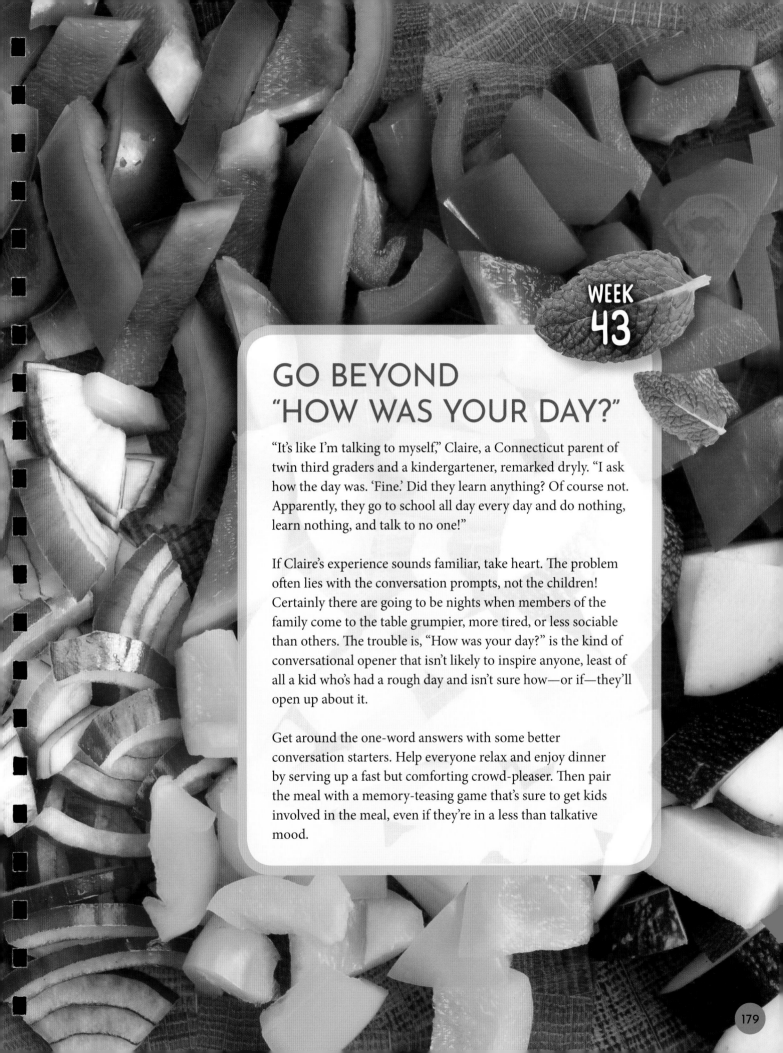

GO BEYOND "HOW WAS YOUR DAY?"

"It's like I'm talking to myself," Claire, a Connecticut parent of twin third graders and a kindergartener, remarked dryly. "I ask how the day was. 'Fine.' Did they learn anything? Of course not. Apparently, they go to school all day every day and do nothing, learn nothing, and talk to no one!"

If Claire's experience sounds familiar, take heart. The problem often lies with the conversation prompts, not the children! Certainly there are going to be nights when members of the family come to the table grumpier, more tired, or less sociable than others. The trouble is, "How was your day?" is the kind of conversational opener that isn't likely to inspire anyone, least of all a kid who's had a rough day and isn't sure how—or if—they'll open up about it.

Get around the one-word answers with some better conversation starters. Help everyone relax and enjoy dinner by serving up a fast but comforting crowd-pleaser. Then pair the meal with a memory-teasing game that's sure to get kids involved in the meal, even if they're in a less than talkative mood.

FOOD

Liven up the family dinner staples of chicken and rice with these easy, time-tested, and family approved recipes that will get dinner on the table in under 30 minutes. Any remaining tension at your dinner table will surely melt away when you finish the meal with old-fashioned ice-cream sundaes.

LIGHTNING FAST LEMON PEPPER CHICKEN

SERVES 4

Cooking instructor April Hamilton of April's Kitchen Counter (Aprilskitchencounter.com) shared this recipe, which pairs nicely with simply steamed broccoli or a big salad for a fast and tasty dinner.

INGREDIENTS

1 pound boneless, skinless chicken breasts

3 tablespoons olive oil, divided

Coarse salt and black pepper

1/4 cup white wine, chicken broth, or water

Zest and juice of 1 lemon

1 tablespoon cold butter (optional)

INSTRUCTIONS

Cut the chicken breasts into thin cutlets. Place the boneless chicken breast halves on a cutting board and mash the top with the heel of your hand, arching your fingertips up so they are out of the way. Using a long sharp knife, carefully cut each into three thin cutlets. If this method is daunting to you, you can also cut each piece of chicken in thirds and use a meat mallet to gently pound the pieces into cutlets.

Brush the chicken cutlets on both sides with 2 tablespoons of the olive oil and sprinkle with salt and pepper.

Heat the remaining tablespoon of olive oil in a large heavy skillet over medium-high heat.

Add the chicken cutlets in a single layer. (Depending on the size of your skillet, this may have to be done in batches—it is best not to crowd the chicken.)

Turn after 2–3 minutes, when the chicken is light golden.

Cook the second side for another couple of minutes until the chicken is just cooked through.

Remove the chicken to a platter and turn the heat off.

Add the wine or broth, lemon zest, and lemon juice to the hot skillet. Gently scrape any browned bits into the sauce.

Whisk in the butter, if desired, for a silky sauce.

Serve the chicken with the sauce.

CHICKEN RICE

SERVES 6-8

Plain white rice gets a flavor boost from poultry seasoning, making it the perfect partner for a chicken dinner.

INGREDIENTS

2 cups long-grain white rice

4 cups chicken stock

1 tablespoon butter

1 1/2 teaspoons poultry seasoning

1/2 teaspoon salt

INSTRUCTIONS

Combine the rice, chicken stock, and butter in a large saucepan. Cover tightly, bring to a boil, and reduce the heat to low.

Cook the rice over low heat for 20–25 minutes (or according to the package directions for your rice) until the liquid is absorbed and the rice is cooked.

Stir in the salt and poultry seasoning. Adjust the salt level to taste and serve.

OLD-FASHIONED HOT FUDGE SUNDAES
SERVES 4-6

Indulge in a special dessert tonight with surprisingly easy homemade hot fudge.

INGREDIENTS

1/2 cup corn syrup

1/2 cup light cream

1/4 cup granulated sugar

1 tablespoon water

1 cup semisweet chocolate chips

1 teaspoon vanilla

Ice cream

Whipped cream*

Sundae toppings, as desired

*If you prefer homemade whipped cream, check out our recipe on page 58.

INSTRUCTIONS

Combine the corn syrup, light cream, sugar, and water in a saucepan over medium heat. Bring to a boil, stirring constantly.

Remove from the heat and add the chocolate chips, stirring until smooth.

Add the vanilla and mix thoroughly. Serve hot over ice cream with toppings as desired.

FUN
Test your family's powers of observation with a game of Can You Remember?

HOW TO PLAY

Have a family member close his or her eyes. Take turns asking them questions about the environment around them. Can they remember the color of the walls, what color shirt another person is wearing, or where their brother's backpack is?

CONVERSATION

Retire the old standby "How was your day?" in favor of these open-ended conversation starters instead!

(AGES 8-13)

- What was the most interesting thing you did today? How about the most boring?
- Did you help anybody with anything today? Tell me about it!
- If you could change one thing about your day, what would it be?
- Tell me one thing you learned today that you think I might not know.
- Name one person who had the biggest positive impact on your day today. How did they make that impact?

FIND ROOM FOR FAVORITES

One of our team members recalls having dinner at the home of an extended family member and watching as one of the teenage children rooted through a drawer for birthday candles. "Is it someone's birthday?"

"Oh no," the teenager responded casually. "It's my half-birthday, so I get a cake."

This particular household made a habit of finding excuses to turn family dinner into an opportunity to celebrate, even on seemingly ordinary days. While you may or may not get into the idea of making cakes for half-birthdays, it's hard to argue with the idea of turning dinner into a party "just because!" After all, how many of us can hang onto a bad mood when we're sitting in front of a big slice of cake?

If celebrating for no particular reason seems like fun to you, a "Favorites" dinner every month or so might be right for your family. You might choose one family member each time who gets to select everything for dinner, from the food to the place settings and conversation starters. Or you might let each person in the family pick just one aspect of the meal: One person chooses a playlist of music, another chooses the main menu, another the dessert, and so on. You can also get creative with the idea and expand it in different ways, like asking family members to choose foods associated with favorite travel destinations, or dedicating a whole menu to someone's favorite color. The goal is to use your "Favorites" dinners as an excuse to make family members feel recognized and give everyone a turn in the spotlight.

FOOD

A favorite color-themed dinner can be a fun way to play with the "favorites" theme, especially for younger children who often really enjoy seeing concepts like sorting and matching played out in real life. This "all red" menu also happens to include some recipes that might become family favorites, like Baked Chicken Parmesan and Berry Crumble.

BAKED CHICKEN PARMESAN
SERVES 6

Forgot to marinate the chicken? No problem. We think the marinade adds a nice flavor boost to this baked Parmesan, but your chicken will still turn out delicious if you accidentally skipped the step. Just make sure to dip unmarinated chicken in a little beaten egg before rolling in breadcrumbs to help the breadcrumbs adhere.

INGREDIENTS

4-6 boneless, skinless chicken breasts

1 cup Italian dressing*

2 cups breadcrumbs

1/2 cup Parmesan cheese

1 teaspoon garlic powder

Salt and pepper to taste

2-3 tablespoons olive oil

4 cups spaghetti sauce, jarred or homemade**

8-10 slices mozzarella cheese

*The marinade recipe for our Easy Grilled Chicken Sandwiches is a perfect homemade Italian dressing substitute. Find it on page 126.

**The Simple Tomato Sauce recipe we recommend with our spaghetti and meatballs would work nicely in this chicken Parmesan recipe too. Find it on page 140.

INSTRUCTIONS

Marinate the chicken breasts in Italian dressing for at least 30 minutes. This can be done in the morning to make the evening preparation quicker.

Preheat oven to 375 degrees F.

Pour breadcrumbs in a large bowl and add Parmesan, garlic powder, and a dash of salt and pepper.

Dip marinated chicken into breadcrumb mixture and coat evenly.

Heat olive oil in a non-stick skillet. Cook chicken until brown on both sides.

After browning, place chicken in a shallow baking pan. Pour spaghetti sauce over chicken.

Layer the mozzarella cheese on top.

Bake until the cheese is bubbly.

BERRY CRUMBLE WITH WHIPPED CREAM
SERVES 4-6

You can use any berries you like in your crumble. We recommend mixed berries because we love the combination of flavors, but you can stick with just one variety if you prefer. Fresh berries will also work perfectly here, but frozen are usually more cost-effective and can be kept on hand so you can whip up this special treat whenever the mood strikes.

INGREDIENTS

6 cups frozen mixed berries

1/4 cup sugar

1/4 cup all-purpose flour

1/4 teaspoon ground cinnamon

1 cup rolled oats

1/2 cup all-purpose flour

1/2 cup brown sugar

Pinch of salt

1/2 cup cold unsalted butter, diced

Whipped cream or ice cream (optional)

INSTRUCTIONS

Preheat the oven to 350 degrees F. Butter a 9-inch glass pie plate.

Gently combine the berries with the sugar, flour, and cinnamon. Place in the prepared pie plate.

Prepare the topping. Combine the oats, flour, brown sugar, and salt in a bowl. Use a pastry blender or two knives to work in the butter until topping resembles coarse meal. Sprinkle evenly over the berries.

Place the pie plate on a baking sheet. Bake in the center of the oven until the fruit is bubbling and the topping is golden brown, about 1 hour. Remove the crisp to a rack to cool slightly. Serve in dessert bowls with whipped cream or ice cream.

BRUSCHETTA

SERVES 6-8

We love making bruschetta with families at our Community Dinner events. This is the classic tomato and basil preparation, but you can always get adventurous with your bruschetta and add whatever toppings you like.

INGREDIENTS

2 cups diced fresh tomatoes

2 cloves of garlic, minced

1 1/2 teaspoons salt

3 tablespoons olive oil

1 baguette, cut into 1/2-inch slices

12 fresh basil leaves, torn

Parmesan cheese (optional)

INSTRUCTIONS

In a medium bowl, stir together the tomatoes, garlic, salt, and olive oil. Let the mixture stand for 5–10 minutes to marinate (the longer it sits, the more flavorful it will become).

Arrange the bread slices on a platter. Spoon the tomato mixture over the top.

Garnish the bread with the torn basil leaves and optional grated or shaved Parmesan.

FUN
Give your "Favorites" dinner a soundtrack with a family dinner playlist!

HOW TO PLAY

Create a compilation of songs and invite the whole family to contribute by sharing their favorite tunes. You can also make this activity a bit more challenging by picking only songs that are food themed, or by picking songs that all contain the same word ("love," "friend," "home," etc.).

CONVERSATION

As long as you're sharing a favorites-themed dinner, why not share more favorite things?

(AGES 2-7, 8-13)

- What's your favorite color? Food? Book? Movie? Animal?
- Are any of your favorite things different now than they were when you were younger?
- Do you ever find it hard to pick a favorite? Why do you think that is?
- Do you and your friends have a lot of favorite things in common? How are your favorites alike and how are they different?
- What is your favorite thing to do as a family? Why is it your favorite?

FORGE A BOND OVER FOOD

Mary and Andrew were involved in a long-distance relationship for some time before deciding that it was time to start establishing a family with Mary's young daughter. Because blending households and establishing new family routines can be tricky and tense, they started off slowly, having regular dinners together as a family unit.

Interacting with one another and with seven-year-old Maggie at mealtimes helped them to learn more about each other and what they might want to establish in their family life together. Letting Maggie take the lead as much as possible helped give her a sense of "ownership and pride" over dinnertime, as she set the tone for everything from conversation topics to menu choices. Her ability to take part in their new ritual together by helping to chop, mix, and serve the meal, choose the games, and ask questions at the table made it easier for her to warm up to Andrew and welcome the change in routine. Andrew, in turn, taught Maggie two valuable family dinner skills: how to make sushi and how to sing his family's special blessing song.

All families can benefit from taking a step back from time to time and getting hands-on with a dinnertime activity to lighten the mood and enhance family bonding. Andrew's idea of making homemade sushi together was a great one due to its fun, creative, and intricate nature, but any cook-together activity would work equally well. The point is to work toward a finished product together and to enjoy the results!

FOOD
Homemade sushi is fun, but it can also feel a bit daunting if you don't have an expert to guide you through the process. These Do-It-Yourself Sushi Bowls follow the same idea without requiring the same level of skill. Dress them up with a homemade teriyaki sauce for drizzling and save the rolling for crispy, fruit-filled dessert sushi.

DO-IT-YOURSELF SUSHI BOWLS
SERVES 4

TFDP team member Bri and her young sons enjoy making these sushi bowls together on busy nights. Sometimes they substitute fresh tuna or bake-and-serve tempura shrimp from the grocery freezer section.

INGREDIENTS

4 cups cooked sushi rice

16 ounces smoked salmon, cooked shrimp, crab stick, or a combination

1 large sweet potato, baked

1 cucumber, diced

1 avocado, cubed

6 green onions, diced

Soy sauce or teriyaki sauce

Toasted nori sheets (optional)

Toasted sesame seeds (optional)

INSTRUCTIONS

Arrange the seafood on a platter.

Using a small spoon or melon baller, scoop out the baked sweet potato flesh in bite-sized pieces and place in a small bowl.

Place the diced cucumber, green onions and avocado cubes in separate dishes.

Slice or crumble the nori sheets, if using, and place in a small bowl.

Divide the sushi rice among four individual bowls.

Serve each person a bowl of rice and let them choose from the toppings, with soy sauce or teriyaki and toasted sesame seeds for garnish.

EASY TERIYAKI SAUCE
SERVES 8-10

This easy homemade version of teriyaki sauce can be kept in a jar in the refrigerator for up to a month. Use leftovers to marinate chicken or salmon for another simple meal.

INGREDIENTS

1 cup tamari (dark soy sauce)

3/4 cup water

6 tablespoons honey

4 tablespoons brown sugar

2 cloves of garlic, minced

1 tablespoon finely grated fresh ginger

INSTRUCTIONS

Combine all ingredients in a medium saucepan. Bring to a boil.

Reduce the heat to a simmer and cook, stirring frequently for about 15 minutes or until the sauce has begun to thicken and lightly coats the back of a spoon.

Allow the sauce to cool before using.

DESSERT "SUSHI"

`SERVES 8`

This fruit-filled "sushi" is a fun hands-on activity for kids!

INGREDIENTS

1 10-ounce package marshmallows

3 tablespoons butter

6 cups Rice Krispies-style cereal

1 cup sliced strawberries

2 bananas, cut into matchsticks

1 mango, cut into matchsticks

Chocolate syrup (optional)

INSTRUCTIONS

Line a rimmed baking sheet with foil or parchment paper. Lightly grease the lining to provide extra insurance against sticking.

In a medium saucepan, melt together the butter and marshmallows, stirring until smooth.

In a large bowl, combine the melted marshmallow mixture with the cereal, tossing until well coated.

Using wet hands to keep the cereal from sticking, scoop the cereal mixture onto the prepared baking sheet and press down firmly to make an even, thin layer that covers the whole pan.

Let the cereal mixture set for 10–15 minutes before making the "sushi".

To cut the "sushi", use a sharp knife to cut the cereal mixture in half lengthwise, then in quarters crosswise (you should end up with eight equal rectangles).

Give each person a rectangle of cereal treat and set out the sliced fruit. Each person can fill their own "sushi" rolls by lining up sliced fruit along one of the short edges of their rectangle, then rolling the whole thing up inside the cereal treat. This can be messy—you might want to lightly but firmly squeeze as you go, to make sure the roll stays together.

Use a sharp knife to slice the "sushi" rolls into four pieces. Serve with chocolate syrup "soy sauce" for dipping, if desired.

FUN

With plenty of bright colors and textures on the table for your hands-on, sushi-inspired dinner, you'll have the perfect opportunity to play a classic game of I Spy.

HOW TO PLAY

Start with one person choosing an object and saying, "I spy with my little eye, something . . ." and then describing the thing. For example, "I spy with my little eye, something . . . purple!" The other diners have to guess what the person is looking at.

CONVERSATION

Keep the mood casual with these conversation starters designed to help you get to know one another a bit better—no pressure or deep thoughts required.

(AGES 2-7, 8-13)

- If you were an animal, which animal would you be and why?

- If you could choose any superpower, like flying or being invisible, what would you choose?

- What's one thing you really love about being you?

- Finish this sentence: "One day, I will be the first person in the world to_____."

- If you could trade places with any person in the world (or any person from history) for just one day, who would you pick?

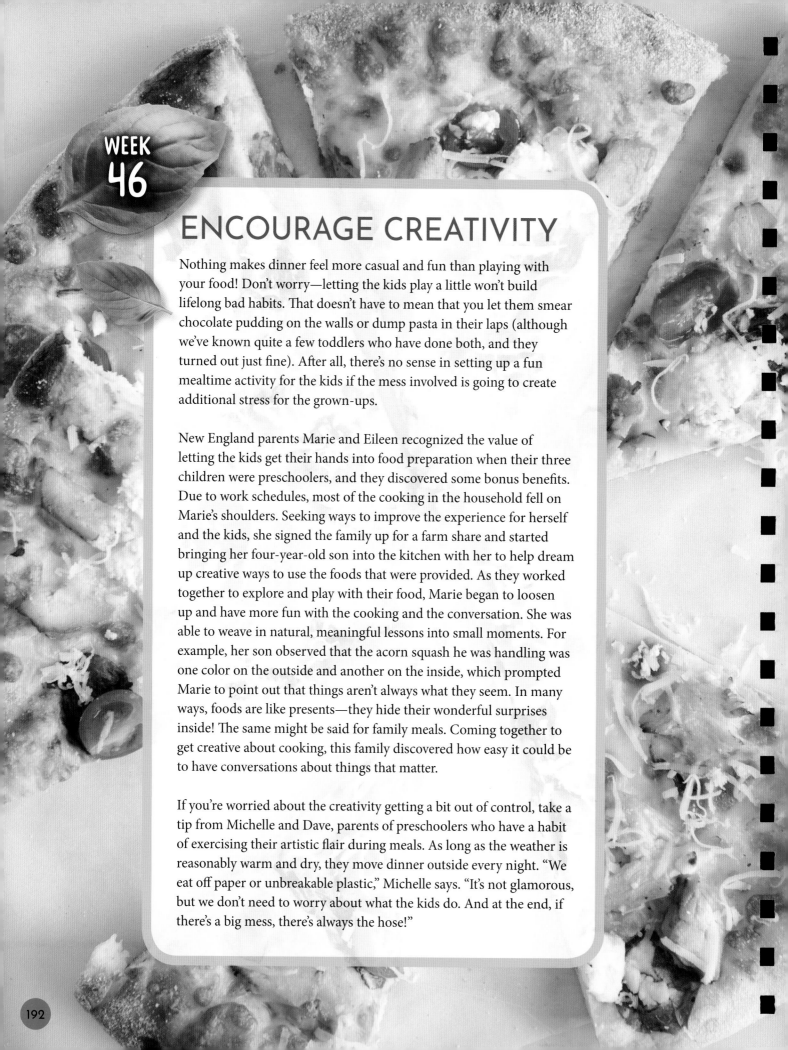

ENCOURAGE CREATIVITY

Nothing makes dinner feel more casual and fun than playing with your food! Don't worry—letting the kids play a little won't build lifelong bad habits. That doesn't have to mean that you let them smear chocolate pudding on the walls or dump pasta in their laps (although we've known quite a few toddlers who have done both, and they turned out just fine). After all, there's no sense in setting up a fun mealtime activity for the kids if the mess involved is going to create additional stress for the grown-ups.

New England parents Marie and Eileen recognized the value of letting the kids get their hands into food preparation when their three children were preschoolers, and they discovered some bonus benefits. Due to work schedules, most of the cooking in the household fell on Marie's shoulders. Seeking ways to improve the experience for herself and the kids, she signed the family up for a farm share and started bringing her four-year-old son into the kitchen with her to help dream up creative ways to use the foods that were provided. As they worked together to explore and play with their food, Marie began to loosen up and have more fun with the cooking and the conversation. She was able to weave in natural, meaningful lessons into small moments. For example, her son observed that the acorn squash he was handling was one color on the outside and another on the inside, which prompted Marie to point out that things aren't always what they seem. In many ways, foods are like presents—they hide their wonderful surprises inside! The same might be said for family meals. Coming together to get creative about cooking, this family discovered how easy it could be to have conversations about things that matter.

If you're worried about the creativity getting a bit out of control, take a tip from Michelle and Dave, parents of preschoolers who have a habit of exercising their artistic flair during meals. As long as the weather is reasonably warm and dry, they move dinner outside every night. "We eat off paper or unbreakable plastic," Michelle says. "It's not glamorous, but we don't need to worry about what the kids do. And at the end, if there's a big mess, there's always the hose!"

FOOD

Homemade pizza has got to be the ultimate creative dinner experience. We love the crust recipe here, but if you haven't got time to make your own, store-bought dough or even individual pizzas made with bagels, English muffins, or pitas work fine. A "Raggedy Ann" salad makes a healthy side dish with an imaginative flair, topped off with a wholesome version of a banana split bar for dessert.

HOMEMADE PIZZA

MAKES 2 12-INCH PIZZAS

Thanks to our friends at the Home Baking Association for this great pizza crust recipe. It's simple to put together, but on particularly busy nights, feel free to use store-bought dough instead.

INGREDIENTS

Crust

1 1/2 cups all-purpose flour

1-1 1/2 cups whole-wheat flour, divided

1 tablespoon sugar

1 package fast-rising yeast

1 1/2 teaspoons salt

1 cup water

2 tablespoons olive oil, plus additional for topping dough

Toppings

3-4 cups marinara sauce, jarred or homemade*

24 ounces mozzarella cheese, shredded

1 cup freshly grated Parmesan cheese

Meats, cheeses, and vegetables of your choice

*The Simple Tomato Sauce recipe we recommend with our spaghetti and meatballs would work nicely in this pizza recipe, too. Find it on page 140.

INSTRUCTIONS

In a large bowl, combine all-purpose flour, 1/2 cup whole-wheat flour, sugar, undissolved yeast, and salt.

Heat water and oil until warm (90–105 degrees F). Stir into dry ingredients. Stir in only enough remaining whole-wheat flour to make a rough ball of dough. Turn out onto a floured surface or knead in the bowl. The flour may not all be used. If dough is too dry or stiff, knead in 1–2 tablespoons of water.

Cover and let rest 10 minutes. (Or, refrigerate in an oiled, sealed container overnight, punching once and reforming the dough after an hour.)

Divide dough in half. Shape each half into a ball. Roll or press each into a 12–14 inch circle. Place on greased pizza pans or baking sheets.

Brush or rub with garlic and oil. Prick dough with a fork, then let rest for 10 minutes.

Par-bake crusts at 450 degrees F for 5–7 minutes.

Spread sauce on the prepared crusts and top with a mixture of Parmesan and mozzarella cheeses, along with any preferred toppings.

Bake the pizzas for an additional 10 minutes, or until the crust is crisp and the cheese is bubbly.

"RAGGEDY ANN" SALAD
SERVES 4

One of our team members recalls making these salads frequently with her great grandmother when she was a small child. At that time, hummus was not a common ingredient in her part of the world—she and her great-grandmother typically used either tuna or egg salad and ate their creations for a light lunch. We've updated the concept using hummus, which makes a nice dip for the vegetables.

INGREDIENTS

1 cup hummus*

4 large romaine lettuce leaves

2 hard-boiled eggs, cut in half lengthwise

1 medium carrot, cut into sticks

1 stalk celery, cut into sticks

1/2 cup finely diced red bell pepper

Raisins or dried cranberries

Favorite salad dressing, for dipping (optional)

*Our hummus recipe can be found on page 66.

INSTRUCTIONS

On each of four individual plates, place a scoop of hummus in the center. Use a spreader or butter knife to smooth it into a triangle shape for the "body."

Cover the hummus "bodies" with lettuce leaves, torn as needed, for the "dress."

Give each "Raggedy Ann" a head with half of a hard-boiled egg. Use raisins or dried cranberries to make faces and carrot and celery sticks for arms and legs.

Finish the "Raggedy Ann" salads with a sprinkling of diced red peppers around the faces to create the "hair."

If desired, serve with small cups of salad dressing for dipping and drizzling.

YOGURT BANANA SPLIT BAR
SERVES 4

Making banana splits with yogurt and a variety of toppings means you control just how healthy or decadent you want dessert to be. These are also fun for an after-school snack or even for breakfast.

INGREDIENTS

4 bananas, peeled and sliced in half lengthwise

2 cups vanilla or plain yogurt

Toppings of your choice: chocolate chips, marshmallows, chopped nuts, granola, sprinkles, sundae syrups, or fresh and dried fruits

INSTRUCTIONS

Arrange the halved bananas in four individual serving dishes, as you would for a banana split.

Place spoonfuls of yogurt down the center of each split.

Provide an assortment of toppings and let everyone make their own banana split creations.

FUN
While you're mixing pizza dough or while the pizzas are baking, set the kids up with a kitchen art activity to lend festive flair to your dinner decor.

HOW TO PLAY

Assemble two eyedroppers, several small dishes filled with water and different food colorings, and a pile of paper towels. Fold the paper towels into squares, or keep folding them into a tight pile. Then apply drops of different colors. When the towels are unfolded, get ready for colorful patterns that will surprise and delight your little culinary artists! You can hang them up to dry on a clothesline strung around the kitchen.

CONVERSATION

As long as everyone's getting creative, try these conversation starters about imagination and creativity.

(AGES 2-7, 8-13)

- If you created your own museum, what kind of museum would it be? What kinds of things would you put in it?

- If you could learn to make, build, or create anything at all, what would you choose?

- Many great inventors, artists, and innovators have failed more times than they've been successful. Have you ever failed at something and been inspired to try a different creative approach because of it? Tell us about it.

- What inspires you?

- Do you think having art that can be seen by the public—like sculpture gardens, statues in parks, and art galleries in places like banks and schools—is important? What does having art visible to everyone add to the world?

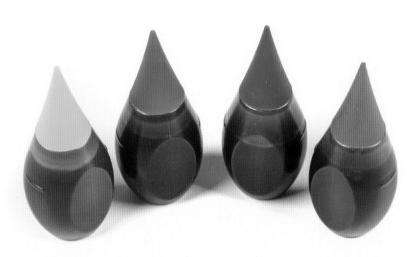

PART VI
THERE'S TOO BIG A CROWD!

So far, the majority of this book has dealt with the types of family dinners most of us strive for each day—just the immediate household, gathered around the table to pause and take a breath together in the midst of the daily routine. But family dinners aren't always small weeknight events. Often, the ones we remember most fondly are the big gatherings of family, and sometimes friends who feel like family. Dinners can mean holidays, celebrations, and sometimes just Sundays with as many people as can fit at Grandma's house.

Crowded dinners can be joyful, like the annual buffet for over one hundred friends and neighbors that has one family we know eagerly cooking and freezing items for a meticulously planned menu a month ahead of time. They can also catch us off guard—just ask Jane, who was asked to prepare dessert for her new partner's family dinner and showed up with an 8-inch pan of brownies only to find a driveway filled with cars and twenty-five guests crammed into the dining room. But in the end, those big, noisy, and sometimes confusing dinners for a crowd can be the essence of what family dinner is really about: Showing up to be together however, whenever, and wherever you can make it happen. In this section, you'll be cooking enough, so we've only focused on the main dish. You can ask your guests to bring the sides, potluck style!

SKIP THE TAKEOUT

When you're hosting a big crowd, it's tempting to just order takeout and let someone else handle the hard work for you. But as one family we know shared with us, the decision to order in for guests can have its own challenges. "My brother-in-law has sometimes relied on takeout to feed everyone during family gatherings, but it always seems like that stresses him out even more. First he worries about whether he's getting enough food, then he worries that he won't have the things everyone likes so he feels compelled to take individual orders, and then he's overwhelmed by the size of the bill for all that food—which is always either too much or too little. I'd rather help out with a potluck dinner than watch him be uncomfortable when he's trying to be kind!"

Why not try a takeout-inspired one-dish meal that's easy to make and easy to scale up or down, depending on how many diners will be joining you? That way, you'll always be sure to have the right amount of food—and choosing an easy recipe means you'll still have plenty of time with your guests.

FOOD

Anne's Simple Chicken Sesame Noodles are a real crowd-pleaser. She used to make a double batch for her husband and two sons so there would be plenty for dinner and lunch the following day. Since this dish is even better cold than hot, it was a great food to bring to a school picnic or to a baseball game. Her sons liked the way they could trade it for other foods, like a slice of pizza at those outings, since their friends liked it too. Years later, Anne makes Simple Chicken Sesame Noodles for her students when they come to dinner.

SIMPLE CHICKEN SESAME NOODLES
SERVES 8-10

as written; double the recipe (or more!)
to feed a crowd

This recipe was provided to us by TFDP co-founder Dr. Anne Fishel. As an added bonus, the short ingredients list makes these noodles relatively budget-friendly. The whole dish can be made in advance and served cold, or you can roast and shred the chicken a day in advance and assemble the rest at dinnertime.

INGREDIENTS

For the Noodles:

2 cups snow peas

1 tablespoon olive oil

2 bone-in chicken breasts

Salt and pepper to taste

1 3/4 pounds linguine

1/2 cup sesame seeds

For the Sauce:

3 cloves of garlic, minced

3/4 cup sesame oil

3/4 cup soy sauce

6 tablespoons balsamic vinegar

2 tablespoons hot pepper oil

1 teaspoon minced ginger

2 bunches green onions, minced (white parts only)

INSTRUCTIONS

Bring a large and a small pot of water to a boil.

Preheat oven to 375 degrees F.

Add the snow peas to the small pot. Cook for 5 minutes.

Drizzle olive oil on the chicken breasts and season with salt and pepper. Roast in the oven for about an hour.

Add the linguine to the large pot. Cook until al dente, about 8 minutes.

Spread the sesame seeds in a single layer on a baking sheet. Toast the sesame seeds in the oven for 5 minutes. Set aside.

While the snow peas, chicken, and linguine are cooking, prepare the sauce.

Whisk together garlic, sesame oil, soy sauce, vinegar, hot pepper oil, ginger, and green onions.

When the snow peas are done (bright green and tender but not mushy), plunge them in a bowl of cold water and set aside. Once cooled, cut them into thin strips.

Divide the sauce into two small bowls.

When the chicken is done, let it cool a bit. Shred the chicken into bite-sized pieces and add it to one of the sauce bowls. Let marinate for 10–15 minutes.

When the linguine is ready, place in a large serving bowl and toss with the remaining sauce. Add the toasted sesame seeds and toss.

Add the chicken and the remaining sauce. Top the noodles with the sliced snow peas.

FUN
Have a little fun testing how well everyone at the table knows each other with a round of Top Four.

HOW TO PLAY

Before the meal starts, every guest is given at least four slips of paper. Each person writes a phrase or item on each slip (for example, "Clean Sheets," "Snakes," "The Grateful Dead," "Remembering a word you forgot"). The slips all go into a jar for the middle of the table.

At dinner, one person starts as the leader. The leader randomly draws four slips of paper from the jar and reads them aloud. Then the leader privately puts the slips in order of preference, from most favorite to least. At the same time, the other guests write down the order in which they think the leader would place things. The leader reads his list, and whoever guesses the leader's list order perfectly gets a point.

CONVERSATION

Take advantage of a bigger gathering as an opportunity to talk about traditions you value.

(AGES 8-14, 14-100)

- What family traditions do you enjoy the most? Which are the most important to pass on to the next generation?

- In what ways have you seen traditions evolve over the years?

- What is a tradition from your childhood or from years past that you would like to see rekindled? How could we do that?

- What's one traditional food or idea from another culture that might be fun for us to try at our next gathering?

- Have you ever found following a specific tradition to be challenging for any reason? How did you decide to handle it? Did you ultimately feel that the rewards of keeping with tradition outweighed the challenge?

KEEP LITTLE HANDS OCCUPIED

Even the best-behaved children can make big family dinner gatherings a challenge. Some of the antics of little ones are sure to become family legend: Finding and eating the whole cake that was meant for dessert, accidentally flooding the bathrooms during an innocent "experiment" while the adults were cooking, burying Grandma's good jewelry in the backyard as pirate treasure. ("We quit having big family gatherings at their house for a while after that one!")

If you can't beat 'em, join 'em—or let them join you! These meal preparations and hands-on activities will keep the kids in the kitchen with the adults and away from Grandma's jewels!

FOOD

Lasagna is the perfect feed-a-crowd solution, and it's great for young helpers. Here, we've provided two different ideas—one for a traditional large-pan lasagna, and the other for individual lasagnas that everyone can customize to their own tastes. Both have been hits with the guests at our Community Dinner events! Depending on the size of your gathering, oven space, and the personalities and tastes of your guests, you can choose whichever works best for your crowd.

TFDP COMMUNITY DINNER LASAGNA, TRADITIONAL STYLE

`SERVES 8`

This lasagna is a staff favorite for our Community Dinner Series because it's so easy to make for a crowd! You can make a basic dish by skipping the garlic, spinach, and fresh basil, or you can go the whole nine yards. If you want to make your dinner for a crowd really easy, you can make a lasagna (or two or three) ahead of time and refrigerate or freeze it. Then all you have to do is reheat on the day of your dinner.

INGREDIENTS

15 ounces ricotta cheese

2 large eggs

1/2 cup grated Parmesan cheese

4 cups shredded mozzarella cheese, divided

1/4 teaspoon salt

1/4 teaspoon pepper

2 tablespoons chopped fresh basil (optional)

3 cloves of garlic, minced (optional)

45 ounces tomato-basil pasta sauce, jarred or homemade*

8 ounces no-boil lasagna noodles

3 cups fresh baby spinach (optional)

*The Simple Tomato Sauce recipe we recommend with our spaghetti and meatballs would work nicely in this lasagna recipe too. Find it on page 140.

INSTRUCTIONS

Preheat the oven to 375 degrees F.

Combine ricotta, eggs, Parmesan cheese, and a 1/2 cup of mozzarella in a bowl.

Mix in salt, pepper, and, if you're using them, basil and garlic.

Spread about 1 cup of tomato sauce at the bottom of a 9 by 13–inch pan.

Arrange a layer of lasagna noodles on top of the sauce. Depending on the size of the noodles, three or four will cover the pan.

Next, layer 1/3 of the ricotta cheese mixture, 1/3 of the spinach (if using), and 1 cup of mozzarella cheese. Then layer about 1 cup of sauce on top.

Repeat layers in this order (noodles, ricotta mix, spinach, mozzarella, sauce) twice more.

Top the last layer with noodles. Then cover with remaining sauce and mozzarella.

Cover with aluminum foil. Bake for 40–50 minutes. Remove foil and bake 5 minutes longer to brown the cheese on top.

Let stand for 5 minutes before serving.

TFDP COMMUNITY DINNER PERSONAL PAN LASAGNAS

SERVES 8

These personal pan lasagnas are a fun way to get the whole crowd involved in making dinner. The basic recipe is very similar to our traditional lasagna, but allows for add-ins and personal preferences. To make cleanup easy, consider using disposable mini-loaf tins for each person.

INGREDIENTS

15 ounces ricotta cheese

2 large eggs

1/2 cup grated Parmesan cheese

1/4 teaspoon salt

1/4 teaspoon pepper

4 cups shredded mozzarella cheese, divided

45 ounces tomato-basil pasta sauce, jarred or homemade*

128 wonton wrappers

Add-ins: chopped fresh garlic, baby spinach leaves, sautéed eggplant or zucchini, crumbled cooked sausage, miniature pepperoni rounds, fresh basil

*The Simple Tomato Sauce recipe we recommend with our spaghetti and meatballs would work nicely in this lasagna recipe, too. Find it on page 140.

INSTRUCTIONS

Preheat oven to 400 degrees F.

Combine ricotta, eggs, Parmesan cheese, and a 1/2 cup of mozzarella in a bowl. Add salt and pepper and stir well.

Set out ricotta mixture, sauce, add-ins, and 3 1/2 cups of mozzarella cheese where guests can easily reach them.

Give each person a miniature loaf tin and 16 wonton wrappers. Instruct guests to begin by coating the bottoms of their tins with a few spoonfuls of sauce, then layer in four wonton wrappers, overlapping them slightly to fit.

Each person can then continue building a personal lasagna by adding some of the ricotta mixture, any add-ins they like, and another layer of sauce and wonton wrappers. Finish the personal lasagnas with the final four wonton wrappers, a top layer of sauce, and a generous sprinkling of mozzarella cheese.

Set the loaf tins on baking sheets lined with parchment paper. Use a pencil to mark each guest's name next to their personal creation.

Bake the lasagnas for 20–30 minutes until the wonton wrappers are cooked and the cheese is bubbly.

FUN

Let the kids handle the side salad with this food collage activity adapted from some of our family workshops.

HOW TO PLAY

Set out salad fixings such as lettuce leaves, bell peppers, cucumbers, carrots, avocados, cherry tomatoes, bean sprouts, and any other vegetables, fruits, nuts, and seeds you can think of. Instruct children to wash their hands well. Ask them to create pictures with the vegetables. Faces are an easy idea to start with, but you might move on to animals, trains, boats, or flowers. If you're really feeling brave, you might ask all the children to collaborate on one big salad collage on a large platter to serve as your family dinner centerpiece (and side dish). There's only one rule: Anything you create, you should eat!

CONVERSATION

Engage all ages with a conversation about special memories.

(ALL AGES)

- What is your favorite family memory? Why is it special to you?
- What's the funniest thing that has ever happened at one of our gatherings?
- A week, a month, or a year from now, what will you remember most about today? Why?
- What is your earliest memory?
- Sometimes memories are sparked for us by our senses, like certain smells or sounds. What's one sensory experience that always brings back memories for you?

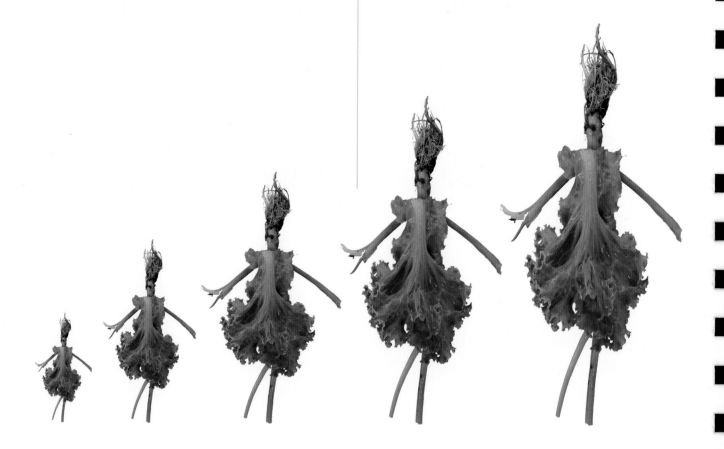

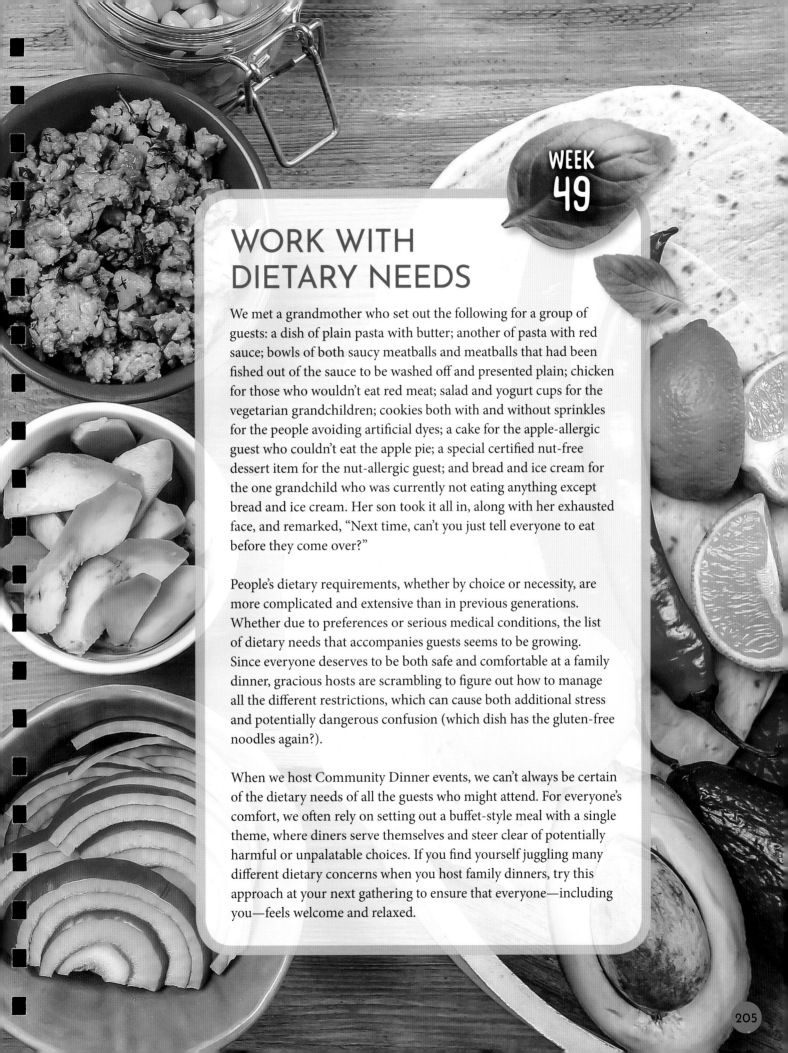

WORK WITH DIETARY NEEDS

We met a grandmother who set out the following for a group of guests: a dish of plain pasta with butter; another of pasta with red sauce; bowls of both saucy meatballs and meatballs that had been fished out of the sauce to be washed off and presented plain; chicken for those who wouldn't eat red meat; salad and yogurt cups for the vegetarian grandchildren; cookies both with and without sprinkles for the people avoiding artificial dyes; a cake for the apple-allergic guest who couldn't eat the apple pie; a special certified nut-free dessert item for the nut-allergic guest; and bread and ice cream for the one grandchild who was currently not eating anything except bread and ice cream. Her son took it all in, along with her exhausted face, and remarked, "Next time, can't you just tell everyone to eat before they come over?"

People's dietary requirements, whether by choice or necessity, are more complicated and extensive than in previous generations. Whether due to preferences or serious medical conditions, the list of dietary needs that accompanies guests seems to be growing. Since everyone deserves to be both safe and comfortable at a family dinner, gracious hosts are scrambling to figure out how to manage all the different restrictions, which can cause both additional stress and potentially dangerous confusion (which dish has the gluten-free noodles again?).

When we host Community Dinner events, we can't always be certain of the dietary needs of all the guests who might attend. For everyone's comfort, we often rely on setting out a buffet-style meal with a single theme, where diners serve themselves and steer clear of potentially harmful or unpalatable choices. If you find yourself juggling many different dietary concerns when you host family dinners, try this approach at your next gathering to ensure that everyone—including you—feels welcome and relaxed.

FOOD

Please every palate at a large gathering with our totally customizable taco bar, which easily accommodates food preferences and dietary needs.

TFDP COMMUNITY DINNER TACO BAR
SERVES 8-10;
CAN BE SCALED UP OR DOWN AS NEEDED

This is less a recipe and more a template for how we set up taco bars at our events. You can add or subtract items based on your own preferences and feel free to do as much or as little cooking as you like. Store-bought items are a big help when you're setting up a buffet with lots of variety!

INGREDIENTS

For Taco Meat:

2 tablespoons olive oil

2 pounds ground beef or turkey

1 medium onion, chopped

2 tablespoons chili powder

1 1/2 tablespoons cumin

2 teaspoons garlic powder

2 teaspoons paprika

2 teaspoons salt

1 teaspoon oregano

For the rest of the buffet:

2 15-ounce cans refried beans, black beans, or vegetarian chili

1 pre-cooked rotisserie chicken, shredded

6 medium tomatoes, diced

2 heads romaine lettuce, shredded

1 8-ounce can sliced black olives, drained

1 8-ounce can pickled jalapeño slices

1 1/2 pounds shredded cheddar or Monterey Jack cheese

24 flour or corn tortillas

24 hard taco shells

Sour cream

Salsa

Guacamole

INSTRUCTIONS

In a large skillet over medium heat, warm the olive oil. Add the ground beef or turkey and the chopped onion. Cook, breaking the meat up with a wooden spoon or spatula, until the meat starts to brown.

Add the spices (chili powder through oregano). Stir well and continue cooking until the meat is well browned all over and cooked through. Taste and adjust seasoning as needed. Keep the taco meat warm.

Heat up the refried beans, black beans, or vegetarian chili. Keep warm.

If desired, warm up the rotisserie chicken meat. This is best done gently in a little bit of chicken broth to keep the meat moist.

Set out a buffet of all your fillings and toppings and let people make their own tacos.

FUN

Add a little lighthearted suspense to dinner by assigning each guest a secret task!

HOW TO PLAY

Before dinner, the host secretly gives each person a word or phrase. Their secret task is to find a way to use that word or phrase during dinner, without another diner calling them out for it! Sample phrases might be "That's the way the cookie crumbles" or "That's a real knee-slapper." See how many people can accomplish their secret task without giving the game away.

CONVERSATION

Keep the fun going with a lighthearted conversation that's perfect for everyone.

(ALL AGES)

- Name three things that are fun for you.
- What has been the happiest day of your life so far?
- What's your most unusual talent? Demonstrate it!
- If you could start a school dedicated to fun, what would it be like? What kinds of things would you teach?
- Describe your perfect day. Where would you go? What would you do? Who would you want with you?

MAKE STRANGERS FEEL LIKE FAMILY

Not every big dinner gathering includes just family, of course. Sometimes our tables expand to greet new guests, especially as our families themselves expand with new relationships and friends who feel like actual relatives. Particularly during the holiday season, we often throw open our doors and share our festivities with newcomers, but a welcoming spirit isn't always enough to make an outsider feel like one of the family.

It's to be expected that both hosts and guests might feel awkward at first, but that doesn't mean you have to resign yourselves to a whole meal filled with discomfort. Instead, plan ahead to break the ice. One thoughtful suggestion that a team member's mother-in-law employed during their first shared Thanksgiving was to make the meal a potluck. She invited all of the family sons- and daughters-in-law to bring a side dish that was meaningful to their own family traditions. Having a concrete way to contribute to the meal and a natural entry to point to conversation—"Tell us about what you've brought!"—helped everyone at that holiday dinner feel more at ease.

FOOD

A simple recipe like this Apricot Glazed Ham will easily feed a crowd, and it's likely to go well with whatever potluck side dishes your new guests bring. The minimal attention it needs also means you'll have much more time to devote to making everyone feel comfortable and getting to know newcomers, instead of spending every minute leading up to dinner in the kitchen.

APRICOT GLAZED HAM

`SERVES 8-10`

For a smaller gathering, you could use a small boneless ham of about three pounds. However, a large spiral-sliced ham feeds lots of people easily and can often be found on sale, making this a very cost-effective way to host a potluck gathering.

INGREDIENTS

1 spiral-sliced ham, about 6-7 pounds

3/4 cup apricot preserves

2 tablespoons Dijon mustard (optional)

INSTRUCTIONS

Preheat oven to 350 degrees F.

Place the ham in a foil-lined roasting dish. Pour an inch of water in the bottom to help prevent the ham from drying out.

Bake the ham for an hour.

Mix the preserves and Dijon mustard (if using) in a small bowl. Remove the ham from the oven and thoroughly spread the glaze over the ham.

Return the ham to the oven and cook for another 30–40 minutes, until the ham is heated through and the glaze is sticky and caramelized.

FUN
Make a game out of getting to know one another with the Hat Game!

HOW TO PLAY

Before dinner, have each dinner guest write their answers to one or more of the following questions on slips of paper and place them in a hat. At dinnertime, the host reads the answers aloud, and everyone tries to guess which guest gave which answers!

What is a book that transformed your life?

What character in a children's book did you most identify with as a child?

What was your favorite toy as a child?

What do you feel most grateful for?

What do you love most about being a part of your family?

What animal would you most like to be?

CONVERSATION

Invite your guests to tell you more about the special dishes they're sharing with these questions.

(AGES 14-100)

- Where did this recipe come from?
- Who do you remember making this for you? Who taught you to make it?
- When and where did you typically eat this food growing up?
- Was this a special occasion food only or an everyday food?
- What kinds of memories does this dish bring up for you?

CREATE FAMILY BONDS WITH "FRAMILY"

Beyond family dinners, we know many groups who gather for shared mealtimes and create a community. In our minds, this definitely counts as its own type of family dinner! Young people away at college or just starting out in their own apartments away from home, couples seeking a network of support in a new city, like-minded people gathering to bond over a shared interest or idea—are all examples of "framily dinners" (friends who feel like family).

The number one rule of "framily" dinners is to start off by making things feel as casual and homey as possible. We suggest kicking things off with a budget-friendly homestyle baked pasta dish and a guessing game that's just the right mix of fun and challenge. When everyone's engaged, you can move on to a conversation about a shared interest or goal. Before you know it, you'll have created a "framily."

FOOD

TFDP team member Cindil shared this recipe for her aunt's Midwestern-style mostaccioli, which can easily be scaled up or down depending on how many people you're inviting to the table.

FAMILY-STYLE MOSTACCIOLI

SERVES 6-8

This budget-friendly baked pasta is the pinnacle of comfort food. You can make it a day in advance and just pop in the oven before company arrives.

INGREDIENTS

16 ounces penne pasta

Olive oil

1 medium onion, chopped

4 cloves of garlic, minced

1 pound ground beef

Salt and pepper to taste

1 teaspoon dried basil

1 teaspoon dried oregano

1 14.5-ounce can diced tomatoes with juice

24 ounces spaghetti sauce, jarred or homemade*

2-4 cups shredded mozzarella cheese

2 tablespoons brown sugar (optional)

*The Simple Tomato Sauce recipe we recommend with our spaghetti and meatballs would work nicely in this recipe too. Find it on page 140.

INSTRUCTIONS

Cook pasta according to package directions; drain and set aside.

Preheat oven to 350 degrees F. Lightly grease a 9 by 13–inch baking dish.

Coat the bottom of a large pot with olive oil. Sauté the onion and garlic until softened.

Add the ground beef and cook, breaking it up with a spoon until lightly browned. Add salt, pepper, basil, and oregano.

Once the beef is fully browned all over, add the diced tomatoes and spaghetti sauce. Bring to a low boil, reduce the heat, and simmer for 15 minutes.

Stir in the brown sugar, taste, and adjust seasonings as desired.

Mix the meat sauce with the cooked penne pasta. Pour into the prepared baking dish and top with mozzarella cheese—2 cups if you are only feeling somewhat "cheesy," up to 4 cups if you're a cheese fan.

Cover with foil and bake for 40 minutes, then uncover and bake for an additional 10–15 minutes to brown the cheese.

FUN

One fun ice-breaker is to have someone ask everyone to go around the table to take a guess at how to spell "mostaccioli." Then get things going with a round of Advanced Celebrity, a brain teasing guessing game.

HOW TO PLAY

This is a guessing game that goes both ways. First, the leader thinks of a famous person and gives the group their initials. For example, "CD." Then the rest of the group takes turns asking questions about famous people with the same initials, like this:

"Is this person a 19th century scientist?"

"Are you thinking of a famous lawyer?"

To answer them, the leader must be able to guess who they're thinking of as well. So the leader might answer:

"No, it's not Charles Darwin."

"No, I'm not thinking of Clarence Darrow."

If the leader can't figure out who the guesser is talking about, the leader is officially "stumped." That entitles the guesser to one free yes or no question, such as "Is this person a woman?" or "Did this person act in a 1990s TV show?"

The game continues until someone is able to correctly guess who the leader is thinking of:

"Is this person the actress from *Homeland*?"

"Yes, I'm thinking of Claire Danes!"

CONVERSATION

Shared interest in the community where you live can be a great starting point for meaningful conversation. Try these conversation starters about community at your "framily" dinner.

(AGES 14-100)

- What are the elements of a strong community? What makes people feel included and connected to each other?

- Are there any efforts or initiatives going on to improve our community right now? How much do we know about them and how can we help?

- What's one thing you wish could happen in our community? Is there a way for us to make it happen?

- What is one action we can all take in the next week that would have a positive impact on our neighborhood?

- Is there anyone in our community that needs additional support or help right now? How can we reach out?

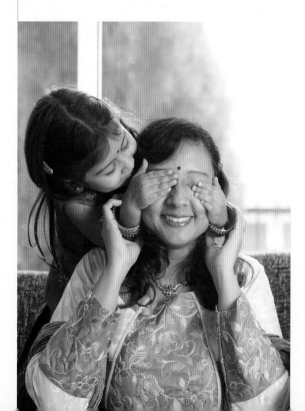

THE MORE, THE MERRIER!

When a crowd's expected, there's no reason everyone can't pitch in to contribute to the food, fun, and conversation. At least, that's the approach Meredith and her family take to big family gatherings.

Every year or so, about fifteen members of the family take a weeklong vacation together. While the many planned daytime activities are participation-optional, family dinners are not. "We call it 'free to be you and me,' inspired by Marlo Thomas, where everybody does their own thing and joins when they want to," Meredith says. "But we all get together for dinner. That's non negotiable."

You might imagine that a whole week of big dinners would be a lot of work, but that's part of the fun for Meredith's family. Before the vacation, they all decide together which nights will be out-to-eat nights and which will be stay-in-and-cook nights. Then the family members vote on what kinds of meals they'd like to cook, and they form "Dinner Committees." Each committee—comprised of a mix of ages and experience levels with cooking—is assigned one night of the vacation. Then the fun begins.

The Dinner Committees don't just plan menus. They plan an entire evening of food, fun, and conversation for all ages, along with taking care of the cleanup at the end of the meal. Because there is a wide range of ages and appetites in the group, the committees plan meals that can go all night, beginning with an array of snacks and progressing through to main dishes that can be served anytime (little ones first, to keep hunger-related meltdowns at bay) and fun dessert options available when people are ready for their sweet treat. The important part, Meredith says, is that no matter when people choose to eat, they all stay together for the whole evening, sharing the different courses and enjoying games, activities, and conversations together while munching. There might be a collaborative puzzle built by family members who huddle around it with a plate of appetizers, a group of people sharing funny videos with each other at the counter while they build their burgers, or the whole group challenging one another to Minute to Win It–style games between courses.

This casual and fun menu would fit in perfectly at one of Meredith's family dinners, with a dippable appetizer for munching, a barbecue main dish that can feed the whole crowd whenever they're hungry, and a creative twist on a vacation classic for dessert.

FOOD

ESPINACA DIP
SERVES 8-10

This dip recipe is a hit at Meredith's family gatherings, especially since it's a rich, indulgent, once-in-a-while treat! It's modified from an original recipe from the Village Church Mini Chef Summer Camp.

INGREDIENTS

2 8-ounce blocks light cream cheese, cubed

1/2 pint heavy whipping cream

2 14.5-ounce cans diced tomatoes with green chiles, drained

1/2 white onion, chopped (optional)

1/4 cup jalapeños (optional)

5 ounces chopped frozen spinach

1 chicken bouillon cube, crushed

8 ounces pasteurized processed cheese product (such as Velveeta), cubed

1/2 cup milk

INSTRUCTIONS

Mix all ingredients and heat in a slow cooker or on the stove over medium heat.

Heat until melted and serve with tortilla chips.

SLOW COOKER APPLE BARBECUE PULLED PORK
SERVES 8-10

This recipe is adapted from team member Bri's blog, "Red, Round, or Green." Cooking the pork and then keeping it warm in a slow cooker means that family members can assemble their own sandwiches whenever the mood strikes.

INGREDIENTS

4-5 pounds boneless pork shoulder

Salt and pepper to taste

2 medium onions, peeled and quartered

3 apples, cored and quartered

2 cups water

1/2 cup apple cider vinegar

8 ounces of ketchup

1/2 cup brown sugar

1 tablespoon ground cumin

2 teaspoons dry mustard

1 teaspoon ground cloves

1 teaspoon ground allspice

Sandwich buns, for serving

Slaw and/or pickles, for topping sandwiches (optional)

INSTRUCTIONS

Sprinkle the pork shoulder liberally with salt and pepper.

Place in a slow cooker. Nestle the onions and apples around the pork.

In a medium bowl, mix together the sauce ingredients (water through allspice). Pour over the pork.

Cover and cook on low for 10 hours, until the pork is very tender. Remove the pork from the slow cooker and shred with two forks.

Use an immersion blender to puree the sauce in the slow cooker, or transfer in batches to a blender and blend until smooth.

Return the pork and sauce to the slow cooker and keep warm.

S'MORES BAR
SERVES AS MANY AS YOU LIKE

Everyone knows how to make a classic s'more: toasted marshmallow, graham crackers, and chocolate. But have you ever made a s'mores bar? Swap graham crackers for cookies, chocolate for candies, and more to create personalized twists on the well-known treat.

INGREDIENTS

2 bags marshmallows

1 box graham cracker sheets, broken in half

1 sleeve chocolate sandwich cookies

1 sleeve fudge striped or mint-chocolate cookies

1 bag chocolate peanut butter cups

1 jar chocolate hazelnut spread

1 bag caramel-filled chocolate bars

INSTRUCTIONS

Lay out all of your ingredients on separate platters and be sure to remove all wrappers before you begin.

Toast marshmallows. Ideally this would be done over a campfire, but when a campfire isn't available, they can be toasted over the flames of a grill, the burner flame of a gas stovetop, or even under an oven broiler for 30 seconds or so. Put them on a foil-lined baking sheet and watch them carefully!

Let everyone use their toasted marshmallows to make their own gourmet s'more creations.

FUN

As long as you've got cookies available for your s'mores bar, why not use them for a hilarious—and challenging—game of Cookie Face Race?

HOW TO PLAY

Each player tips his or her head back. Place a cookie on each person's forehead. Then set a timer for one minute, say "On your marks, get set, go!" See who can get the cookie from his forehead to his mouth first—using no hands, only facial muscles!

CONVERSATION

Remember the reason you've all gathered with these conversation starters about shared meals.

(AGES 8-14, 14-100)

- If you could learn to cook any family recipe, what would it be?
- Besides the food, what do you enjoy most about our family dinners?
- If you could invite anyone to join us for dinner—living or dead—who would you invite? What would you want to talk about with that person?
- What is one thing you wish we could do at our next meal together?
- If you could sum up our family dinners in just three words, what words would you choose?

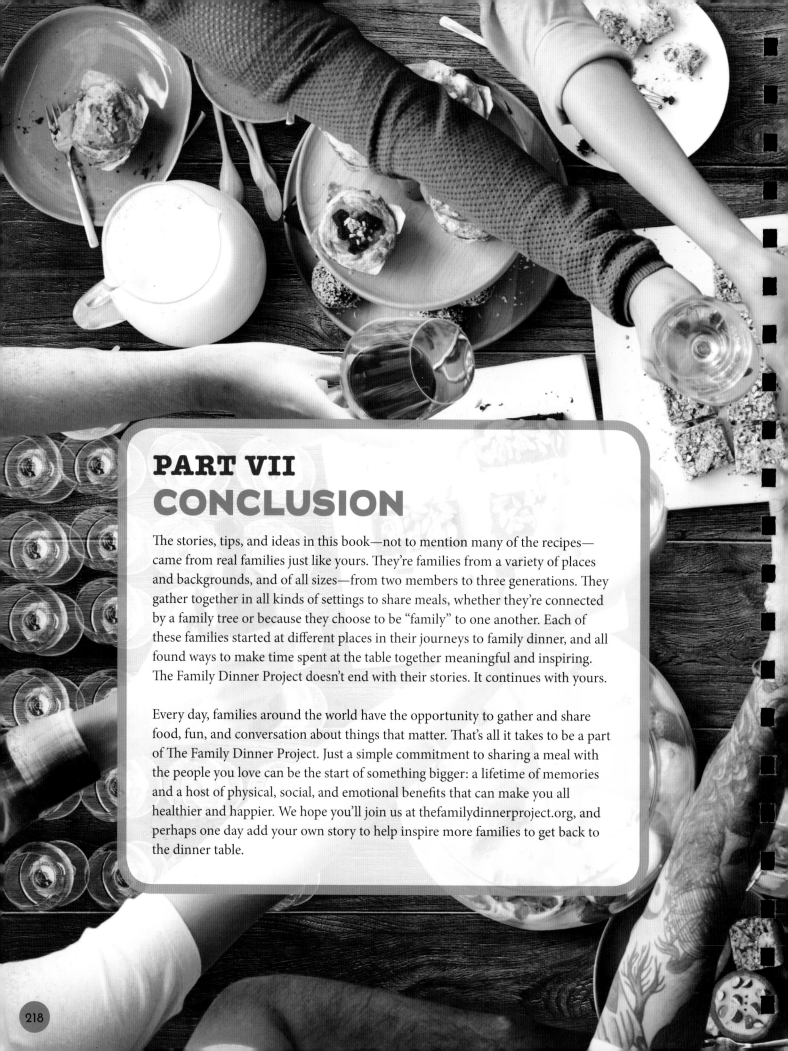

PART VII
CONCLUSION

The stories, tips, and ideas in this book—not to mention many of the recipes—came from real families just like yours. They're families from a variety of places and backgrounds, and of all sizes—from two members to three generations. They gather together in all kinds of settings to share meals, whether they're connected by a family tree or because they choose to be "family" to one another. Each of these families started at different places in their journeys to family dinner, and all found ways to make time spent at the table together meaningful and inspiring. The Family Dinner Project doesn't end with their stories. It continues with yours.

Every day, families around the world have the opportunity to gather and share food, fun, and conversation about things that matter. That's all it takes to be a part of The Family Dinner Project. Just a simple commitment to sharing a meal with the people you love can be the start of something bigger: a lifetime of memories and a host of physical, social, and emotional benefits that can make you all healthier and happier. We hope you'll join us at thefamilydinnerproject.org, and perhaps one day add your own story to help inspire more families to get back to the dinner table.

ACKNOWLEDGMENTS

We first want to thank the Familius team members who suggested that we write this book and then held our collective hands every step of the way. Kate Farrell, Katharine Hale, Brooke Jorden, Zach Marell, David Miles, Christopher Robbins, and Peg Sandkam—we're grateful to each of you for your unique talents, contributions, and kindness.

To Heather Won Tesoriero: We thank you for your invaluable feedback and thoughtful edits on an early draft of our manuscript.

To all the people who shared their recipes: Some recipes came handed down through the generations as cherished heirlooms and others were created out of necessity to feed a family on the run. Above and beyond the recipes, this book draws upon so much more that we've learned from all of you. Thanks for enriching the fun and conversation as much as the food.

To the special friends and advisors of The Family Dinner Project: From the earliest days, you believed in our work and provided motivating, candid feedback. We give special thanks to the Harvard University Advanced Leadership Initiative (Rosabeth Moss Kanter, founding chair and director), where The Family Dinner Project idea began. And we'll always be grateful to Harvard's Howard Gardner for his wise counsel from the beginning.

To all our partners, as well as past and present team members of The Family Dinner Project: Over the past 10 years, many people have contributed to our knowledge of family dinners and the creation of evidence-based resources used by hundreds of thousands of families. We thank you for everything you've done to nurture our collective labor of love and make a difference for families. We give a special shout-out to Jessie Magyar and Shannon Frederick Meneses, who kept everything moving as we wrote this book.

RECIPE INDEX

MAIN DISHES

NOTES

1. Duke, M.P., Fivush, R., Lazarus, A., Bohanek, J. (2003). Of ketchup and kin: dinnertime conversations as a major source of family knowledge, family adjustment, and family resilience. The Emory Center for Myth and Ritual in American Live, Working Paper, no. 26.

2. Fishel, A. (2015) Home for Dinner: Mixing Food, Fun, and Conversation for a Happier Family and Healthier Kids. NY: Harper Collins

3. Gillman, M.W., Rifas-Shiman, S.L., Frazier, A.L., Rockett, H.R., Camargo, C.A., Field, A.E., Berkey, C.S., Colditz, G.A. (2000). Family dinner and diet quality among older children and adolescents. Arch Fam Med. 9:235-40.

4. Berge, J.M., Wall, M., Hsyed, T-F, Fulkerson, J.A., Larson, N., Neumark-Sztainer, D. (2015). The protective role of family meals for youth obesity: 10-year longitudinal associations. The Journal of Pediatrics, 166: 296-301

Wolfson, J.A. Bleich, S.N. (2015). Is cooking at home associated with better diet quality of weight loss intention. Public Health Nutrition, 18: 1397-1406.

5. Fiese, B.H., Winter M.A., Botti J.C. (2011). The ABCs of family mealtimes: Observational lessons for promoting healthy outcomes for children with persistent asthma. Child Development. 82 (1): 133-145.

6. Khoury, M., Manlhior, C., Gibson, D., Stearne, N., Chahal, N., Dobbin, S., McCrindle, B. (2015). Evaluation of the associations between buying lunch at school, eating at restaurants, and eating together as a family and cardiometabolic risk in adolescents. Canadian Journal of Cardiology, 31: S266-S267.

7. Berge et al. 2015

8. Snow, C.E., Beals, D.E. (2006). Mealtime talk that supports literacy development. New Directions in Child and Adolescent Behavior, 111: 51-66.

9. Snow and Beals, 2006

10. Hofferth, S.L., Sandberg, J.F (2001). How American children spend their time. Journal of Marriage and Family, 63: 295-308

11. Hofferth, and Sandberg, 2001.

12. CASA (2007). The importance of family dinners, IV. Retrieved on 10/31/18: The-importance-of-family-dinners-IV%20(9).pdf

13. Eisenberg, ME, Neumark-Sztainer, D, Fulkerson, JA and Story, M. (2008). Family meals and substance abuse: Is there a long-term protective association? Journal of adolescent health, 43:151-145.

14. Neumark-Sztainer, D., Eisenberg, M.E., Fulkerson, J.A., Story, M., Larson, N. (2008). Family meals and disordered eating in adolescents. Archive Pediatric and Adolescent Medicine 162(21): 17-22.

Neumark-Sztainer, D., Wall, M., Story, M., Fulkerson, J.A. (2004). Are family meal patterns associated with disordered eating behaviors among adolescents? Journal of adolescent health. 35:350-359.

15. Sen, B. (2010).The relationship between frequency of family dinner and adolescent problem behaviors after adjusting for other family characteristics. Journal of Adolescence, 33: 187-196.

Fiese, B.H., Schwartz,M. (2008). Reclaiming the family table: Mealtimes and child health and wellbeing. Social Policy Report, Vo. XXII: No. IV, 3-20.

Fulkerson, J.A., Kubik M.Y., Story, M., Lytle L., Arcan C. (2009). Are there nutritional and other benefits associated with family meals among at-risk youth? Journal of Adolescent Health, 45: 389-395.

Fulkerson, J.A.,Story, M.,Mellin, A., Leffert, N.,Neumark-Sztainer,D., and French, S.A.(2006). Family dinner meal frequency and adolescent development: Relationships with developmental assets and high-risk behaviors, Journal of Adolescent Health, 39:337-345.

16. Eisenberg, M.E., Olson, R.E., Neumark-Sztainer, D., et al. (2004). Correlations between family meals and psychosocial well-being among adolescents. Archives Pediatric Adolescent Medicine, 158: 792-796.

17. Bradshaw, C. (2014). The role of families in Preventing and Buffering the Effects of Bullying. JAMA Pediatrics, 168:991-993.

Elgar, F., Napoletano, A., Saul, G., Dirks, M., Craig, W., et al. (2014). Cyberbullying victimization and mental health in adolescents and the moderating role of family dinner. JAMA Pediatrics, 168, 1015-1022.

18. CASA 2007

19. Eisenberg et al, 2004.

Utter, J., Denny, S., Robinson, E., Fleming, T., Ameratunga, S., Grant, S. (2013). Family meals and the well-being of adolescents. Journal of Pediatrics and Child Health, 49: 906-911.

20. Harbec, M.J. & Pagani, L.S. (2018). Associations between early family meal environment quality and later well-being in school-age children. J Dev Behav Pediatr, 39: 136-143.d

21. Duke, M.P. Lazarus, A., & Fivush, R. (2008). Knowledge of family history as a clinically useful index of psychological well-being and prognosis: a brief report. Psychotherapy Theory, Research Practice, Training, 45: 268-272.

22. Gable, S., Chang Y., Krull, J.L. (2007). Television-watching and frequency of family meals are predictive of overweight onset and persistence in a national sample of school-age children. Journal of the American Dietetic Association, 107:53-61.2000

Coon K.A., Goldberg J., Rogers B.L., Tucker K.L. (2001). Relationships between use of television during meals and children's food consumption patterns. Pediatrics,107: e7

23. Smith, L.P., Ng, S.W., Popkin, B.M. (2013). Trends in US home food preparation and consumption: analysis of national nutrition surveys and time use studies from 1965-1966 to 2007-2008. Nutrition Journal, 12: 45

24. Fiese, B., Fishel, A., Doherty, B., Roberts, J. (2015). Expert roundtable: the psychological benefits of our Thanksgiving rituals, Theconversation.com, https://theconversation.com/expert-roundtable-the-psychological-benefits-of-our-thanksgiving-rituals-50716

25. Fiese et al. 2015

26. Mascola AJ, Bryson SW, Agras WS (2010). Picky eating during childhood: a longitudinal study to age 11 years. Eat Behav. 11(4):253–257

27. Satter, Ellyn (2008). Secrets of Feeding a Healthy Family, 2nd edition. NY: Kelcy Press.

28. Galloway, A.T., Fiorito, L.M., Francis, L.A., Birch, L.L. (2006). 'Finish your soup': Counterproductive effects of pressuring children to eat on intake and affect. Appetite, 46: 318-323.

29. Menella, J., Jagnow, M., Beauchamp, G. (2001). Prenatal and postnatal flavor learning by human infants, Pediatrics, 107:88-94.

30. Sullivan, S.A. & Birch, L.L. (1990). "Pass the sugar, pass the salt: experience dictates preference. Developmental Psychology, 26: 546-551.

31. Coulthard, H., Thakker, D. (2015). Enjoyment of tactile play is associated with lower frequency of neophobia in preschool children. Journal of the Academy of Nutrition and Dietetics, 115: 1134-1140.

32. Liquori, T., Koch, P.D., Contento, I.R., Castle, J. (1998). The cookshop program: outcome evaluation of a nutrition education program linking lunchroom food experiences with classroom cooking experiences. Journal of Nutrition Education, 30: 302-313.

33. Information shared in 2 Focus groups with about a dozen pediatricians. Pediatricians were from the Boston area with inner-city and suburban practices. Spring 2012, https://thefamilydinnerproject.org/food-for-thought/doctors-order-have-family-dinners/

34. Steinberg. L. (2001) We know some things: Parent-Adolescent relationships in retrospect and prospect. Journal of Research on Adolescence, 11:1-19

35. CASA 2007

36. CASA 2007

CASA (2012). Retrieved on 10/31/18:The importance of family dinners, VIII, The-importance-of-family-dinners%20 VIII%20(10).pdf

37. Fishel, A., Gorrindo, T. (2014). Should you turn off tech at dinner? Psychologytoday.com, https://www.psychologytoday.com/us/blog/the-digital-family/201410/should-you-turn-tech-dinner10/21/2014.

ABOUT FAMILIUS

VISIT OUR WEBSITE: WWW.FAMILIUS.COM

Familius is a global-trade publishing company that publishes books and other content to help families be happy. We believe that the family is the fundamental unit of society and that happy families are the foundation of a happy life. We recognize that every family looks different, and we passionately believe in helping all families find greater joy. To that end, we publish books for children and adults that invite families to live the Familius Nine Habits of Happy Family Life: *love together, play together, learn together, work together, talk together, heal together, read together, eat together,and laugh together.* Founded in 2012, Familius is located in Sanger, California.

JOIN OUR FAMILY

There are lots of ways to connect with us! Subscribe to our newsletters at www.familius.com to receive uplifting daily inspiration, essays from our Pater Familius, a free ebook every month, and the first word on special discounts and Familius news.

GET BULK DISCOUNTS

If you feel a few friends and family might benefit from what you've read, let us know and we'll be happy to provide you with quantity discounts. Simply email us at orders@familius.com.

CONNECT

Facebook: www.facebook.com/paterfamilius
Twitter: @familiustalk, @paterfamilius1
Pinterest: www.pinterest.com/familius
Instagram: @familiustalk

The most important work you ever do will be within the walls of your own home.